ENGLISH

NEXT

B 1/1

Myriam Fischer Callus
Ingrid Gürtler
Gareth Hughes
Judith Mader

Hueber Verlag

English NEXT B1/1

Autorenteam

Student's Book
Myriam Fischer Callus
Ingrid Gürtler
Gareth Hughes
Judith Mader

Übungen Internet
Alexandra Haas
Brigitte Köper
Judith Mader

Companion
Gareth Hughes

English NEXT Team
Myriam Fischer Callus (Fachbereichsleiterin Englisch, VHS Aschaffenburg), Dr. Ingrid Gürtler (Autorin und Fortbildnerin), Alexandra Haas (Fachbereichsleiterin, VHS Rhein-Sieg), Gareth Hughes (Autor und Fortbildner, UK), Brigitte Köper (Kursleiterin und Fortbildnerin, Nürnberg), Judith Mader (Head of Languages, Frankfurt School of Finance and Management)

| 3. 2. 1. | Die letzten Ziffern |
| 2014 13 12 11 10 | bezeichnen Zahl und Jahr des Druckes. |

Alle Drucke dieser Auflage können, da unverändert,
nebeneinander benutzt werden.
1. Auflage
© 2010 Hueber Verlag, 85737 Ismaning, Deutschland

Verlagsredaktion: Rolf Brüseke, Karen Emmendorfer, Hueber Verlag, Ismaning
Umschlag und Gestaltungskonzept: Alois Sigl, Hueber Verlag, Ismaning
Layout/Herstellung: Büro Sieveking, München
Reproarbeiten: Lorenz & Zeller, Inning a.A.
Druck: Aprinta Druck GmbH
Bindung: Ludwig Auer GmbH, Donauwörth
Printed in Germany
ISBN 978-3-19-002934-1

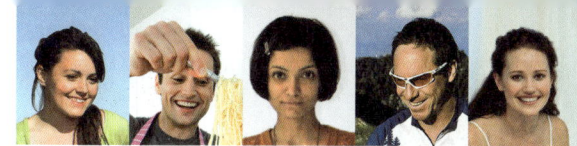

Welcome to English NEXT!

Sie erhoffen sich von Ihrem Englischkurs spürbare Lernfortschritte? Sie möchten Ihr Lerntempo mitbestimmen können und mit Freude am Unterricht teilnehmen? Und jederzeit sicher sein, dass Sie das, was Sie gelernt haben, auch tatsächlich können? Mit English NEXT ist das kein Problem. Unterhaltsame Themen machen neugierig, vielfältige Übungen sorgen für erfrischende Abwechslung und regelmäßige Tipps zeigen auf, wie Sie persönlich am besten lernen können. Doch orientieren Sie sich zunächst einmal, was English NEXT Ihnen alles zu bieten hat:

Woraus besteht mein Lernpaket?

Aus Student's Book, 2 CDs und einem Companion.

Das Student's Book enthält:
- 10 thematische Einheiten (Units)
- mit jeweils 4 Aspekten A, B, C, D als unterrichtliches Kernmaterial
- und einem weiteren Aspekt E als Zusatzmaterial für den Unterricht (Plus)
- sowie 4 Wiederholungseinheiten (Consolidation)
- und zusätzlichen Lesetexten im Reading Club.

Der Anhang enthält die Texte zu den Tonaufnahmen (Tapescripts), den kompletten Lösungsschlüssel (Key) und die alphabetische Wortliste mit Lautschrift.
Zu den 10 Units gibt es zusätzliches Übungsmaterial für die häusliche Nacharbeit (Homestudy).
Auf den beiliegenden Audio CDs finden Sie das gesamte kursbegleitende Hörmaterial.

Das zusätzliche Booklet
- NEXT Companion
  enthält einen Unit-Lernwortschatz, eine Phrasebank, eine Kurzgrammatik sowie Hinweise zum Europäischen Sprachenportfolio.
- Und wenn Sie Internet-Zugang haben, dann finden Sie weiteres Übungsmaterial und interessante Links unter www.hueber.de/next.

Wie lerne ich im Kurs?

Ihre Kursleiterin/Ihr Kursleiter führt Sie sicher durch die Units des Student's Book. Hier die wichtigsten Merkmale einer Unit:
- Das Thema wird in den Aspekten A – E aus unterschiedlichen Blickwinkeln beleuchtet.
- Innerhalb der Übungen finden Sie Kästchen Focus on ... (z.B. S. 11, 12). Diese Kästchen unterstützen Sie bei den Übungen und geben Ihnen wertvolle Tipps mit Blick auf Grammatik, Wortschatz oder gesprochene Sprache. Die Kästchen mit der Bezeichnung Remember wiederholen wichtige Aspekte der Grammatik und nützliche Ausdrücke aus vorangegangenen Units (z.B. S. 21).
- In der linken schmalen Spalte einer Seite zeigt Ihnen das CD-Symbol den Einsatz von Hörmaterial an, z.B. auf S. 10: Die Zahlenkombination 1/1 sagt Ihnen, dass der Hörtext auf Spur 1 der CD 1 zu hören ist.
- Außerdem finden Sie in der Randspalte Verweise auf andere Teile Ihres Lernpakets, z.B. auf S. 11: Zur Übung A1d gibt es die zusätzliche Übung H1 für zu Hause im violett gekennzeichneten Homestudy-Teil der Unit 1, S. 114/115. Der Querverweis auf Seite 11 auf den NEXT Companion deutet an, dass es dort noch weitere Erläuterungen zu Focus on Grammar gibt.
- Die in der Randspalte blau hinterlegten Kästchen Exploring learning (z.B. S. 11) verweisen auf die letzte Seite jeder Unit, auf der Sie Tipps zum Lernen finden.

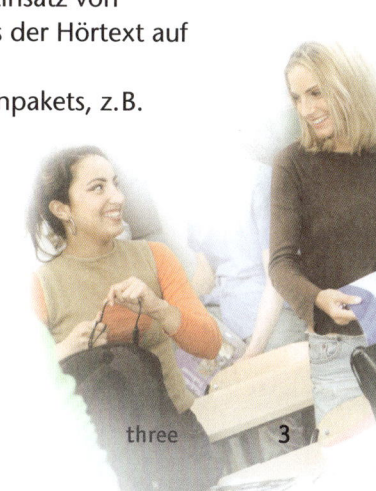

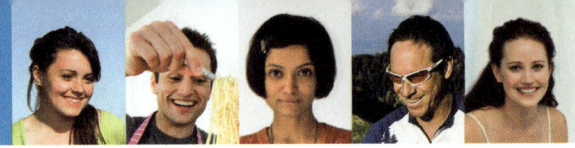

- Die Symbole Erdkugel (z. B. S. 21) und @work (z. B. S. 13) signalisieren, dass etwas landeskundlich bzw. beruflich bedeutsam ist.
- Die Consolidation-Units ermöglichen es den Kursleitenden, nach jeweils drei Units und im Anschluss an Unit 10 den Lernzuwachs ihres Kurses zu bestimmen und flexibel das Lerntempo darauf abzustimmen.

Wie lerne ich zu Hause?

Die Nacharbeit des im Kurs Gelernten gibt Ihnen zusätzliche Sicherheit und zeigt Ihnen auch, was Sie schon richtig gut können – oder hilft Ihnen festzustellen, dass ein wenig mehr Übung nicht schaden könnte.

- Im Student's Book enthalten ist der mit violettem Balken gekennzeichnete Homestudy-Teil. Ihn sollten Sie zu Ihrer eigenen Absicherung regelmäßig bearbeiten.
- Der NEXT Companion begleitet Sie mit einem unitweisen Wortschatz, der zur besseren Merkfähigkeit mit Lerntipps zum Vokabellernen und in überschaubaren Lernportionen aufbereitet ist. Your link to the Portfolio hilft Ihnen, Ihre Lernfortschritte zu planen und zu dokumentieren. Im Companion finden Sie ebenfalls eine systematische Grammatikübersicht und eine Phrasebank mit nützlichen Wendungen.
- Wenn Sie darüber hinaus ein wenig auf Englisch lesen wollen, dann schmökern Sie entspannt im Reading Club (s. S. 110). Die Texte sind unterhaltsam, überfordern nicht und schenken Ihnen zusätzliches Selbstvertrauen.
- Wenn Sie Internet-Zugang haben, dann klicken Sie auf www.hueber.de/next und Sie entdecken nicht nur weitere Übungen, sondern auch Links zu interessanten landeskundlichen Phänomenen.

Wie kann ich meinen persönlichen Lernfortschritt einschätzen?

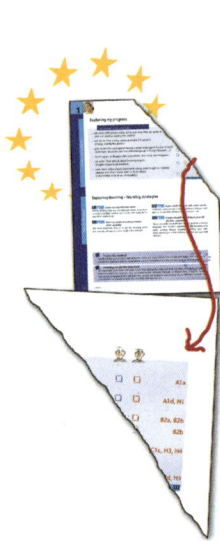

Im Sinne der europäischen Integration hat der Europarat einen „Gemeinsamen Europäischen Referenzrahmen" für den Fremdsprachenerwerb entwickelt, um Sprachenlernen innerhalb Europas vergleichbar zu machen. In 6 Stufen (A1, A2, B1, B2, C1, C2) wird konkret beschrieben, was Lernende auf der jeweiligen Stufe in der Fremdsprache können müssten. Damit können auch Sie selber sich in Ihrer Fremdsprachenkompetenz einschätzen. English NEXT ist Ihnen dabei eine große Hilfe, indem am Ende einer jeden Unit (z. B. S. 16 in Unit 1) unter Exploring my progress aufgezeigt wird, was konkret in der Unit vermittelt wurde.

Was ist, wenn Sie sich nicht sicher sind? Kein Problem mit English NEXT. Die roten Buchstaben- / Ziffern-Kombinationen rechts im Kasten zeigen Ihnen, wo Sie nochmals nachlernen können: in der Unit, im Homestudy-Teil oder im NEXT-Portal (z. B. Code für Unit 1: XB1101) im Internet. Ihren persönlichen Lernprozess und -erfolg steuern Sie letztendlich auch, indem Sie darüber nachdenken, welche der Lerntipps für Sie besonders hilfreich sind und wie Sie besonders erfolgreich lernen können. Treffen Sie darüber eine bewusste Entscheidung, indem Sie den Abschnitt Your link to the Portfolio im NEXT Companion durcharbeiten. So planen Sie Ihren Lernfortschritt bewusst und erfolgreich.

Wir wünschen Ihnen viel Freude und Erfolg mit English NEXT!
Ihr NEXT Team

Contents

Core aspects A–D It's a small world; If I won a million euros; Crime doesn't pay; Modern times
Plus aspect E More or less technology?

Communication
compare information about life in different countries; say what surprised you most or least about something you've read; give tips about how to behave in a new country or how to prevent crime; say what you would do if you won a lot of money or witnessed a crime;

compare the past, present and future and say how things have changed and will change

Grammar
comparative and superlative forms (more, the most, less, the least); "-ing" form; imperatives; "nobody, everybody"; sentences with "if"

Vocabulary
different countries and customs; jobs; crime and criminals; modern words

★**Exploring my progress,**
★**Exploring learning**
– comparing and contrasting

Core aspects A–D The way things used to be; What if?; Global warming; Back to the basics
Plus aspect E The most beautiful place on earth

Communication
talk about how things used to be and compare that with today; read and understand a longer text by guessing unknown words from the context; talk about possible changes and imagine what the effects of these changes would be; talk about what you think

is certain in the future and what you think is possible; talk about and share ideas for a different lifestyle; talk in a simple way about ideas for recycling

Grammar
"used to"; passive with "be"; sentences with "if"; "will" vs. "may / might"; "going to"

Vocabulary
the way people used to live; things made with oil; global warming and recycling

★**Exploring my progress,**
★**Exploring learning**
– reading

Core aspects A–D Your body; Looking after your body; Holiday problems; The worst holiday
Plus aspect E Water

Communication
talk about some basic medical problems or accidents; read advertisements to find specific information; make a phone call to make a reservation at a health spa; give somebody advice to avoid illness or accidents; report what somebody said

Grammar
reflexive pronouns; passive with "get"; "should", "need to", "ought to"; indirect speech

Vocabulary
parts of the body; health problems; body treatments and exercise

★**Exploring my progress,**
★**Exploring learning**
– strategies and techniques for better communication

Contents

Communication
tell people what you do not or cannot eat; write a short email to organize a party; listen to a conversation about a party and understand important information from it; ask people to choose between a number of possibilities; hold a short meeting with someone to organize a party; deal with situations at a party; explain what you've learnt on the course; give a short speech

Grammar
time expressions; "get something done / get somebody to do something"; "what" vs. "which"; present perfect vs. past simple

Vocabulary
food and drinks; organizing a party; at a party; a short speech of thanks

**Exploring my progress,
Exploring learning**
– making progress

Language and learning

What are you good at?

Do you talk to yourself in English sometimes?

Do you think there should be only
one official language in Europe?

1

A What are you good at? Languages? Sports?

A1a John and Vanessa are at a summer peace camp in Estonia with other people from all over Europe. It's the first evening and there's a welcome party. Work with a partner and imagine that you're talking to John or Vanessa. Write some questions that you would like to ask one of them.

Examples: Where are you from?
Are you good at learning languages?
Do you like going to the cinema?

Where _____?
What _____?
When _____?
How _____?
Are _____?
Do _____?

A1b Now listen to John and Vanessa. Which questions do they ask? Compare with the ones you wrote down.

A1c Look at these people and the different things they're good at or enjoy doing.

"I enjoy playing the piano, but I'm not very good."

"I'm keen on painting, but I'm still not very good at it."

"I'm good at solving sudokus."

"I like writing little stories."

"I'm a pretty good cook and I'm making a curry for my friends."

"I like tap dancing."

What about you? What do you like doing? Fill in the gaps.

Companion: Grammar 2.10

a. I'm pretty good at _____
b. I'm interested in _____
c. I'm not very good at _____
d. I'm hopeless at _____
e. I like _____
f. I enjoy _____

> **Focus on grammar**
>
> I'm **interested in** tap danc**ing**.
> I **like/enjoy** rid**ing** my bike.
> I'm (not very) **good at** play**ing** the piano.

Homestudy H1

A1d Write a few words or draw a picture about something you like doing on a Post-it.
Walk around and tell others about your Post-it.
Example:

A1e Tell the class about something interesting you've just heard. Together make a list of all the "class skills" and write them on the board.
Example: Hans is good at gardening.

A2a Do you know any words or phrases from other languages or dialects, besides your mother tongue and English? Fill in the table. Compare with a partner.

		language A	language B	language C
a.	I'm (quite) fluent in …			
b.	I can say a few words in …			
c.	I can write several words in …			
d.	I can read a little …			
e.	I can understand a bit of …			

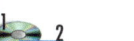 2 **A2b** Listen to these people at the summer peace camp.
They are all saying the same thing in different languages.
Can you guess what they are saying?

Exploring learning p. 16 **TIP 1** Listen for international words.

2 **A2c** Work in pairs and listen again.
Can you guess the languages?
Compare your answers.
You may also look at the tapescript.

	language
Speaker 1	
Speaker 2	
Speaker 3	

A2d How many languages can people in your class say "hello" or "goodbye" in?
How many other words in that language do people know?
Walk round the class and find out.

B The languages of Europe

B1a The welcome party at the summer peace camp starts with a quiz. Work in groups and see if you can answer the questions. You've got five minutes. The group with the most correct answers is the European champion!

a. How many countries are in the Council of Europe? ☐ 47 ☐ 27 ☐ 60

b. Approximately how many languages are spoken in Europe? ☐ 50 ☐ 250 ☐ 100

c. What percentage of people in Europe speak English as a first **or** second language? ☐ 25% ☐ 51% ☐ 38%

d. What percentage of Europeans speak two foreign languages? ☐ 50% ☐ 15% ☐ 28%

B1b Can you name ten European languages and the countries where they are spoken?

> English   England, Ireland, Malta
> German   Germany, Austria, Switzerland, Belgium
> ...   ...

B2a The theme of the summer peace camp is "Languages in Europe".
Would it be a good idea to have only one official language in the European Union?
Make two groups.

Group 1: You think there should be only one official language in the European Union.
Group 2: You don't think there should be just one official language in the European Union.

Collect as many arguments as there are people in your group.
You've got fifteen minutes to prepare.

B2b Now present your arguments. Each group member presents one argument.
Do you agree or disagree with all the statements? Use the phrases in the box *Focus on spoken English*.
Examples: I think there should be only one official language in Europe because …
I don't think there should be just one official language in Europe because …

Exploring learning p. 16 **TIP 2**   Don't be afraid of making mistakes when speaking.

Focus on spoken English
I (don't) think … because …
It's a good idea because …
I agree (disagree) …
I'm sorry, but I disagree …

B2c

What do you need other languages for? Talk with a partner.

Examples: For me, translating is very important because my boss asks me to
translate emails for him.

I like travelling and I use English a lot. It's an international language.

		me	my partner
a.	translating		
b.	interpreting		
c.	making phone calls		
d.	writing emails		
e.	writing letters		
f.	making presentations		
g.	negotiating		
h.	entertaining visitors		
i.	travelling		
j.	…		

B2d

Collect the results from the whole class on the board. What's most important?
You can also record your personal needs in the language biography of your
"Europäisches Sprachenportfolio für Erwachsene".

C   The rocky road to learning a language

omestudy
2

C1a

At the summer peace camp there's a forum about problems people have with language
learning. John talks to two other participants, Asko and Maria, about learning English.
Listen and write down the names next to what they say.
Which of the problems is not mentioned? Check with a partner.

	Asko/Maria?	me
a. English is hard to pronounce.	Maria/Asko	☐
b. The spelling is difficult.	_____	☐
c. Grammar is hard.	_____	☐
d. Words are hard to remember.	_____	☐
e. I don't have enough time to practise.	_____	☐
f. Native speakers talk too fast.	_____	☐
g. I'm afraid to speak.	_____	☐
h. I'm afraid of making mistakes.	_____	☐

C1b

What do you find difficult about learning English?
Tick the comments in C1a that are true for you.

omestudy
3

C1c

Work with a partner and talk about what you find difficult about learning English.
Examples: I find grammar very hard.

Well, I think that English is very hard to pronounce.

I forget lots of words.

1

C2a **Work in groups and decide whether you agree with these statements or not.**

	agree	disagree	unsure
a. You ought to learn the grammar rules first.	☐	☐	☐
b. It's more important to know words than grammar.	☐	☐	☐
c. You ought to try and speak even if you make mistakes.	☐	☐	☐
d. You don't need to worry about your grammar.	☐	☐	☐

C2b **One of the language experts at the camp wrote down a few ideas for learning a language like English. Read them. How do they compare with what you ticked in C2a?**

IDEA ONE	It's important to communicate, so you ought to learn everyday expressions and phrases and use them as much as possible.
IDEA TWO	You ought to practise speaking as much as possible, but you don't need to worry about making mistakes.
IDEA THREE	You need to learn some basic grammar and the irregular verbs. It makes your English sound better and you're more confident when speaking to people.
IDEA FOUR	You don't need to learn everything at once and you don't need to worry if you forget something. Learning a language well takes time.

Homestudy
H4

Companion:
Grammar 2.7.3

C2c **Work with a partner and sort the ideas into two groups.**

You ought to / need to …   You don't need to …

_____   _____

_____   _____

> **Focus on grammar**
>
> You **ought to / need to** practise some English every day.
> You **don't need to** be afraid of making mistakes.

C2d **Work in groups. What do you need to do to practise English?**
Write down five sentences using *ought to* and *need to*.
Examples: We ought to speak English all the time during class.
        We need to read the NEXT Reading Club.

D Practising language outside the classroom

D1a **After the forum on the problems of language learning, Asko, John, Maria and Vanessa exchange learning tips. Listen and match the pictures with the names.**

☐ a. Vanessa
☐ b. Asko
☐ c. Maria
☐ d. John

D1b Do you do any of the things they talk about in D1a?
Discuss with your partner and make a list.
Example: Yes, I love going to the cinema to watch
English and American films in English.

D1c Vanessa practises Russian at the gym.
Why? Find out by reading the blog entry she wrote on
www.peacecamp.eu.

> I've always talked to myself, just like most people,
> and I've always used this technique to practise language.
> I'm learning Russian at the moment, so when I go to the
> gym, I practise Russian in my head while I work out on the
> machines. I name things that I see in the studio, I count,
> I practise verb forms, I say things about myself and other
> people that I see there. It's great.
> It makes working out less boring. In fact I almost enjoy
> myself. When I'm alone, I even talk out loud. It's all
> in my head and I can take my head everywhere. I can really
> recommend talking to yourself.

D1d Read the text again and underline all the phrases that contain *myself* and *yourself*.
Example: … <u>talked to myself</u> …

Exploring learning p. 16

TIP 3 Learn words together with other words.

homestudy 15

D1e Work with a partner and complete the sentences with *myself, yourself, herself* and *himself*.

Companion: Grammar 3.18

a. Vanessa often talks to _____ .
b. She really enjoys _____ at the gym.
c. Sometimes I talk to _____ when I'm alone.
d. Do you talk to _____ ?
e. My partner taught _____ Italian.

> **Focus on grammar**
> I almost enjoy **myself.**
> Do you talk to **yourself?**

D2a Now work in groups of four.
When could you talk to yourself in English?
Discuss and make a list.
Example: I often talk to myself in English
when making my shopping list.

> when making a shopping list
> when checking what's in the fridge
> before making a phone call in English

D2b Can you think of other new and enjoyable ways of practising English outside the
classroom? Exchange ideas with the others and decide which idea is the most creative and
which one you would like to try.
Examples: Cooking and having dinner with my American friends is a good idea.
I'd like to try that.
Reading simple stories sounds great. I'll try it.

Exploring learning p. 16

TIP 4 Practise English by talking to yourself, anytime, anywhere.

1

Exploring my progress

… ask what other people enjoy doing and what they are good at.
(Are you good at learning languages?) ☐ ☐ A1a

… talk about what I enjoy doing and what I'm good at.
(I enjoy playing the piano.) ☐ ☐ A1d, H1

… give reasons for and against having a single language in Europe. (I don't
think there should be just one official language in Europe because …) ☐ ☐ B2a, B2b

… say if I agree or disagree with a statement. (I'm sorry, but I disagree.) ☐ ☐ B2b

… say what I find difficult about learning English.
(English is hard to pronounce.) ☐ ☐ C1c, H3

… write down a few simple statements saying what I ought to / need to
practise and what I don't need to worry about.
(I don't need to be afraid of making mistakes.) ☐ ☐ C2d, H4

Online-Übungen ▶ S. 115

Exploring learning – learning strategies

A2b TIP 1 Listen for international words
Almost all languages use international words. If you hear or read something familiar, use it to try and guess about any other information.

B2b TIP 2 Don't be afraid of making mistakes when speaking
The most important thing is to get the meaning across and nobody will care if you've made a few mistakes.

D1d TIP 3 Learn words together with other words
Underline useful phrases in the English texts that you read and try to use these phrases as often as you can.

D2b TIP 4 Practise English by talking to yourself, anytime, anywhere
This is one of the most effective ways to practise a foreign language. You can do it anywhere – while brushing your teeth, cooking dinner, jogging or riding your bike. Inner monologue and movement together are especially effective.

Do you like reading?
Reading helps you to learn and remember more and more words. You should read things that are easy to understand and then look for useful phrases. If you find a phrase you like, try and use it as often as possible.

Learning outside the classroom
It's important to sit down with your course book during the week, but there are many other ways to practise English outside the classroom. You can watch English television channels, or English films, or buy an English newspaper or magazine now and then. You can practise English in your head all day, by talking to yourself. Try out different techniques and use the ones that work best for you.

Right, let's write

What are the latest online trends?

How do you find a partner?

What's your favourite soap?

2

A What's new?

A1a What are the latest Internet trends? Look at the following possible trends.
Work with a partner and decide if the trend is real or not.

a. Older people are joining social networking sites like Facebook.
b. Young people are not using social networking sites so much.
c. The number of people online in the US has increased ten times in the last thirteen years.
d. The number of hours that Internet users spend online is not increasing.
e. More people are using their mobile phones to go online.

A1b Read the article about Internet trends.
With your partner, check your answers from A1a.

The Internet revolution continues

When the first Harris Poll in the US was conducted thirteen years ago, just under eighteen million adults accessed the Internet at work, at home or at the library. Today, there are 184 million Americans who are online. The amount of time spent online is also increasing: in Britain today, the average number of hours spent online in a week is now standing at fourteen this year, compared with nine hours in 2005. People are spending about a third of their free time online.

And what are people doing online these days?
Two to three years ago social networking sites were only really popular with young people, but there has been a big shift recently. Worldwide, twice as many people aged 50 to 64 years are joining online communities like Facebook than young people under eighteen.

Teenagers use sites like Facebook to share pictures and chat with their school friends, but older people are now using Facebook to find old childhood friends or communicate with family members who live far away.

People are also forming online "clubs", for example, groups on Facebook that share a special interest. There are communities of fans, such as soap opera fans. And some radio and television programmes have Facebook sites: it's like joining a club where you get information about the programme and you can share your opinions and stories with other people.

Another important global trend is that more and more people are now using their mobile phones to access the Internet. In the UK about a quarter of the people with mobile phones are using them to go online. On the other hand, it's estimated that seventeen million people in Britain aged over fifteen are still not using the Internet. And this number is not falling as fast as it was before. A large number of people are deciding that they don't want the Internet, it seems.

A2a Match the sentences with their meanings.

1.
> People in the UK **use** their mobile phones to access the Internet.

2.
> More people in the UK **are** now **using** their mobile phones to access the Internet.

a. This is a new trend, something that people in the UK have started to do recently.

b. This is something that people in the UK often do, something that they have done for some time.

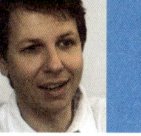

A2b

Complete the following sentences about modern trends with the best form
of the verb in brackets.

a. More and more people today _are using_ (use) the Internet to watch TV.

b. People in Britain today _____ (spend) almost a third of their leisure time online.

c. A lot of older people _____ (join) online communities. They _____ (use) the
Internet to contact old friends.

d. The amount of time that people spend online
_____ (increase).

e. The number of people in the UK who don't
use the Internet _____ (not fall) now as
fast as before.

companion:
Grammar 2.1.2

> **Focus on grammar**
>
> **Talking about trends**
> More and more people **are using**
> their mobile phones to access the Internet.

Homestudy
1

A3a With your partner, write two trends that you can see where you live. Use the topics below.

housing | transport | work | leisure | shopping | computers

Examples: More people are now building houses.
People today are spending more and more time on their computers.

A3b Compare your trends with the rest of the class. Do you agree with the others?

B Surfing for a partner

B1a How would you like to meet a new partner? Here's another paragraph
from the article in A1b.

Other people are using Facebook to look for a
partner. The Internet is becoming the favourite
"place" to meet people. People are reading
Facebook profiles and looking at the photos
to see if they can find someone attractive. In
this way you can find out a lot about somebody
before you meet them in person.

B1b Listen to Judy and Matt talking about how they found their partners.
Who used "chemistry" and who used "mathematics"?
Which do you prefer and why?
Compare your ideas with the rest of the class.

nineteen 19

Homestudy
H2

B2a

On most dating websites you have to write a personal profile.
The following sentences come from profiles.
Tick what you think the highlighted words mean in these sentences.

1. "I work a lot, but I know how to **balance** well."

☐ a. My hobby is gymnastics and I can balance on one foot very well.

☐ b. I can share my time and energy between work and leisure (hobbies, sport, socializing, etc.)

2. "Knows how to **treat** a lady."

☐ a. He pays for a lady.

☐ b. He knows how to behave with a lady: how to talk to her, make arrangements with her, etc.

3. "What are your greatest **pet hates**?"

☐ a. What animals do you hate most?

☐ b. What special things do you hate? What gets on your nerves?

Exploring learning p. 24 **TIP 1** Look at words in their context.

B2b

Now read the three personal profiles from an American Internet dating site.
Check the words from B2a. Which person has written the best profile: the profile
that makes you want to meet the person? Discuss in pairs.

PROFILE 1

I've been in this area for a few years now and I'm always looking to meet new people. I'm a very hard worker and love my job. I work a lot, but I know how to balance well. I enjoy meeting new people and going to new places. I'm very spontaneous and I love the outdoors, watching movies, dancing, and travelling. A great date can be staying at home with a movie and popcorn, or a night on the town. Every year I try to visit somewhere new on vacation. Asia is now top of the list of the places that I'd like to see next.
Well, that's a little about me. If you're interested, say hello and we'll chat. Talk to you soon!!

PROFILE 2

100% Italian-American, fun-loving, affectionate young lady who knows what it takes to make a relationship work. Tired of meeting BOYS who tell me what I want to hear, make and break promises, and aren't ready for something serious.
You: Honest, mature gentleman. Emotionally, mentally, financially secure. Knows how to treat a lady, ready for a long-term relationship. Please ... mean what you say and say what you mean. I'm looking to meet someone in this area and see what happens ☺

PROFILE 3

I don't like most guys, but ... I'm not interested in most guys and perhaps that's why those few unique individuals that I do like are really special. Me – restless, analytical, lots of opinions about everything. I'm not shocked by a dirty joke. I'm independent but not a feminist. Sarcasm is a spice of life, so bring it on. Books and movies that make you think for days about what's right and what's wrong put great flavour into many of my evenings.
What's your story? What are your greatest pet hates and what makes you weak at the knees from happiness?

Homestudy
H3

B2c

We showed these three profiles to Randy Goldbloom, an expert on Internet dating.
Listen to what he had to say and take notes. Do you agree with him?

Profile 1 – *5 out of 10, not much fun to read ...*

Profile 2 –

Profile 3 –

B3a In pairs, write a personal profile for an Internet dating site. Use the following guidelines.

- Write about one of you or imagine a person (man or woman).
- Write an interesting first sentence.
- Write something about "yourself".

- Write something about what sort of person "you" are looking for.
- Write an interesting last sentence (for example about what should happen next).
- Give your profile a name.

Exploring learning p. 24

TIP 2 Make a plan before you write.

B3b Exchange your profile with another pair. Read the other pair's profile and write some comments. Then give it back with your comments.

- What do you like about the profile?
- Can you understand everything?
- Do you think other people will want to meet this person?

- Does the profile have interesting first and last sentences?
- Is there any other information that you would like to read?

Exploring learning p. 24

TIP 3 Check your writing.

B3c When you get your profile back, you can change it, if you like.

C What's your favourite soap?

C1a The word "soap" has two meanings in English. Which meaning is right for the text on the right? Tick.

☐ a. (a bar of) soap: something that you use to wash yourself

☐ b. a soap (opera): a television drama series about a group of people

C1b What soap operas do you have on TV where you live? Are they popular?

C2a For and against. Divide into two groups.

Group 1: You think that soap operas are good television. Look at some reasons why people like soap operas on page 97.

Group 2: You think that soap operas are bad television. Look at some reasons why people hate soap operas on page 98.

Prepare to talk about soap operas with the other group. Each person in your group should have one argument. Use the ideas from the back of the book or find your own ideas.

omestudy 4

C2b Now present your arguments for and against. Each group member presents one argument. Use the phrases in the *Remember* box.

What's Britain's favourite soap?

The oldest soap opera in Britain is *Coronation Street* – the story of the people who live in that street in Manchester. It started in 1960, and there are now five shows of thirty minutes each every week. The other most popular soap in the UK is *EastEnders* which is about the people who live near a square in the East End of London. There are four half-hourly episodes a week.

Soap operas are extremely popular. If you watch a soap, you have to watch every week because the stories never really end and there's always a "cliffhanger" at the end – something exciting or a question that needs to be answered and you have to watch the next show to see what happens next.

CORONATION STREET

Remember

I think that … because …
I don't think … because …
I agree …
I disagree …
I'm sorry, but I disagree …

2

D   Write your own soap opera

D1a   The following ad appeared on a website for soap opera fans.
Take part in this interactive experiment. Discuss the question and make
your choices with the class. Write the names under the photos.

A WEBSITE FOR SOAP OPERA FANS

Help to create a new interactive soap

Hello, all you soap fans out there! We're a new TV production company and we're developing
a new soap, but we need your help. You decide what happens. Every week you can help us
write the next episode.

Our soap opera is called *Hope Hospital* and it takes place,
of course, in a hospital. Here are the characters and
photos of some actors. Who do you want to play which role?
Send your suggestions to www.hopehospital.eu.

List of characters
Amanda Price (40),
            head doctor
Stuart Winton (45),
            doctor
John Skorsky (36),
            head nurse
Dawn Simpson (20),
            trainee nurse
Felicity Granger (35),
            hospital manager

_____ _____ _____ _____ _____

D1b   *Hope Hospital* fans get emails regularly. Here's another message.
Choose your answers with the class.

Hi, all you *Hope Hospital* fans! We loved all your ideas for the characters.
Now we need some ideas for the first episodes. Give us your ideas by filling in the gaps below.

The story so far at *Hope Hospital*

Stuart hates _____ because she got the job as head doctor and he didn't.

Dawn's having a secret love affair with _____.

John's in love with _____ but she doesn't know.

_____ has a secret problem. She left her husband and little daughter more than ten
years ago when she got her job at Hope Hospital. Her ex-husband and daughter, Jenny, live in
another city. Her job as the head doctor in the hospital has always taken a lot of her time, so
the ex-husband brought up the little girl and _____ never sees her.

D1c And here's another update from *Hope Hospital*. Discuss it with the class and fill in the gaps.

Hi *Hope* fans everywhere!
Glad you're enjoying the story so far. Next week, we've got a new episode.
A new patient arrives in the hospital. Who is she? Give us your ideas!

The new episode
Jenny, the little girl who is now 18, arrives at the hospital. She has a serious problem with her heart and only Amanda can help her.

How does the story go on?
One day Jenny, the new patient, arrives in the hospital. _____ comes into the room where the patient is lying. She sees the girl and is very shocked to see who it is. The girl is asleep and doesn't see her.

_____ tries to avoid the new patient for several days, but in the end she has to go and see her. The girl knows immediately who she is and gets really furious. They have an argument and shout at each other. They think they are alone, but _____ is listening behind the curtain.

Companion:
Grammar 2.1.3

Focus on grammar

Amanda **comes** into the room where the patient **is lying** on the bed.
They **think** they are alone, but Stuart **is listening** behind the curtain.

Homestudy
15

D2 Read the most recent email from *Hope Hospital*.
With a partner, write the rest of the story on a piece of paper.

It's up to you to invent the rest of the story. The questions might help you.

• How does Jenny feel about her mother leaving the family for a career?
• Who's going to operate on Jenny and save her life?
• Will the other people in the hospital find out that Jenny is Amanda's daughter?
• Will Amanda give up her job and look after her sick daughter?
• Will Jenny ever forgive her mother?

Exploring learning p. 24

TIP 4 Writing can help you learn.

Focus on grammar

The girl **knows** who she is and **gets** furious.
After Amanda **sees** her sick daughter,
she **gives up** her job to take care of her.

Companion:
Grammar 2.1.1

D3a Exchange your story with another pair.
Read the other pair's story.
Can you understand it? Is it clear?
Do you need any more information?
Give the story back and tell the other pair what you think.

D3b Make the last changes to your story.

Homestudy
16

D3c Either each pair reads their story to the rest of the class or you stick all the stories on the wall and everybody reads them. Which story does the class like best?

Exploring my progress

At the end of this unit I can ...

... describe simple trends.
(More people are accessing the Internet. The number is increasing.)   ☐   ☐   A2b, H1

... work out new meanings of words from their context.   ☐   ☐   B2a, C1a, H2

... write a personal profile (for an Internet dating site) with the help of a plan.   ☐   ☐   B3a–c

... read a short text to get the general meaning.   ☐   ☐   C1a, H3

... give an opinion in a discussion, for example about soap operas.
(I think that soap operas are good television because people enjoy them.)   ☐   ☐   C2b, H4

... write a story with the help of guiding questions.   ☐   ☐   D2

Online-Übungen ▶ S. 117

Exploring learning – reading and writing

B2a TIP 1   Look at words in their context

In all the examples in this activity the words have at least two meanings. So we have to guess what the writer wanted to say. In these personal profiles, it's the second answer each time that is the better meaning. It makes more sense in the context. Sometimes you know one meaning of a word but not two. Always look at the context and be prepared for a word to have a new meaning!

B3a TIP 2   Make a plan before you write

Before you write something such as this or a letter, it's good to have a plan. It makes it easier because you can write one or more sentences for each point on your plan. Think about your readers: what do your readers need to know and what should they feel?

B3b TIP 3   Check your writing

It's always good to check your writing. Firstly, make sure that your message is clear. It's important that your text is clear and good to read. It's good to have questions like the ones here to help you check. It's very good to ask someone else to read your text because it's difficult to check something that you've written yourself. They can tell you if it's clear and interesting.

D2 TIP 4   Writing can help you learn

When you're writing you have more time to think about what you want to say than when you're talking. So it's a good way to practise your English. Don't try to translate everything – that's very difficult. Use the words that you already know as much as possible. You can say a lot with simple words. And if you're writing a story like here, you can keep it very simple!

Why writing is good for you

A lot of people need to write things in English these days: emails, text messages, filling in forms online, etc., but a lot of people also don't like writing. They think that writing is very difficult. Remember that models can help you. Also remember that your writing doesn't always have to be perfect in real life: it just has to be clear. And if you can write simple, clear English, that's great!

Companion →   You can find more tips about writing in the section
Your link to the Portfolio – Mehr zu Unit 2.

Learning outside the classroom

When you write, you can take your time: think about what you want to say and check what you write. In this way, it's a very useful way to consolidate your learning. So it's a good idea to write a little bit every week: a blog or diary, emails, little stories or anything you like. If you would like somebody to read it and check if it's clear, give it to somebody in your class, to another person that you know who speaks English, or to your teacher.

Changing places

Why do people travel?

How do I get to City Hall from here?

Does this sound impolite or polite to you?

3

A   Why travel?

A1a   What does travel mean to you? Work with a partner and add your ideas to the word wheel.

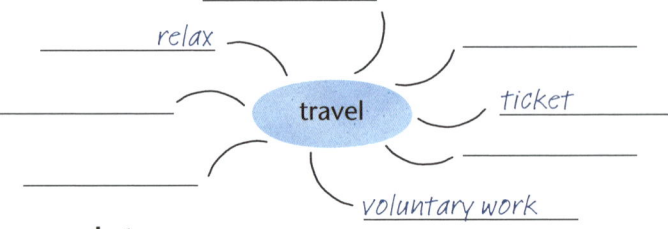

relax — travel — ticket — voluntary work

Homestudy H1

A1b   People travel for different reasons, for example to go to university in a different country. Fill in the gaps. Sometimes there are several possibilities.

do | find | meet (2x) | get away from | go to | go on (2x) | visit | see | speak | take

a. _____ university
b. _____ a business trip
c. _____ different languages
d. _____ the daily routine
e. _____ interesting people
f. _____ interesting places

g. _____ holiday
h. _____ a job
i. _____ time off
j. _____ something different
k. _____ family and friends
l. _____ business partners

A1c   Tell a partner why you travel.
Use phrases from A1b or make up your own reasons.
Examples: I travel because I want to get away from my daily routine.
         I like to see interesting places.

1 · 7

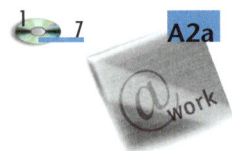

A2a   Suzanne is doing research for an international travel agency. She wants to find out why people travel and how much they travel. Today she's interviewing five people. Listen. Work in pairs and write down their reasons for travelling.

Irene _____

Murat travels to work at a holiday hotel in Turkey.

David _____

Sylvia _____

Pierre _____

1 · 8

A2b   Listen again to what Murat told Suzanne in A2a and fill in the gaps.

Companion:
Grammar 2.6.2, 2.7.6

I'm _____ do a hotel management course here in Germany and one day I _____ have my own little hotel in Turkey.

Focus on grammar

He**'s going to** do a hotel management course.
One day he **may** have his own little hotel.

A2c Listen to the interviews in A2a again. Listen for the phrases in the box below. Are they things that the people *are going to* do or things they *may* do in the future?

> have his own little hotel ▌ meet the team in Istanbul ▌ do a hotel management course
> work on an aid project in India ▌ hike part of the trail from the North Sea to the Baltic
> go to China ▌ stop working as a flight attendant ▌ relax next week

A2d Work in pairs. Test your memory. One of you chooses something from A2c. The other person has to remember the name.

Example: A: One day he may have his own little hotel.
B: That's Murat.

A2e After the interviews Suzanne reports to her supervisor.
Work with a partner and fill in the right form of the verbs.

Supervisor: So, how was the interview, Suzanne?

Suzanne: Fine. There were five people there, two ladies and three men.

Supervisor: OK. Anything interesting?

Suzanne: Well, the usual, I guess. One of the ladies (1) _mentioned_ (mention) that she often (2) _goes_ (go) on business trips. And the other lady (3) _____ (explain) that she (4) _____ (be) going to work on an aid project in India.

Supervisor: Right. And the men?

Suzanne: Well, there was one from North London who (5) _____ (mention) that he and his wife (6) _____ (go) hiking every year. Then there was a flight attendant from France. He (7) _____ (explain) that he (8) _____ (enjoy) travelling which (9) _____ (be) good since it (10) _____ (be) his job.
And the third one, a young man from Turkey, (11) _____ (say) that he (12) _____ (go) to southern Turkey every summer. He (13) _____ (explain) that he (14) _____ (work) there in a big holiday hotel.

Companion:
Grammar 1.7.1

> **Focus on grammar**
>
> Sylvia answer**ed** that she **is** going to work on an aid project in India.
> David **said** that they **go** hiking every year.

A3 Listen to the expressions from A1b. When people speak they stress some words or parts of words. Work with a partner and underline the parts in A1b that are stressed. Then practise saying each phrase out loud. Try to sound like the speakers.

Exploring learning p. 32   **TIP 1** Practise saying whole phrases more naturally.

A4a Work in groups and make a questionnaire with eight to ten questions about why people travel. Use the questions Suzanne asked in A2a and add others.

3

	A4b Now interview some people in your class.
Homestudy H2	**A4c** Report something interesting to the class. Example: Susie said she's going to find a job in Ireland.

B   Making plans

B1a Work in groups. Choose a country that you'd like to travel to with your group, for example Uzbekistan, South Africa, Iceland, Argentina.

B1b Make a list of things you need to remember to do before you go on your trip. Look at the ideas in the box. Find at least three more things.

> buy medicine/books **|** book a flight/train
> change money **|** look up travel information
> rent a car **|** get a visa **|** pack clothes
> learn more English **|** get a vaccination

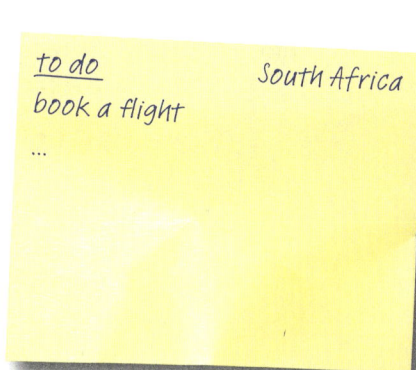

to do
book a flight
...   South Africa

B1c Tell the class where your group is going to and give a couple of examples of what you need to do before you go.
Example: We're going to Uzbekistan and we think we need to get some vaccinations.
We also need to find a driver and a guide to show us the country.

 1 ▬ 10

B2a Sylvia, David and Pierre were all delayed when they were travelling recently. Listen to the announcements and fill in the reasons for the delays. Check with a partner.

a. owing to _____   b. due to _____   c. owing to _____

B2b Sylvia, David and Pierre sent text messages about the delays. Work with a partner and write the complete messages on a piece of paper using less formal language.

a.
> Hi. Flight
> delayed
> _____.
> Will let you know
> when we board.
> Sylvia

b.
> Hi there.
> Train delayed
> _____. Go
> ahead and eat.
> David

c.
> Hi Maria.
> M 25 closed
> _____.
> Will stay in L
> tonight. Pierre

Companion:
Grammar 5.6

> **Focus on grammar**
> This flight will be delayed **owing to/due to** bad weather.
> The plane is late **because of** a snowstorm.
> owing to / due to (formal) = because of (less formal)

B2c With a partner, read the following news items.
Then complete the dialogues using less formal language.

> Due to the rising cost of petrol, many employees are forming car pools instead of driving alone.

> Due to the recession, more people are spending their holidays at home and buying books.

> Sales in July were up. Owing to the very rainy July, many people went shopping instead of going to the beach. Shopkeepers are optimistic.

(Speech bubble) What are your plans for the summer?

(Speech bubble) We're staying at home this year because of our budget, but I'm going to buy the new Dan Brown book to read in the garden.

(Speech bubble) Did you go to the beach every day?

(Speech bubble) No, ...

_____

_____

_____

(Speech bubble) Do you still take the car to go to work?

(Speech bubble) _____

_____

_____

B3 Did you do your English homework this week? Did you have a look at the Reading Club? Did you arrive on time to class? With a partner, write a text message to your teacher to explain why you didn't do one of these things.
Example: No time to read the text because of my business trip to Vienna.

C Helping somebody find the way

C1 Look at the pictures. What do you use when you want to find the way. What is the most popular in your class?

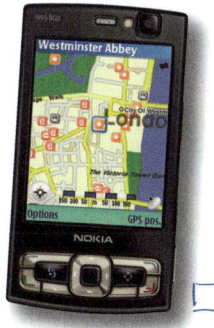

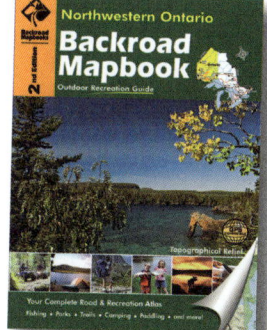

C2 Sort the following sentences into directions for somebody on foot (F), for somebody in a car (C), or both (FC).

a. Carry on till you see a small café.   F / C / <u>FC</u>
b. Drive on to the next traffic lights.   F / C / FC
c. Walk three blocks.   F / C / FC
d. Go straight on at the roundabout.   F / C / FC
e. Turn left.   F / C / FC

f. Take the second exit.   F / C / FC
g. Turn right at the big church.   F / C / FC
h. Follow the signs to Reutlingen.   F / C / FC
i. Walk through the market.   F / C / FC

3

C3a **Listen to three people asking for directions.**
Which phrases from C2 do you hear?

Donna (driving in Britain): _b_____

David (walking in a US city): _c_____

Lizzie (driving in Germany): _h_____

C3b **Listen again.**
How do Donna, David and Lizzie ask for help?

Donna: _Excuse me, ..._____

David: _____

Lizzie: _____

Homestudy
H4

C4 **Work with a partner and add more words**
or phrases that people
use when asking for or
giving directions.
The pair with the most
words and phrases
wins.

D	_drive,_____
I	_____
R	_____
E	_excuse me,_____
C	_corner,_____
T	_____
I	_I'm lost,_____
O	_on the right,_____
N	_____
S	_____

C5a **Work with a partner.**
Write directions from your
school to another place –
by car or on foot.

Companion:
Grammar 5.6

Focus on grammar
by car   **on** foot

C5b **Read out your directions and let the others guess**
where you're going. Which pair has the best directions?

D   Complaining

D1a **Listen to the complaints. Where do they take place?**
Which one in each pair sounds more polite? Tick.

		a.	b.			a.	b.
1.	_hotel_____	☐	☒	4.	_____	☐	☐
2.	_____	☐	☐	5.	_____	☐	☐
3.	_____	☐	☐				

D1b Now underline the words the speakers in D1a use to make the complaints sound more polite.

1. a. This room's a mess.
      It needs to be cleaned now.

   b. This room's not very tidy. Could you please send someone to clean it?

2. a. I'm sorry, but the shower in my room doesn't work. Are there any other rooms available?

   b. The shower doesn't work. I want another room.

3. a. The air conditioning in the conference room is far too noisy. Can't you switch it off?

   b. The air conditioning in the conference room is a bit loud. Would you mind switching it off?

4. a. Excuse me, I ordered a veggie burrito, not a beef burrito.

   b. You've got my order wrong. I want a veggie burrito.

5. a. My soup is cold. Bring me another one.

   b. I'm afraid this soup is cold.

> **Focus on spoken English**
>
> Excuse me, … / I'm afraid … / I'm sorry, but …
> Would/could you … ?
> Would you mind (switch)**ing** (it off)?

| Exploring learning p. 32 | **TIP 2** It's not just words. |

D2a The following letter was written by a British family after a holiday in Greece. Underline three things that the writer complains about.

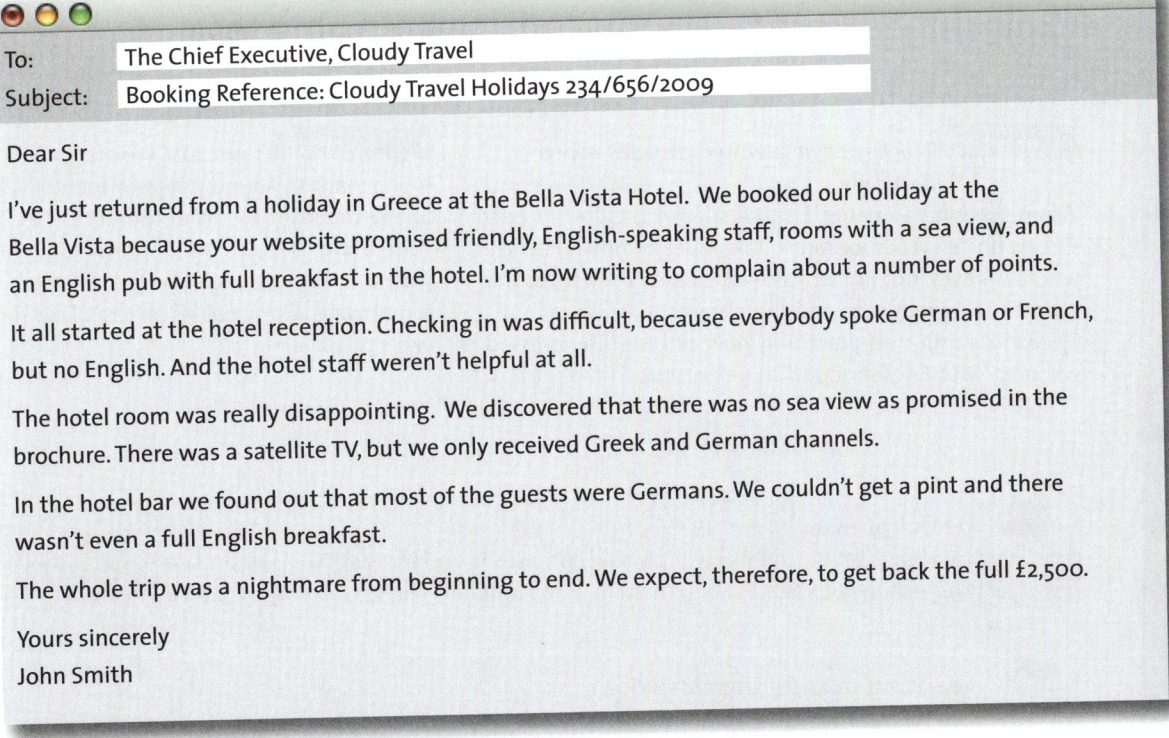

To: The Chief Executive, Cloudy Travel

Subject: Booking Reference: Cloudy Travel Holidays 234/656/2009

Dear Sir

I've just returned from a holiday in Greece at the Bella Vista Hotel. We booked our holiday at the Bella Vista because your website promised friendly, English-speaking staff, rooms with a sea view, and an English pub with full breakfast in the hotel. I'm now writing to complain about a number of points.

It all started at the hotel reception. Checking in was difficult, because everybody spoke German or French, but no English. And the hotel staff weren't helpful at all.

The hotel room was really disappointing. We discovered that there was no sea view as promised in the brochure. There was a satellite TV, but we only received Greek and German channels.

In the hotel bar we found out that most of the guests were Germans. We couldn't get a pint and there wasn't even a full English breakfast.

The whole trip was a nightmare from beginning to end. We expect, therefore, to get back the full £2,500.

Yours sincerely

John Smith

Homestudy
H5

D2b Imagine you're on holiday and have problems in your hotel.
With a partner, make a list of possible problems. What would you say to the hotel manager?
Example: Excuse me, but there's no coffee maker in my room.
        Could you please bring one to my room?

Exploring my progress

At the end of this unit I can …			
… give reasons why I travel. (I like to see interesting places.)	☐	☐	A1, A2a, H1
… talk about plans and possibilities. (I'm going to work in India. I may then go to China.)	☐	☐	A2, H2
… ask other people why they travel. (Why do you travel?)	☐	☐	A4b
… report why other people travel. (Susie said she's going to find a job in Ireland.)	☐	☐	A4c
… plan a trip with other people. (We need to book a flight.)	☐	☐	B1b
… write a short text message when delayed.	☐	☐	B2b, H3
… give directions. (Drive on to the next roundabout.)	☐	☐	C5, H4
… hear the difference between a rude complaint and a polite complaint.	☐	☐	D1a
… complain about poor service, food and accommodation. (Excuse me, could you send someone to clean the room?)	☐	☐	D2b, H5

Online-Übungen ▶ S. 118

Exploring learning – dealing with whole phrases

A3 TIP 1 Practise saying whole phrases more naturally

When listening to native English speakers, either in person or on television or radio, take note of how they say whole phrases, not just words. Notice how they stress the phrases and practise saying the phrases that way.
Thinking about and practising how phrases are stressed will help your English sound more natural.

D1b TIP 2 It's not just words

If you want to sound polite or friendly, etc. it's important to say the right words in the right way. The way you say something is often as important as what you say. So practise saying things like the complaints in D1b in different ways. Copy voices on the CD as models of different ways of speaking.

 Useful phrases

Start making a list of useful travel phrases, phrases for asking directions and phrases for complaining politely. Practise them in your head saying them in many different ways. That way, when you need them they'll be there to use.

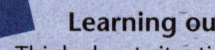 **Learning outside the classroom**

Think about situations that might come up when travelling and that might be important for you, for example asking for details at the rental car desk. Could you manage, or is there something that you need to practise more? Use the dictionary to prepare yourself.

The next time you are planning a holiday or business trip, you can choose and book your hotel online. There are many websites, for example www.tripadvisor.com, where you can search for hotels in destinations all over the world, and read descriptions and even customer reviews of them.

C1 You and your partner want to meet people and practise your English.
Think of all the different ways you can do this. Compare your ideas with another pair.
Example: We can go to see an English film.

C2a You are thinking about joining an English club to practise your English.
Look at these advertisements for English clubs. Match the name to the club.

☐ a. Cosi fan tutte
☐ b. English Discussion Club
☐ c. Walk and Talk Your Way in English

We meet once a week and talk about different important questions.
Members can decide what topics they want. Some of our next topics are:
There should be only one official language in Europe. • You can't make real friends on the Internet. • The best way to travel is on foot.
The discussions are in easy English for Germans and speakers of other languages.
Come and meet us next Tuesday!
①

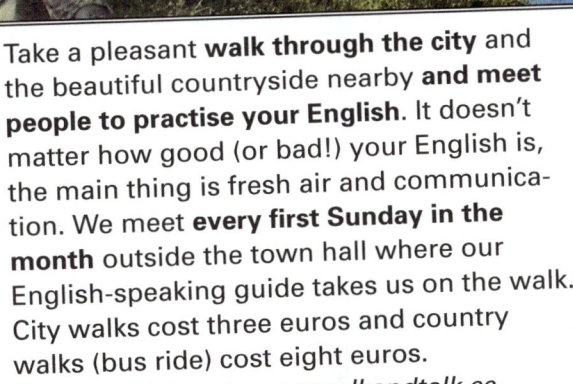

②

Take a pleasant **walk through the city** and the beautiful countryside nearby **and meet people to practise your English**. It doesn't matter how good (or bad!) your English is, the main thing is fresh air and communication. We meet **every first Sunday in the month** outside the town hall where our English-speaking guide takes us on the walk. City walks cost three euros and country walks (bus ride) cost eight euros.
Please register at www.walkandtalk.cc.

③

Opera fans of all nationalities are invited to join us for a visit to the opera and a discussion in English afterwards at the opera house. We decide together which opera to see and when. Not all the operas are in English but all the discussions always are!
English native speakers are also welcome.
Call 0211 38 71 39 for details of membership and prices.

C2b Decide which club you would like best and why. Tell your partner.

C2c What would you like to know about the clubs? Work in pairs and write five to ten questions.

 16 **C2d** Listen to a member of one of the clubs. Which club is she talking about?
What are the good and bad things about the club? Would you like it?
Example: I would like to join this club because I like operas.

C3a You decide to start your own English speaking club. Work in small groups. Talk about your ideas for the club. Think about your questions in C2c.

Discuss …
… who the members should be.
… what you want to do.
… how often to meet.
… what level of English members must have.
… how many members you want.
… how much money you need.
… if you want food and drink.
… where the meetings can take place.
…

> We must / should / ought to / need to …
>
> … collect money.
>
> … make an advert.
>
> … talk to the newspaper.
>
> … book a room.
>
> … design a website.
>
> … write emails.
>
> …

C3b Make a list of things to do.

C3c Decide in your group who can do what.
Examples: I'm good at working with numbers
so I can look after the money.
Hans is good at painting so he can design a poster.
Jenny is good at presentations so she can talk to the newspaper.

 17

C4a You need a good name for your club. Listen to these people talking about a name for an English club. What names do they talk about? What do you think are the advantages and disadvantages of these names?

name	advantages	disadvantages
The English Club		

C4b Decide on a name for your club.

C5a Here are three ways of advertising your club.
Decide which is the best for your club and say why.

> email invitation **|** poster **|** newspaper advertisement

Example: I think an email invitation is best because it
doesn't cost anything and it's fast.

C5b Write the text and design the invitation, poster or advertisement in your group. Present your club to the class.

C6 In pairs, interview someone else about their club. Decide which club you want to join.

I'm fed up with my job

What's your job like?

What sort of person are you?

What would you like to learn?

4

A Are you happy in your job?

Homestudy H1

A1a Here are some adjectives to describe jobs. In pairs, group them into adjectives to describe a good job, a bad job, and adjectives that could be good or bad.

> tiring **|** stressful **|** stimulating **|** dangerous **|** quiet **|** well-paid
> noisy **|** comfortable **|** exciting **|** boring **|** dirty **|** badly paid

good job	good or bad job	bad job
_____	_____	_____
_____	_____	_____
_____	_____	_____
_____	_____	_____
_____	_____	_____

A1b Choose one of the words in A1a and find another word that belongs to the same word family. Use your dictionary if you need help.
Examples: tiring – tired
exciting – excitement

A1c Compare with the rest of the class. Do you know what all the words mean?

Exploring learning p. 42 **TIP 1** Word families

Homestudy H2

A2 What's the difference between a secure job and a safe job?
With your partner, look at the sentences below and make a guess.

secure/security
A lot of people are losing their jobs at the moment so you're lucky if you have a **secure** job.
The **Security** Officer makes sure people don't steal things from the company, or that people outside don't get private information about the company.

safe/safety
This machine is very old.
It's not **safe**.
It's too dangerous to use it.
The Health and **Safety** regulations are there to make sure that people are healthy at work and that they don't have accidents.

Exploring learning p. 42 **TIP 2** One word in German, two words in English

Homestudy H3

A3 Here are some more words to describe a job.
Underline the part of the word that you stress when you say the word.
Use your dictionary to help you and to check the meanings if you're not sure.

a. <u>in</u>teresting   c. challenging   e. monotonous
b. rewarding   d. varied   f. exhausting

Exploring learning p. 42 **TIP 3** A good dictionary can help you in lots of ways.

1 ● 18

A4a Listen to Nigel and Becky talking about their jobs. Which job would you prefer?

1 ● 18

A4b Listen again in pairs. What adjectives do Nigel and Becky use to describe their jobs? Make a list and compare.
Examples: *Nigel:* badly paid
Becky: stressful

A5a Choose the best adjectives to describe your dream job and your nightmare job. Put them on word wheels as below.

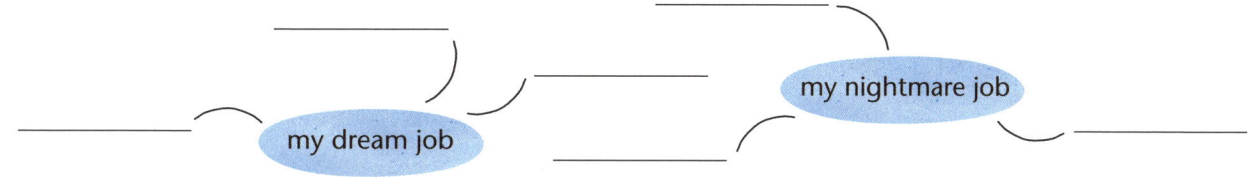

my nightmare job

my dream job

omestudy 4

A5b Compare your word wheels with other people in the class.

B Tina is fed up with her job

1 ● 19

B1 Tina is a young German woman who lives in Britain and works for Conducta, an engineering company. Listen to her talking to a workmate in the factory canteen one day. What's her problem?

> **Focus on spoken English**
> I'm fed up. I'm bored.
> Life's boring. I can't stand my job.

omestudy 5

B2 Tina decides to write to the HR department to ask about training possibilities. Fill in the gaps in her email with the phrases below.

> enjoy working for **|** I've worked in the production department
> if you need more information **|** look forward to hearing
> more challenging **|** you let me know about

To: Mr Patten

Subject: Training courses

Dear Mr Patten,

My name is Tina Neuhaus and _____ (1) of Conducta for four and a half years. I came to Britain from Germany in 2003 and I want to stay in this country.

I _____ (2) Conducta but I think I could do a _____ (3) job.

Could _____ (4) any training courses that I could do?
I can send you my CV _____ (5) about my education and experience.

I _____ (6) from you.

Best wishes,

Tina Neuhaus

37

4

B3a Two weeks later Tina has an interview with Ed Patten from HR.
What questions do you think he asks? Can you unjumble the following?

a. How / you / for the company / have / long / worked / ?
b. How / you / long / here / lived / have / ?
c. What / in Germany / did / education / have / you / ?
d. What / like / would / sort of / to do / thing / you / ?
e. Why / you / come / to Britain / did / ?
f. Why / your job / to change / want / you / do / ?

B3b Listen to the interview. In what order does Ed ask his questions?

B3c Listen again. What answers does Tina give?

B4a With a partner, look at the example sentences. Then put the other phrases in one of the columns.

I've lived here since 2003.
I've worked here since last Monday.
I've lived here for three years.
I've worked here for six months.

since	for
2003	three years
last Monday	six months

1998	two days	June
10 minutes	a long time
6 o'clock	seven years
four weeks	my birthday

Companion:
Grammar 2.3.1, 5.4.2

Focus on grammar

I've lived here **since** 2003.
I've worked here **for** six months.

B4b Match the items below.
Check your answers with the rest of the class.

1. for   a. the beginning of a period of time
2. since   b. a period of time

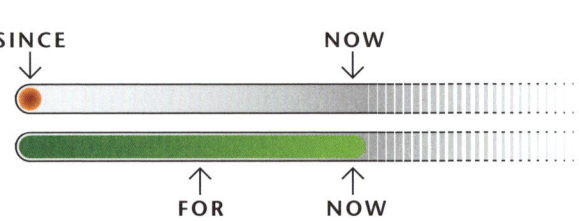

Exploring learning p. 42   **TIP 4** Rules or examples?

Homestudy
H6

B4c Think about your life and write down some dates and times using *for* and *since*. Here are some ideas.

How long have you lived in your house / flat / town, etc.?   *Since 1999. / For 10 years.*
How long have you been married / been with your partner, etc.?   _____
How long have you been on this course?   _____
How long have you worked in your job?   _____
How long have you been in your college / school, etc.?   _____
How long have you not smoked?   _____
…   _____

B4d Work in pairs.

Student A says a date or time: Since 1984.
Student B guesses: You've been married since 1984.
Student A answers: Yes, that's right. I've been married since 1984.
    No, that's not right. I haven't smoked a cigarette since 1984.

C   How do you describe yourself?

C1a   Work with a partner. Match the words with the phrases.

1. ambitious	a. I don't get too excited or too worried about things.
2. calm	b. I feel sure that I can do this.
3. confident	c. I have lots of new ideas about how to do things.
4. creative	d. I like to talk with other people.
5. dependable	e. I want to be a top manager one day.
6. hard-working	f. I'm good at understanding what other people feel.
7. outgoing	g. I'm never late.
8. punctual	h. I'm not lazy: I'm strong and I do a good job.
9. sensitive	i. If I say that I will do something, I do it.

C1b   Compare your answers with another pair and underline the part of the word (1–9) that you stress. If you're not sure of some words, check them in a dictionary.

C1c   Test your partner. Read the example and your partner has to say the word.

Student A: I don't get too excited or too worried about things.
Student B: Calm.

C2a   In pairs, use the phrases below to complete Ed's message to Tina after the interview.

apply for
are interested
attaching
coming to see
let me know

C2b   Tina found question 6 on the application form difficult to answer. Can you think of a tip that might help her? Discuss with a partner.

To: Tina Neuhaus
Subject: Re: Training courses

Dear Tina,

Thanks for _____ (1) me and I'm pleased that you _____ (2) in a career with Conducta.
I'm _____ (3) an application form for a team leader training course that you could _____ (4).

If you have any questions, please _____ (5).

Best wishes,
Ed

5. How long have you worked for Conducta?   _____
6. How would you describe yourself?   (1) _____
   Choose three things that tell us what sort   (2) _____
   of person you are?   (3) _____
7. How would you describe your relationship   _____
   with your colleagues?

Tina decided to ask Ed for help and got the following reply.

...
The training organization wants to know if you are the right sort of person to become a team leader. Think about what you need to do as a team leader. Here's a tip for you: ask family or friends to give you some ideas. They know you very well!
Best wishes,
Ed

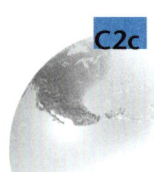

4

C2c Tina texted her partner, Liam, to ask him.

hi liam.
what sort of
person am i?
give me 3
things for the
application.
xxx tina

Tina finishes her message with *XXX*.
An *X* in English means a kiss.
How do people in your area end a
message to their partner?

 21

C2d Liam left a voicemail message for her.
Listen and fill in what Liam says.

a. _____ : good with people,
made lots of friends
b. _____ : learnt English
very fast
c. _____ : worked all day
and went to class in the evening
d. good at _____ : organized lots of
activities at school

C2e Which three things do you think Tina should write on her application form?

Companion:
Grammar 5.2.2

C3a Write three things about your neighbour in the class on
a piece of paper and send it to him.
Example: You're punctual. You're never late for our English class.

C3b Read the message from your neighbour.
Do you agree with the description?
What adjectives would you choose for yourself?

> **Focus on grammar**
>
> **Irregular adverbs**
> You learnt English **fast**.
> You worked **hard**.

D | Why do you want to do this course?

D1a Tina goes for an interview for the training course to become a team leader.
The interviewer is Sharon Walford. You're going to hear part of the interview.
What questions do you think Sharon will ask?

> Why …? | What sort of …? | How …? | Do you …?

 22

D1b Listen and check the questions.

22

D1c Listen again and with a partner complete the
word wheels with Tina's answers.

Homestudy
H9

(I like)

(I'm)

Companion:
Grammar 2.7.4

(I'd like)

> **Remember**
>
> **I'd like to** go on the course.
> **I like** people and **I like to**
> learn new stuff.

D2a Tina wants to learn something new. Read about the following competition. Choose what <u>you</u>'d like to learn.

Win a two-week working holiday in Britain.

The British Education Service is offering a limited number of free working holidays in Britain this summer for people from other countries. Come to Britain and learn something new while you work. **Choose from the following subjects:**

Gardening: work with British gardening experts and learn new skills | **Holiday camps for disabled children:** help organize activities for children with learning difficulties **Cooking:** work in the kitchen of a famous British TV chef | **Television:** work in the studio of a famous British soap opera and learn how the programme is made

Do you want a challenge? We're looking for people who'd like to learn about something new in a new place and in a new language. Write to us. Tell us where you'd like to work and why you think you're the best person for this holiday offer.

Grace Perkins
British Education Service
PO Box 8553
York YO6 7CF
grace.perkins@bec.org

D2b With a partner, write a short letter or email to Ms Perkins in answer to the advert. Include the following points.

a. Explain where you saw the advert.
b. Say which holiday you're interested in.
c. Explain why. (What sort of person are you? Why are you interested in this holiday?)
d. Finish the letter / email with what you hope.

D3 Form groups of three. Two of you work for the British Education Service. You interview the third person about the holiday offer. Then change roles. Read the letter that the person wrote and use some of the following questions for the interviews.

Where do you come from? **|** Where did you go to school? **|** Where do you work?
What sort of person are you? **|** How would you like to describe yourself?
Why are you interested in this working holiday? **|** Do you have any questions?

D4 Choose a winner from your group (the person with the best reasons for going to Britain). All the winners can be interviewed again in front of the class. Choose a class winner.

mestudy
0

Exploring my progress

At the end of this unit I can …

... describe a good job and a bad job with simple adjectives.
(A good job is well-paid.) □ □ A5a, H1

... write a short letter or email to ask for information or help. □ □ B2, H5

... describe my recent life using *since* and *for*.
(I have lived in my flat for three years.) □ □ B4c, H6

... describe a person's character.
(You're hard-working. You're good at organizing things.) □ □ C3a, H7

... take part in an interview where I have to talk about myself and explain
why I want to go on a course, for example. □ □ D3

Online-Übungen ▶ S. 120

Exploring learning – vocabulary

A1c TIP 1 Word families

When you know a word it's easy to learn other words in the same "word family". For example, if you learn the word *exciting (The film was exciting.),* it's easy to learn the word *excited (I was excited when I got the news.).* You can use a dictionary to look at and learn word families, e.g. *excite, exciting, excited, excitement.*

A2 TIP 2 One word in German, two words in English

Sometimes when translating a word you have to be careful, because there may be two words for it in the other language. In English we have the word *go,* but in German we sometimes say *gehen* and sometimes *fahren.* In German we have the word *Schwein,* but in English we have the word *pig* for the animal but *pork* for the meat.

A3 TIP 3 A good dictionary can help you in lots of ways

Dictionaries can help you with the meaning of a word, the pronunciation and the spelling. They can also help you with examples of how to use the word. There's more about dictionaries in the Companion (Your link to the Portfolio), and Unit 4 Plus is about dictionaries.

B4b TIP 4 Rules or examples?

Do you like rules or explanations about grammar and vocabulary, or do you prefer examples? In this activity about the difference between *for* and *since,* you have both a rule (We use *for* to talk about a period of time and we use *since* to talk about the beginning of a period) and some examples *(since 2003, for three years).* If you find rules difficult to remember, try to remember an example or two.

How to increase your vocabulary
In this unit we've seen that words can have different meanings and that words belong to families. Words also often come in phrases, so you need to learn two or three words together. A good dictionary can help. It's a good investment for the language learner!

Companion → You can find more tips for choosing and using a dictionary in the section Your link to the Portfolio – Mehr zu Unit 4.

Learning outside the classroom
As your English gets better, you need lots of reading and listening practice. So try to read and listen to as much English as possible. There are simple "readers" at your level. There's a version of Wikipedia in simple English. There are English podcasts in simple English. They can all help.

Imagine

What's the strangest thing that ever happened to you?

Do you read in bed?

What kind of films do you like? What kind of music?

5

A You won't believe this, but ...

A1a Look at the picture with a partner and talk about how you think Tom got into this situation.
Example: I think the box fell on his foot.

A1b Listen to three different versions of Tom's story.
Try to note down as much of it as you can.

> I'm in the _____
> _____ 's stuck.
> _____ the pain.
> My toes _____
> _____
> _____ too heavy.
> _____ tool.
> _____
> Nobody's _____

A1c Compare your notes with a partner.
Did you complete the text?

Companion:
Grammar 2.4.1, 2.2.1

> **Focus on grammar**
> Last week I **was** in the garden.
> I **needed** a tool.
> Nobody **was** at home.

A2a Tom shouted for help. His neighbour was in the garden. Listen to what she told a friend the next day. Fill in the gaps.

1. ... I _____ just _____ the paper
   in the garden when I _____ someone.
   He _____ for help.

2. ... I _____ just _____ some coffee
   when I _____ the shouting again.

Companion:
Grammar 2.2.3

> **Focus on grammar**
> I **was** just **reading** the paper
> when I **heard** someone.

A2b How do you think Tom's accident happened? With your partner think of an explanation.
Examples: He was working in the garden when …
He was carrying a box of … when …
He was trying to lift a heavy box of … when …
He was trying to put … when …

Homestudy H1

A2c Compare your explanations with the rest of the class.

A3a It's now the day after Tom's accident. You are Tom and you want to tell your friend the story of your accident. Choose one of these beginnings and add one or two details to the story. Mumble your story to yourself a few times. You can stay seated or walk around the classroom.

> The strangest thing happened to me last week. I was working in the garden when …
> One of the funniest things that ever happened to me was when …
> A funny thing happened last week while I was working in the garden. I was lifting a heavy box …
> You won't believe this, but last week a heavy box fell on my foot while I was working in the garden. I was just giving up hope when my neighbour …

Exploring learning p. 50

TIP 1 Practise your English by making up little stories.

Homestudy H2

A3b Now sit in a circle or a horseshoe and count off A, B, A, B …

Student A: Tell your version of the story to student B on your left.
Student B: Listen and then tell your version to student A.

Each student talks for exactly two minutes. Then student A stays seated and B moves clockwise to the next B seat. The new partners repeat their own stories and continue in this way around the circle clockwise until they return to their original seat.

Focus on spoken English
One of the funniest things that ever happened to me was when …
You won't believe this, but … /
You'll never believe this, but …

B

The story of my reading

B1a Do you read? What do you read? How often? Tick what's true for you.

	regularly	often	occasionally	seldom	never
a. newspapers	☐	☐	☐	☐	☐
b. books	☐	☐	☐	☐	☐
c. magazines	☐	☐	☐	☐	☐
d. comics	☐	☐	☐	☐	☐
e. blogs	☐	☐	☐	☐	☐
f. Internet forums	☐	☐	☐	☐	☐
g. advertisements	☐	☐	☐	☐	☐
h. book and film reviews	☐	☐	☐	☐	☐
i. cookbooks	☐	☐	☐	☐	☐
j. online news	☐	☐	☐	☐	☐
…	☐	☐	☐	☐	☐

Companion:
Grammar 3.10

B1b In groups, compare your results and report something
to the class.

Examples: All of us read the newspaper.
Two of us often read blogs and two
occasionally read book reviews.
None of us read cookbooks.

Homestudy
H3

B1c Talk to a partner about the following points.

> why you read **|** why you don't read **|** where you read
> when you read **|** if you like to read

Examples: John, do you like to read?
– Well, yes, but I don't have much time to read.

Focus on grammar
All of us / we all read a lot.
Two of us read cookbooks.
None of us go to the cinema.

B2a Look at these statements from recent surveys of book reading habits
in the UK and decide in groups if you think they are true or not.

A RECENT SURVEY FOUND *that* …	True	False
a. … women read more than men.	☐	☐
b. … men sometimes bluff about reading to impress someone.	☐	☐
c. … few of the people interviewed read in bed.	☐	☐
d. … 25% read in the bath.	☐	☐
e. … 10% – mostly men – read on the toilet.	☐	☐
f. … only men are "serial shelvers", that is, they buy lots of books and never read them.	☐	☐
g. … 12% of men and women are "double bookers", that is, they read more than one book at the same time.	☐	☐

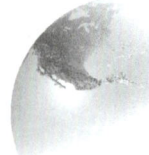
28

B2b Listen to the following radio report and check your guesses.
Is there any information not mentioned in B2a?

B2c Now do a class survey like the one in B2a.
Find out how your class compares with people interviewed in the UK.

Our class survey found that …	True	False
a. … the women read more than the men.	☐	☐
b. … some people bluff about reading to impress someone.	☐	☐
c. … many people in our class read in bed.	☐	☐
d. … some read in the bath.	☐	☐
e. … a few read on the toilet.	☐	☐
f. … some are serial shelvers.	☐	☐
g. … a few are double bookers.	☐	☐

Companion:
Grammar 3.13.1, 3.10

Exploring learning p. 50

TIP 2 Reading is important for language learning.

Focus on grammar
not **many**, only **a few**
some, but not **all**

C Let's go to the cinema

C1a Do you go to the cinema? Sometimes? Often? Why? Why not? Talk to a partner.

C1b Sally, John and Ben enjoy going to the cinema together.
They've just been to a film festival and have seen different films.
Some are quite old. Now they're in the pub chatting.
Which films and characters are they talking about?

C1c Compare with a partner.

C1d The titles of foreign films are often translated differently from the original.
Why is this? Brainstorm some reasons and collect them on the board.
Example: The original title is hard to translate …

C2a What kinds of films do you like?
Tick what is true for you and then compare with a partner.

	Yes	No
a. I like adventure films with lots of action.	☐	☐
b. I enjoy thrillers and suspense.	☐	☐
c. I like fantasy films.	☐	☐
d. I prefer romantic comedies.	☐	☐
e. I really like love stories.	☐	☐
f. I enjoy films based on novels.	☐	☐
g. I prefer biopics (films based on a real person's life).	☐	☐
h. I like animated films.	☐	☐

C2b Where do you like to watch films: at the cinema or at home on TV, on DVD or on the computer? Compare with your partner.

C2c Have you seen a good film recently? Collect the film titles on the board.
Do any need translating?

5

C2d What is your all-time favourite film? Find one or two people who also like that film. With your partner(s), prepare a short presentation of the film and what you like about it. Use the outline below to help you.

Example: The title of our film is *Titanic*. The actors are Kate Winslet and Leonardo DiCaprio.
The main characters are a young couple. It's the true story of a shipwreck.
It takes place on a huge ship crossing the Atlantic Ocean. I liked …

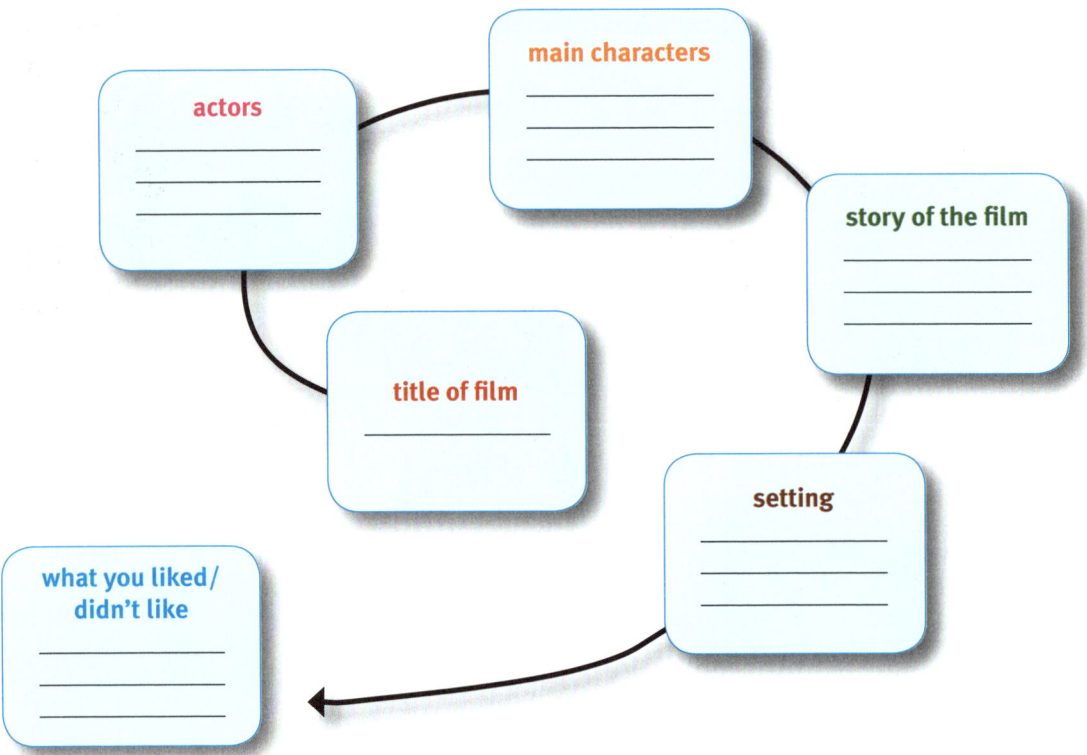

C2e Each group or pair presents its film to the class.

Exploring learning p. 50   **TIP 3** Use outlines to prepare summaries or presentations.

C3 Take a class vote about which film you would like to see together in English.

D   Music in the air

D1a These days we can hear music just about everywhere, but how often do you actually listen to music? Talk to a partner and add to the two word wheels.

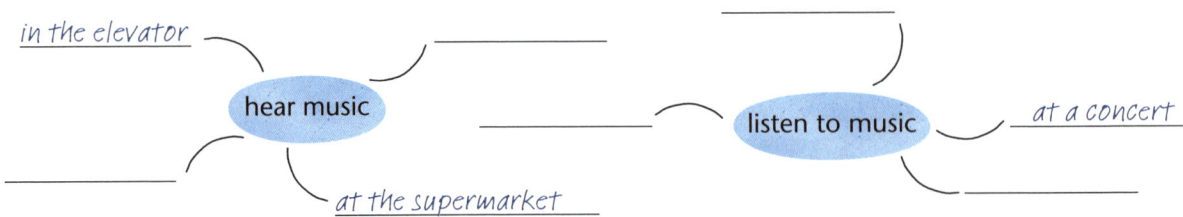

30

D1b How well do you know your partner?
Listen to these bits of music and tick what
you think your partner likes.

1. ☐ jazz
2. ☐ rock 'n' roll
3. ☐ rap
4. ☐ reggae
5. ☐ classical
6. ☐ electro
7. ☐ country
8. ☐ tango
9. ☐ musicals

D1c Now show your results to your partner. Did you get it right?
How well did you guess about your partner? How well did your partner guess about you?

31

D2a Rhythm is important in a lot of music but it's also important in language.
Listen to the following rap. Pay careful attention and when the rap is finished
write down everything that you remember hearing.

> *adventure*   *suspense*
>
>
>   *with ease*
>
>   *news reports*

D2b Choose someone to write on the board and take turns dictating your different
notes until you think you have the whole text. Don't look at the tapescript.

Homestudy
H5

31

D2c Listen again and make any necessary corrections.

D3a Get into two groups and stand opposite each other.
Your teacher will erase every third word.
Group 1 says the first line of the rap.
Group 2 answers with the next and so on.
Pay attention to the rhythm.

D3b Now erase the whole text and do the same thing again.
How much do you remember?

D3c Between lessons try to remember the song whenever you can.
In the next lesson, tell or show the class how much of the rap you remember.

5

Exploring my progress

At the end of this unit I can …			
… understand and tell simple stories, for example about something that happened to me. (You won't believe this, but …)	☐	☐	A3a, A3b, H1, H2
… talk about habits, for example why, where and when people read.	☐	☐	B1c, B2c, H3
… listen for specific information in a short radio report.	☐	☐	B2b
… talk about likes and dislikes, for example which films I like to watch and which music I like to listen to. (I prefer romantic comedies.)	☐	☐	C2a, D1b, D1c
… prepare and give a simple presentation, for example about the characters, setting, and story of a film.	☐	☐	C2d, C2e, H4

Online-Übungen ▶ S. 123

Exploring learning – ways to prepare to tell a story or give a presentation

A3a TIP 1 Practise your English by making up little stories

You can practise your English by making up stories and going over them in your head or talking under your breath. If you get into the habit of doing this, you'll be able to practise English all the time, anywhere, even in those weeks when you don't find time to sit down with your book and paper and pencil. You'll be amazed how effective this technique is.

B2c TIP 2 Reading is important for language learning

Find things to read that you enjoy. Reading is one of the best ways to expand your language knowledge. You will find that it also improves your speaking and writing a lot. Even if you don't enjoy reading books, there are loads of other things to read. Look out for English everywhere you go.

C2e TIP 3 Use outlines to prepare summaries or presentations

This helps you to organize your thoughts and decide what is most important. At least for some people it's more efficient than writing lots of notes. An outline makes presenting easier.

■ Reading

A good way to get into reading English is to read something that you're already read in your own language. That means that you know it and it makes understanding easier. Whatever you do, make sure to read something that you enjoy.

■ Learning outside the classroom

Listen to yourself. We've already mentioned talking to yourself as a way to practise English. As you practise using this technique you can talk to yourself about the story of things that happen to you during the day, the story of a book you are reading or the story of a film. You don't need to be shy because the only person listening to you is you!

All in the family

Do you like family get-togethers?

Did you have a good weekend?

What do you do when you feel sad?

6

A Meet the family

A1a **Answer the following questions with a partner.**

a. What is a family?
b. How many people are there in your family?
c. Do you live with your family?
d. Do you know your family well?
e. How often do you see your family?
f. What are the occasions when you meet them?

Homestudy H1

A1b **Look at this photo. What occasion is this? The two people in the middle of the photo at the front are Janette and Philip. With a partner discuss who the people are.**
Examples: I think he's Janette's brother.
She must be Philip's aunt.
She looks more like Philip's mother, so she's probably his aunt.

Philip

Janette

Focus on spoken English
I think she's …
She must be …
She's probably ….

A1c **Listen to the bride, Janette, telling her friend about her wedding. Were you right?**

Homestudy H2

A1d **Now listen to Janette again and fill in Philip's family tree.**

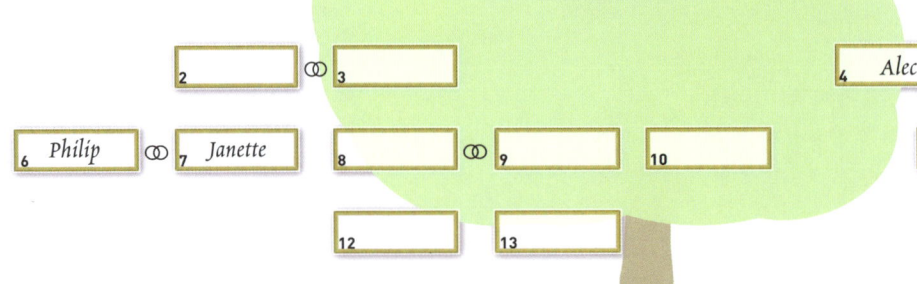

PHILIP'S FAMILY TREE

1 Pam and Alec's parents

2 ⚭ 3
4 Alec ⚭ 5
6 Philip ⚭ 7 Janette 8 ⚭ 9 10 11
12 13

Homestudy H3

A1e **Write down five names of people who are important to you (friends or family) on a piece of paper. Show them to your partner and answer questions about the names.**
Examples: • Who's Jonathan?   • He's my brother.
• Who's Jessica?   • She's one of my daughters.
• Who's Pauline?   • She's a good friend of mine.

Companion: Grammar 3.6.2

Focus on grammar
She's a good friend **of mine/ one of my friends.**
I'm a good friend **of hers.**

A2a **Make three word wheels about families on a piece of paper.**

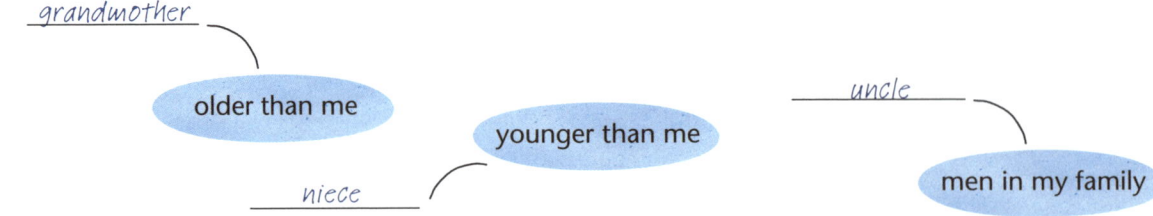

grandmother

older than me

younger than me

uncle

niece

men in my family

Homestudy
14

Companion:
Grammar 3.13.1,
3.9

A2b How big is your family? In pairs, write down four questions. Walk around the class and ask the other students your questions. Make notes on their answers.

Examples: How many aunts have you got?
Do you know all your cousins?

Focus on grammar

- How **many** sisters have you got?
- I've got two. / I haven't got **any**.
- Have you got **many** cousins?
- No, I haven't got **any**. /
Yes, I've got two. / Yes, **lots**.

A2c Report back one interesting bit of information to the class.

Examples: Petra's got five grandchildren.
Jan hasn't got any cousins.

A3a What's a nuclear family? What's an extended family? Which definitions are correct? Match the sentences.

1. A nuclear family is
2. An extended family is

a. a family full of energy.
b. a family consisting of a mother, a father, and their children.
c. a family group that includes grandparents, cousins, aunts, etc.

A3b Read these explanations of nuclear and extended families from an encyclopedia on the Internet. Which kind of family is the most common in your country? Discuss with a partner.

Extended family [edit]

This term is used for people who are members of the same family and not only parents and children. In these families many generations live together and often share their money. This type of family is quite common in India and other parts of Asia, but not so common in western Europe. It's often important to have an extended family to help with work and to earn money. In America the term extended family usually means all the family. It doesn't matter whether they live together or not.

Nuclear family [edit]

This is a family with only a father and mother and children who live together. These families can be big, with many children, or small if there's only one child. In China, this is the most common type of family. In India, the number of these families is growing. In the United States, 70% of children live in this type of family.

A4a Do you know these expressions? Match them to the explanations.

1. stepmum
2. patchwork family
3. an only child
4. silver wedding anniversary

a. the day when people celebrate twenty-five years of marriage
b. a child with no brothers and sisters
c. father's second wife
d. children and partners from two or more families

Exploring learning p. 58

TIP 1 Use words you know to describe words you don't know.

 35

A4b Listen to these young people talking about their families and match the expressions to the person talking.

1. stepmum
2. patchwork family
3. only child
4. silver wedding anniversary

Julian
Belinda
Nadine

A5 Write a text of three or four sentences about your family (without your name on it). Put all the texts on a table and see if you can decide who wrote which text.

6

B "My favorite things"

🎵 36

B1a Do you like these things?
Listen to the song and put the words and pictures in the order you hear them.

dog   kettle ☐   kittens ☐   bee ☐   package ☐   roses ☐

🎵 36

B1b Listen to the song again and fill in the missing words.

Focus on vocabulary
favourite (UK) = favorite (US)

Raindrops on (1) _____ and whiskers on (2) _____
Bright copper (3) _____ and warm woolen mittens
Brown paper (4) _____ tied up with strings
These are a few of my favorite things

Cream colored ponies and crisp apple strudels
Doorbells and sleigh bells and schnitzel with noodles
Wild geese that fly with the moon on their wings
These are a few of my favorite things

Girls in white dresses with blue satin sashes
Snowflakes that stay on my nose and eyelashes
Silver white winters that melt into springs
These are a few of my favorite things

When the (5) _____ bites
When the (6) _____ stings
When I'm feeling sad
I simply remember my favorite things
And then I don't feel so bad

Exploring learning   p. 58 **TIP 2** Decide what and how much you want to learn.

B1c Look at the song again. What makes her happy? Make a list of things that make you happy.

Exploring learning   p. 58 **TIP 3** Make lists.

B2 Write your own verse for the song. Use one of the verses above as a model.
Don't worry about the rhyme.
Put all the verses together and make one class song.

C Kids' stuff

C1a Work in pairs. Do you agree with these sentences? Tell your partner.

a. Thirteen is too young to have children.
b. Parents should look after children themselves.

c. It's OK for women to go to work when their children are young.
d. It's better to have children when you are young.

6

C1b The following texts were all in one English magazine. Which title goes with which text?

> Are grandparents as good as parents?
> Too young to be a father?
> What's the best age to have a baby?

a. _____

He's only four feet tall (1 m 20), his voice hasn't broken and he looks more like eight than thirteen. He's a father, one of the youngest in Britain. His girlfriend, Amy, who's fifteen, had a baby boy last month. The story is in all the newspapers and Brian Sanderson says he feels proud that he's a father. His dad, Kevin, who's forty, divorced his mother three years ago and lives with his girlfriend who's also only seventeen. Brian's father has five other children. He's quite happy to be a grandfather but doesn't want to look after the baby. Brian and Amy want to bring up the baby on their own. ==Many of their friends and family think they are too young== but Amy's mother says she'll help them.

b. _____

Some people say you should have kids when your parents are young enough to look after them. Others say it's not a good idea for grandparents to look after babies, because the children later have difficulties at school and find it difficult to make friends. Experts believe that grandparents are not good parents; they often have no other interests and spend too much time and energy on their grand-children. But mothers who want to or have to work often need grandparents. They can be really positive for children because they are a good mixture of parent, teacher and friend. Most people feel very happy when they remember their grandparents.

c. _____

Sylvia, who's now fifty, tells us about her experience with children. "I had my first baby when I was nineteen and my second when I was forty-two, so I think I know the good and bad sides of both ages. Looking after a baby when you're very young can be difficult, but now my daughter is grown-up and we're good friends. When I had my second daughter, I was much more mature and knew much more about life. I was not so worried about the baby and now she's very inde-pendent. There are really good and bad sides about both ages, so I don't know what I would choose. I had a lot of help from my parents with my first child and from my partner with my second and I'm really grateful to them."

C1c Use a highlighter and mark the opinions in the text.
Compare what you have marked with a partner.

Exploring learning p. 58   **TIP 4** Use colours.

37

C1d Listen to Janette telling Philip about the articles in the magazine.

a. Which text is she talking about?
b. When do Janette and Philip want to have children?

Compare your answers with a partner and then tell the class.

C2a Do a survey. In pairs write sentences about families.
Examples:

> – It's best to have two children.
> – You should have children when you are under thirty.

6

C2b **Walk around and ask other people in the class what they think. Is there anything everyone agrees on?**
Example: Thirteen is too young to become a father.
            What do you think?

C3 **Write a few sentences about the opinions of class members. The title is "What our class thinks about families". Use the following phrases.**

> Most people in the class think …
> Nobody agrees that … | None of us agree that …
> Two of us think …
> In Harald and Maja's opinion, …
> Everyone thinks … | All of us think …

D Never a cross word

D1a **What does it mean if you fall out with someone? Tick.**

- ☐ a. You move in with them.
- ☐ b. You fight with them.
- ☐ c. You go to a party together.

D1b **Ask your partner.**

Have you got a best friend?
Have you ever fallen out with him / her?
What did you argue about?

D2a **Work in pairs. Look at the pictures of important men in Samantha's life. Who do you think they are? Talk to your partner.**
Example: I think this is Samantha's
            brother / cousin / friend / colleague.

Samantha

Don

Robert

Hans-Peter

D2b **Listen to Samantha talking about these men in her life. Fill in the information.**

a. Samantha and Robert:

We (1) _____ each other for twenty years.

We (2) _____ twenty years ago when we were at school.

We (3) _____ after three years.

b. Samantha and Don:

He lives in Australia and we (1) _____.

We (2) _____ to know each other through an online discussion list.

We (3) _____ out.

He (4) _____ me this photo last year.

c. Samantha and Hans-Peter:

He (1) _____ in England for ages.

A colleague (2) _____ this photo last year.

> **Focus on grammar**
> I**'ve never met** him.
> We**'ve known** each other **for five years.**
> We **met** twenty years **ago.**
> He **mailed** me this photo **last year.**

38
Homestudy
17

D2c **Listen again. What's the word for …**

a. … someone you write to?
b. … someone you work with?

c. … someone you are married to?
d. … someone you were married to?

D3a **Have a guess.**

"Grand Hotel Papa" is the title of an article in a women's magazine. Is the article about …
a. a family?   b. a hotel?

Exploring learning p. 58 **TIP 5** Use what you know.

D3b **Read the article and fill in the blanks in the following sentences.**

a. Malcolm is Anne's _____ .

b. Claire is Malcolm's _____ .

c. Anne's never _____ home.

d. Malcolm and Anne have never had
an _____ .

GRAND HOTEL PAPA

Hotel Mama is an expression used for families with grown-up children at home. Their mother looks after them when they are 25, 30 or older. A similar family is called Grand Hotel Papa. This is where the father looks after his adult children. Malcolm (52) and Anne (24) told our reporter about how they live. Here's what they say. Malcolm says, "When my wife Mary died ten years ago I had to look after Anne, our daughter. I worried about her a lot and didn't want her to move out and live on her own or with friends. So she went to university in the town we live in and stayed at home. I am quite content with things and I think Anne is too. We share the housework and we spend a lot of time together and get on very well. I'd be very lonely if Anne moved into her own apartment, so I hope she doesn't do that soon. I now have a partner, Claire, and I think she would like to get married. We've never talked about it, but I know she sometimes thinks of

it and I don't know how Anne would feel about that. I've never asked her. Anne likes Claire but I don't know if she wants her to live with us."
Anne says, "I really love living with Dad. We've never had an argument and I have a really nice life with him, so I don't want to move out. Maybe later if I get married or meet a nice man, but at the moment things are fine. I pay Dad a bit of money and we share the chores. We spend most evenings together but I sometimes go out with friends at weekends. Dad has just met Claire and they've been together for about six months now. This changes things a bit, I suppose. I don't think Dad wants Claire to move in with us but we haven't talked about it."
We talked to Claire, Malcolm's girlfriend. She says, "Malcolm and Anne are very good friends so I some- times feel a bit like an outsider. They spend a lot of time together and I only see Malcolm at the weekends. I would like to spend more time with him but I don't think Anne would like it."

D4a **Write your name in the middle of a piece of paper**
and write the names of three people in your life around it.
Write two true sentences about each person and one sentence which is false.

> This is … ▐ We met … ago. ▐ We've … for … years/months/weeks. ▐ We've never …

D4b **Now talk to your partner about the people in your life.**
Guess which sentences on your partner's paper are true and which are false.

Homestudy
18

companion:
Grammar 2.3.1, 3.18

D4c **Ask questions about your partner's people.**

Have you ever been to the cinema with …?
Have you ever fallen out with …?
How long have you known each other?
Where did you meet …?

> **Focus on grammar**
> We**'ve known** each other **for twenty years.**
> How often **do you see** each other?

Exploring my progress

At the end of this unit I can …			
… talk about my family. (She's one of my daughters.)	☐	☐	A1e, A2b H2, H3
… understand the main points of what somebody says, for example when somebody describes their family.	☐	☐	A4b, C1d, D2b, H2
… understand the main points in short magazine articles about familiar topics, such as family life.	☐	☐	C1b, D3b
… identify the opinions in a short magazine article about a familiar topic.	☐	☐	C1c
… exchange opinions with people, for example about family life.	☐	☐	C2a, C2b
… report other people's opinions.	☐	☐	C3

Online-Übungen ▶ S. 125

Exploring learning – meeting new words

A4a TIP 1   Use words you know to describe words you don't know

Use words you know in English to describe words you don't know. This will help you to learn words in English without always translating them from your own language.

B1b TIP 2   Decide what and how much you want to learn

The song text in B1b probably contains a lot of words that you didn't know, but do you want to learn them all now? Are they words that you like or that are useful to you? When you meet new words decide which ones you really want to learn. Write sentences for these words and try to use them. Don't try to learn too many words at the same time.

B1c TIP 3   Make lists

Decide on your own ways of putting words in groups and make as many different lists as possible. Some ideas could

be: things I can see from my window, how I feel in the morning, what I think of in summer. There are many more. Write down different word types and groups of words and short sentences.

C1c TIP 4   Use colours

Mark words in texts and in your book using different colours. Connect the colours with the words. For instance, you can mark things you like or which make you feel happy in your favourite colour and things you don't like in a colour you hate.

D3a TIP 5   Use what you know

Before you read a new text, look at the title. When you read a text try and understand the main point. Use what you already know to help you. Notice all the words you know first before you worry about what you don't know. You'll be surprised at how much you know!

How to remember new words

Try and connect words with ideas or actions. If you learn new words and phrases on the train to work, try and remember the words next time you're on the train without looking at them. Listen to English texts or songs when you're walking through the country. Take the same walk again and try and remember the words. You can also do this in your head. Just imagine the walk or the train journey and you can think of the words.

Learning outside the classroom

Read something in English just before you fall asleep at night. Read a text from your English book (for example from the Reading Club or a text from the last lesson). See how much you can remember in the morning. Tell a friend or someone in your family about the text you've read (in English!). If you have a pet, talk to your pet in English. Your dog or cat won't mind if you make mistakes!

check your progress

tips for learners

C1a You see this advertisement in a newspaper. Can you do this job?
Would you like to do this job? Compare your ideas with a partner.

Books for the World

We sell second-hand books and use the money to help people all over the world.
We need someone to help us in our shop in the town centre.

volunteer work — free coffee — nice atmosphere — never boring

Do you like books and reading? | Can you speak English?
Can you speak another language? | Are you good with money?
Are you well organized? | Have you got between two and
five hours free time every week?

Come for an interview and meet us!
BFTW ❧ Books for the World ❧ Read and Help
Suzanne Winter

38 Wakefield Road · Leeds LS98 1FD · ++44 (845) 834 1117· suzanne@bftw.info

C1b What do you think the job will be like?
In pairs find five words to describe the job.
Example: interesting

C2a You go to *Books for the World* for an interview
and meet the manager Suzanne Winter.
What questions do you think will she ask?
With a partner think of some questions.
Examples: When can you work in our shop?
What sort of books do you like?
How do you describe yourself?

C2b Now find another partner and ask and answer your questions.

C2c What questions can you ask Suzanne Winter?
With your new partner think of some questions.
Examples: When can I start in your shop?
What are the customers like?

C2d Now find another partner and ask and answer your questions.

C3a One thing you have to do is sort out the books which people bring to the shop.
In pairs think of how books can be sorted into groups.

C3b Here are some examples of groups. In the box below, there are some books which people bring to the shop. Which group do they belong to? Add them to the word wheels.

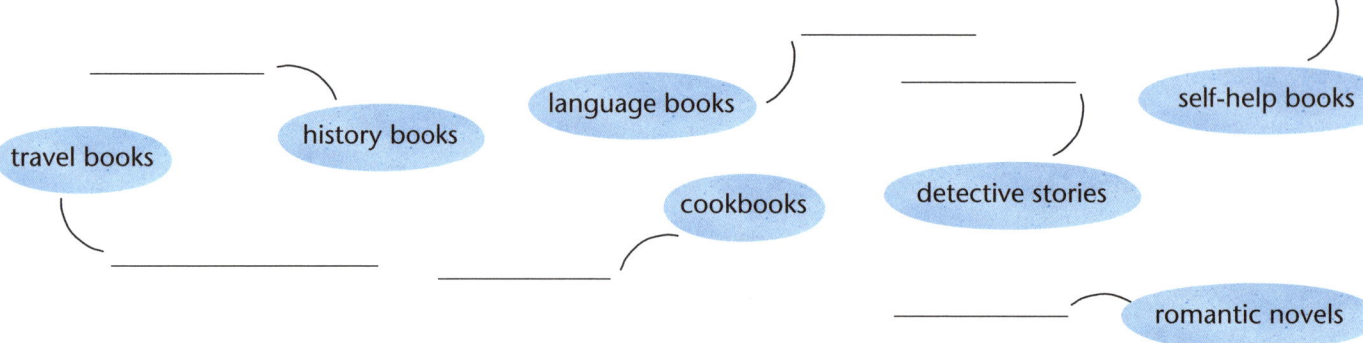

travel books · history books · language books · cookbooks · detective stories · self-help books · romantic novels

> *Baxter's English-French Dictionary* ▌ *My Job is Boring!* by Dennis Smart
> *Tips for Teams* by Frederick Hillmann ▌ *A Chef's Kitchen* by Petronia Grant
> *The Dark Night* by Rodney Bewley ▌ *My Neighbour's Garden* by Carol Flay
> *Love Lasts Longest* by Cordelia Marston-Mead
> *The Decline and Fall of the British Empire* by Piers Brendon
> *Frommer's Alaska 2010* by Charles P. Wohlforth

 41

C3c Listen to these customers and decide which of the books in C3b would be best for them.

C3d Decide which book you think you would like best and why.
Tell your partner.

C4a Work with a partner. Think of as many different books as you can. Write down the titles. Which group do they belong to? Add them to the word wheels in C3a.

C4b You want to buy a book from *Books for the World*. Work with a partner. Think about the sort of book you want.

what sort of book?	for you or as a present?	how long?	what about?
why you want the book?	who for?	how big?	how much?

C4c Work with a partner. One of you wants to buy a book and the other works for *Books for the World*. Try and find the right book.

C5a All the people who work in *Books for the World* have to write a short review of a book they want to recommend to customers. Here is a review by one of your colleagues. Which of the books in C3b is it about?

★★★★☆

I enjoyed this book very much because I have to work with lots of people and sometimes it's not easy to organize everything. So I need lots of tips to help me in my work. This book is well laid out and has lots of interesting information about different personalities and how a good manager can use them so everyone can work well. I like self-help books and this is one of the best!

C5b Now write a review of a book you want to recommend.

Modern times

Is the world getting smaller?

How dangerous is modern life?

What will the world be like in one hundred years?

7

A   It's a small world

A1a How much do you know about the countries of the world?
Do this quiz with a partner and find out how much you know together.

QUESTION **1** Which country does flamenco music come from?

QUESTION **2** What's the capital of Australia?

QUESTION **3** Which countries border on Poland?

QUESTION **4** How many states are there in the USA?

QUESTION **5** Which state is Chicago in?

QUESTION **6** Where (and what) is Uluru?

QUESTION **7** Where do people eat with chopsticks?

QUESTION **8** Where was Barack Obama born?

QUESTION **9** Where do people eat curry?

QUESTION **10** What separates Great Britain and continental Europe?

QUESTION **11** What colour is a European Union passport?

QUESTION **12** In which European country do men do the most housework?

Companion:
Grammar 3.16.3

Focus on grammar
Which country does flamenco come from?
Which countries border on Poland?

A1b Now think of four more questions with your partner. Use the ones above as models. Ask another pair. Can they answer your questions?

A2a Read the article published on a European website. Were you right about the last two questions in A1a?

Even though everyone in the European Union has the same dark red-brown passport and everywhere you go, you think you see the same shops, restaurants and cars, there are still a lot of differences between countries in Europe.

Did you know, for example, that
· *more people in Germany live alone than in Italy or Spain?*
· *more people in Great Britain go to adult education classes than in any other country in Europe?*
· *the Dutch have the most caravans?*
· *Greeks spend less on heating than Germans?*
· *more people in France commute than in Germany?*
· *Sweden is the country with the highest percentage of people who speak English as a foreign language?*
· *men in the Netherlands do more housework than men in any other European country?*

Companion:
Grammar 3.13.2

Focus on grammar
More people in France commute **than** in Germany.
Men in the Netherlands do **more** housework **than** men in Germany.
Greeks spend **less** on heating **than** Germans.
The Dutch have **the most** caravans.

Homestudy
H1

A2b With a partner, write down ten more differences between people in European countries.
Then work together with another group.
Read your statements out and find out which are the same and which are different.
Example: Germans drink more beer than the French.

A2c Were you surprised about the information in the text? What surprised you most? What surprised you least? In small groups discuss your reactions.
Example: What surprised me most / least was that …

Companion: Grammar 3.13.2

Focus on grammar

What surprised me **most** was that more people in Great Britain go to adult education classes than in Germany. What surprised me **least** was that Greeks spend less on heating than Germans.

A3a Do you agree with the following sentences? Discuss with a partner.

Black cats are unlucky.
Tea with milk is a fantastic drink.

Noodles are good for breakfast.
Kissing people is a nice way of saying hello.

A3b Now listen to three people talking about what they found different in another country. What countries are they talking about? Where do they come from?

1. Noelle comes from _____.
   She spent some time in _____.
   She doesn't think _driving on the left_ and
   _____ are strange.

2. Johann comes from _____.
   He spent some time in _____.
   He thinks _____ is strange.

3. Mikito comes from _____.
   She spent some time in _____.
   She thinks _____ is strange.

Companion: Grammar 2.10

Focus on grammar

I think **drinking** tea for breakfast is strange.
I think **shaking** hands is nice.
I don't think **driving** on the left is strange.

A3c What do foreigners think is different about your country? Discuss in small groups.
Example: Well, I guess foreigners might think eating sausage and cheese for breakfast is funny.

Homestudy 2

A3d What tips would you give someone coming to stay in your area for a short time? With a partner make a list of five important tips. Compare them with another pair. Make a class list.
Examples: Don't be late for business meetings / parties.

Companion: Grammar 2.8

Remember

Be on time. / **Don't be** late.

A4a Do a class survey to find out more about students in your class. Choose one question each from the box or think of your own question. Walk around and ask your question. Report back on the result.

Do you have a caravan? ▌ Do you drink tea or coffee for breakfast?
Do you believe that black cats are unlucky? ▌ Do you commute? ▌ Do you do housework?
Do you eat eggs for breakfast? ▌ Do you kiss people to say hello?
Do you shake hands with people? ▌ Do you use chopsticks? ▌ Do you like curries?
Do you have a European passport? ▌ …

Homestudy 3

Companion: Grammar 3.12, 3.13

A4b Write a text or make a poster about the class. Write what you found out.
Example: In our class most people drink coffee for breakfast. There are only a few who drink tea.

Focus on grammar

Most students in our class drink coffee for breakfast, **some** drink tea and **only a few** drink milk.
Nobody uses chopsticks.
Everybody likes sausages, but **not many** like curries.

7

B If I won a million euros

Homestudy
H4

Companion:
Grammar 1.6.2

B1a If you won a million euros, what would you do?
How would your life change? Talk to your partner.
Example: If I won a million euros, I'd buy a nice house with
a big garden.

Focus on grammar
If I **won** a million euros,
I**'d buy** a big car.

B1b If you won a million euros, would you stop working? A radio station in Dublin asked
four people in the street this question. How do you think they answered?

Jan, primary school teacher	Yes ☐	No ☐	Helmut, artist	Yes ☐	No ☐
Melanie, shop assistant	Yes ☐	No ☐	Ellen, cook	Yes ☐	No ☐

Exploring learning p. 68 **TIP 1** Compare what you think you'll hear with what you hear.

  B1c Now listen to their answers. Were you right?

 **B2a** Put the following jobs into groups. Some can go in more than one group.
Discuss with a partner.

blacksmith ▌ bookbinder ▌ bus conductor ▌ bus driver ▌ doctor ▌ film star ▌ gardener
maid ▌ nurse ▌ journalist ▌ investment banker ▌ postman ▌ product manager ▌ secretary
shop assistant ▌ teacher ▌ website designer ▌ IT specialist ▌ HR manager ▌ sound engineer

past	present	future

B2b Where does your job go? Is it a past, present or future job?

B3a Here are some words from an article
called *Two lucky millionaires*. Underline the
ones you think will appear in the text.

win ▌ garden ▌ designer ▌ millionaire
famous ▌ Prince Charles ▌ psychotherapist
university ▌ boss ▌ unemployed

Exploring learning p. 68 **TIP 2** Imagine what words you will read.

B3b Read the first part of the article and see if you were right.

Two lucky millionaires

JUDITH KEPPEL, who's now sixty-two, was the first person to win a million pounds on the famous television show *Who Wants To Be A Millionaire?* She's a trained psychotherapist and garden designer and has just written a quiz book: *1,000 Questions From Britain's First Quiz Millionaire.* She's a member of the same family as Prince Charles's wife, Camilla Parker Bowles. Judith was born in Wolverhampton, England and now lives alone in London. She's been married twice and has three children. What did she do with all the money she won on the quiz show? She bought a car and spent a lot of money on her garden, but invested most of the money which she won. She didn't stop working but became a full-time garden designer.

B3c Now read the second part of the article.
How did Morris become a millionaire?

Morris Tonstick, who's now fifty-three, was the first person to win a million pounds in the South Yorkshire prize draw, which started two months ago. After that he stopped working and started writing novels. He's a trained teacher and guitar player and has just written a story about living in the north of England two hundred years ago. He's a member of a band and plays the guitar at folk music concerts. Morris was born in Huddersfield, England and now lives with his wife in Leeds. He has two children who are twenty-three and twenty. What did he do with all the money he won in the lottery? He bought cars for his wife and his children and spent a lot of money on his house, but invested most of the money which he won. He stopped working as a teacher and became a full-time writer.

Homestudy
H5

B3d What are the differences between
the two people?

Examples: Judith is sixty-two years old
and Morris is …
Judith was born in Wolverhampton and Morris …

> **Remember**
>
> She **is** sixty-two years old.
> He **was** born in England.

B4a Write a few lines about what you'd do
if you won a million euros.

B4b In B1a you talked to a partner about what you'd do if you won a million euros.
Now find a different partner and guess what he or she wrote.
Example: If you won a million Euros, you'd buy a house in the Caribbean.

B4c Now exchange texts and see if you were right.
Read the text about your partner to the class.

C Crime doesn't pay

C1a Look at the pictures and match each of
the following words to one picture.
Compare your answers with a partner.

1. ☐ burglar
2. ☐ mugger
3. ☐ pickpocket
4. ☐ robber

a.

b.

c.

d.

C1b What's the difference between the
following words. Use your dictionary to find out.

1. burglar   *somebody who breaks into a building to steal something*
2. thief   _____
3. robber   _____

C1c Which of the following describes all of the words in C1a and C1b? Tick.

☐ artists ☐ criminals ☐ jobs ☐ players

Exploring learning p. 68

TIP 3 Find out about differences and similarities between words.

C2a The Dublin radio station invited listeners to phone in with their stories about crime. Listen to Sinead talking to three people. Which of the words from C1a describes the criminals in the stories? What happened to each person?

Maeve: *pickpocket, stole her purse* _____

Diarmid: _____

Sheila: _____

C2b Listen again and read the following tips. Fill in the gaps with *always* and *never*.

1. _____ keep your handbag closed.

2. _____ keep your money and credit cards in one place.

3. _____ go with other people in a train.

4. _____ keep valuables in the car.

Homestudy H6

C2c Can you add more tips of your own? What do you always / never do? Discuss with a partner.

C3a Imagine you witness a crime. What would you do? Work with a partner.
Example: If I saw a burglar, I'd ring the police.

C3b Walk round the class and ask how the others would react if they witnessed a crime.
Example: What would you do if you saw a burglar in your neighbour's house?

C3c Report back to the class and discuss what would be the best way to help.
Example: Most students would call the police.

Exploring learning p. 68 | **TIP 4** Work together.

D Modern times

D1a Match each word on the left with one on the right.

1. junk   a. crime
2. cyber   b. marriage
3. same-sex   c. mail

Exploring learning p. 68 | **TIP 5** Combine words.

D1b What do you think of when you hear these words?
Discuss what they mean with a partner.
Compare your definitions with another pair.

D1c Now read the following pieces of news and match each word to one text.

1. Eighty-five percent of all email is spam and some firms have more than ninety percent _____ in their mailboxes every day.

2. Mexico is the eighth country to allow _____. The first seven were Belgium, Canada, Norway, the Netherlands, Spain, South Africa and Sweden. Some US states also allow it.

3. The FBI is investigating a Russian Internet gang because it is suspected of committing _____ and stealing millions of dollars from US banks by using computer programs and finding out passwords.

D2a Look at the following items. Have all these things changed in the last forty years?
Choose one or two and discuss the changes in small groups.
Find as many changes as you can.

> cars ▎ eating in restaurants ▎ houses ▎ letters ▎ money
> speaking English ▎ telephones ▎ television ▎ travel / flying ▎ …

Examples: Now we have more than fifty television channels.
          Now I book all my travel online.

D2b With a partner, write two sentences about the things
you chose in D2a, one beginning with *Forty years ago …*
and one with *Now …*
Example: Forty years ago, we only had three television channels.
          Now we have more than fifty.

Homestudy
17

Companion:
Grammar 5.4.2

D2c What will be different forty years from now?
Change partners and write another two sentences
beginning with *In forty years, we will …*
Example: In forty years, we will create our own
          television on the Internet.

> **Focus on grammar**
>
> Forty years **ago** we **had** three
>   television channels.
> **In** forty years we **will create** our
>   own television on the Internet.

D3a What's a time capsule? Tick.

- ☐ a box of things to show people in the future what life is like now
- ☐ a watch or clock in a box
- ☐ medicine you take more than once a day

Homestudy
18

D3b Here's some information about
time capsule. Were you right?

2 ⟳ 4

D3c Listen to a group of students
planning a time capsule.
Tick the things that they
decide to put in it.

> ◉ ◯ ◯
>
> **Time capsule**   [edit]
>
> A time capsule is a collection of things and / or information
> used to communicate with people in the future. Time
> capsules are sometimes made and buried in the ground
> as a part of celebrations such as a world fair or football
> championship, when a building is opened, or at other
> events.

☐ clothes	☐ a lipstick	☐ a toy	☐ a cinema ticket
☐ a newspaper	☐ a train ticket	☐ an empty can	☐ a photo
☐ an English course book	☐ a letter	☐ a pen	☐ jewellery
☐ a letter opener	☐ a shopping list	☐ stamps	

D4 Get into groups to plan a time capsule. Before you start, think about the following questions.
What else should you think about?

- When will someone open the time capsule?
- What sort of box is best?
- What will you put in the box?
- Where will you put the box?

- How will you explain to people in the future
  what the things in the box are?
- How will you remember where the box is?

7

Exploring my progress

… compare information, for example about life in different countries. (More people in France commute than in Germany.)   □ □   A2b, A4b, B3d, H1, H3

… say what surprised me most or least about something I've read. (What surprised me least was that Greeks spend less on heating than Germans.)   □ □   A2c

… give tips, for example about a country or how to prevent crime. (Always keep your handbag closed.)   □ □   A3d, C2c, H6

… say what I would do in some situations, for example if I won a lot of money or witnessed a crime. (If I won a million euros, I'd buy a big car.)   □ □   B1a, B4a, C3a, H4

… compare the past, present and future, for example how things have changed and will change. (Forty years ago we only had three television channels.)   □ □   B2, D2b, D2c, H7

Online-Übungen ▶ S. 127

Exploring learning – comparing and contrasting

B1b TIP 1   Compare what you think you'll hear with what you hear
If you know you're going to hear something like a radio programme or an announcement at a station, think first about what you expect to hear and then compare what you hear with this. It'll be easier to understand if you have thought about it first.

B3a TIP 2   Imagine what words you will read
Before you read a text, make a short list of the words you expect to read. See if these words are in the text. Some words in the text may have the same meaning as your words but be new for you. In this way you can learn several words for the same thing.

C1c TIP 3   Find out about differences and similarities between words
All the words in C1a are expressions for criminals or thieves but each is a bit different; a pickpocket takes things from pockets, a burglar breaks into a building, etc.

C3c TIP 4   Work together
Often it's easier to work out the answers or to write a text in groups. Ask colleagues and friends to help you if you don't know something. Or write a text and ask a friend or colleague to correct it for you and suggest ways of making it better.

D1a TIP 5   Combine words
When you see English words, see if you can combine them with others to make new words. Use your imagination. It doesn't matter if the words don't really exist, it can be fun!

English around you
When you hear or read English words you already know, try and think of other words with the same meaning or think of the opposites. In this way you can use language you know well to activate more language.

Learning outside the classroom
Before you hear or read something think of questions you want to ask the person speaking or writing. Make these questions as detailed as possible and then see if you hear or read the answers.

Our world

Have you ever used a typewriter?

Would you wear the same outfit for a whole year?

Are you going to throw away that old tin?

8

A The way things used to be

A1a The world is changing all the time. What did your grandparents and parents use to do? What do you do today? Read the questions, fill in the table and talk to a partner.

a. Where did they use to buy milk? – Where do you buy milk now?
b. How often did your grandmother or your mother use to wash clothes? – What about you today?
c. How often did they use to listen to the radio? What did they listen to? – What about you?
d. How did they use to wash dishes? – What about you?
e. How often did they use to travel? – What about you?
f. What else did they use to do? – …

	grandparents	parents	me	partner
buy milk	from the farmer	from the milkman	in a shop	
wash clothes				
listen to the radio				
…				

Example: My mother used to buy milk from the milkman who came to our neighbourhood. Now we buy it in a shop.

Focus on grammar

My parents **used to** listen to the radio.
My grandparents **didn't use to** have a washing machine.
What else **did/didn't** they **use to** do or have?

Companion:
Grammar 2.2.4

A1b What do you know about Native Americans? Look at the photos and name three things they used to do, and things they do now.
Example: They used to live in tepees, but now they live in houses.

A1c Read what a young Lakota Native American woman has to say and circle all the examples with *used to*.

Homestudy H1

A LONG TIME AGO the Lakota used to live in tepees, which were easy to build and to transport. The tepees and some of the clothing were made from buffalo skins. There used to be huge buffalo herds on the Plains. Before the white men came, my people hunted the buffalo on foot with bows and arrows. They used to take only as much as they needed for food, clothing, housing, cooking and heating.

The white men brought my people the horse, which made it much easier to move and to hunt. They also brought the railroad, which we called the iron horse. With the railroad came the people who killed off the buffalo. They used to stop the trains, kill the animals and just leave them. This killing destroyed my people's way of life and the rich plant and animal life that used to be a part of the Plains.

TODAY many of us live in houses on a reservation and drive pickup trucks. We go to school and some of us go to university, but there are no good jobs on the reservation. However, we try to keep some of our old ways, so we still go to pow-wows and dress in our traditional costumes, like we used to do. Now some ranchers are trying to keep buffalo again instead of cattle and bring back some of the richness that used to be on the Plains.

A1d Read the text again with a partner. Underline the words and phrases you don't know and try to guess them from the context. Help each other but don't use a dictionary or the word list yet.
Example: I think "herd" must mean a large group of animals of the same type.

Exploring learning p. 76

TIP 1 When you read try to guess words and phrases.

A1e Now group the expressions that you've underlined.

can guess from context	need to know	nice to know	can do without
herd			

A1f Compare your table with others in the class and check if any unknown expressions are left over. If so, try to guess together, use a dictionary or, finally, ask your teacher.

A2a Did the area where you live use to look different? What about the area where you grew up? Talk to a partner about the changes. Make a sketch if that helps you.
Examples: Next to my house there used to be a lot of trees, but they were cut down ten years ago. They built a shopping centre there.
There used to be a lot of small shops where I live. Most of them have closed.
There didn't use to be a playground here, but the city built one about five years ago.

Companion: Grammar 2.9.1

A2b Work in groups and compare your results. Fill in the table together and decide whether you think the changes are positive or negative.

Focus on grammar
The trees **were cut down** ten years ago.

used to be	trees	...	...	...	...
didn't use to be					
now	shopping centre				
positive					
negative	X				

A2c Who has experienced the most changes in your class?

8

B   What if?

B1a   Do you like to dream? Would you change anything about the way you live, the way you work, the way you relax? Talk to a partner.
Examples: I'd try (= I would try) to stop smoking.
I'd work less and relax more.

Companion:
Grammar 1.6.2

> **Focus on grammar**
>
> **I'd try** (= I would try) to stop smoking.
> We**'d work** less.

B1b   What would happen if ...?
Work with a partner and match the sentence parts.

1. If more people rode bicycles,
2. If we used more wind energy,
3. If we bought food in season,
4. If we stopped cutting down the world's rainforests,
5. If we shared household equipment,
6. If we slowed down and didn't work so much,

a. we'd save fuel and support local producers.
b. life would be more relaxing.
c. there'd be less pollution and we'd be fitter.
d. we'd save money and energy.
e. future generations would have a better chance of a good life.
f. we'd need fewer power stations.

B1c   Do you agree with the statements in B1b?
Work with a partner. If you don't agree with something, change the second part of the sentence to make a statement you both agree with.
Example: If we slowed down and didn't work so much, we wouldn't have as much money to travel.

B1d   Report your changes to the class.

B2a   Label each of the pictures.

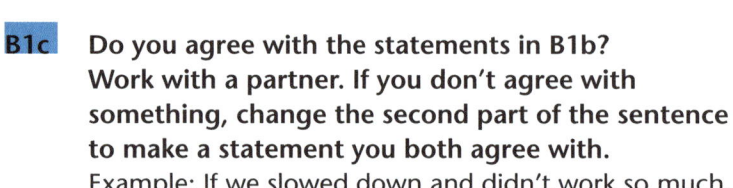

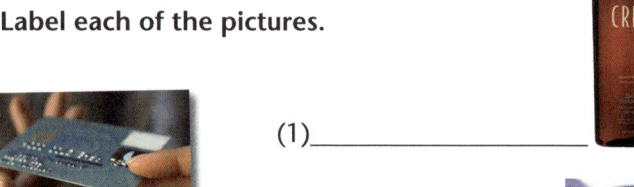

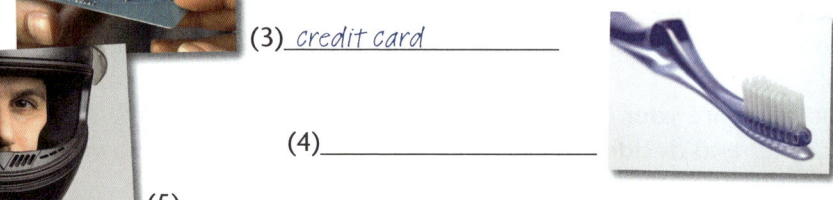

(1)_____

(2)_____

(3) _credit card_____

(4)_____

(5)_____

(6)_____

(7)_____

B2b   What do you think all the pictures have in common?
Talk to your partner and then collect suggestions on the board.

 B2c   Now listen to part of a radio programme and find out what they have in common.

 B2d   Listen again. What other products are mentioned?
Make notes and together with your partner add to the list.

B2e Now work in groups and complete the following statements any way you want. Add some of your own statements and report back the class.

1. If we didn't have credit cards, we'd _pay cash all the time._____
2. If we didn't have nylon umbrellas, we'd _____
3. If we didn't use plastic bottles, _____
4. If we didn't have helmets, _____
5. If _____

Homestudy H2

B2f *Reduce, Reuse and Recycle* was a successful campaign in the UK and the US. Make a class survey and produce a list of ways you can reduce, reuse and recycle.

<u>reduce</u>   <u>reuse</u>   <u>recycle</u>

fuel consumption   shoebox   glass

C Global warming

C1a Many experts are predicting serious changes to our world if we don't control CO_2 emissions. Look at the pictures and talk to a partner about one or two things that you think will happen.
Example: I think we'll have more storms.

C1b Dave studies climate change and this is part of a report that he recently presented at a conference on global warming. Read the text and write down five words or phrases that you don't know.

C1c Now walk around the class with your list of unknown words and phrases and ask other students if they know what they mean.

If the polar ice caps continue to melt at the present rate, sea levels will rise, coast-lines, islands and land below sea level will be destroyed, and people will have to leave these areas. We already have an increase in heavy rainfall and serious flooding in north-ern Europe and this trend will continue. At the same time, in Africa, the Sahara is growing and we will have more serious droughts in southern Europe. Worldwide we already have an increase in serious, destructive storms and this trend will also continue. However, we may be able to slow things down if we reduce CO_2 emissions...

C2a Dave predicts that these changes really *will happen*, but some people only think that they *may happen*.
Make dialogues by matching the left and the right column.

1. As Dave said, ice caps will continue to melt.
2. There'll be an increase in heavy rainfall.
3. Dave believes that we'll have serious droughts in southern Europe.
4. I'm sure that this trend will continue.

a. But we may be able to slow things down if we reduce CO_2 emissions.
b. Or there may be more flooding. Who knows?
c. I'm not sure. There may actually be droughts in some areas.
d. Well, we don't really know. They may stop melting and then things will be all right.

8

C2b   Listen to the dialogues and check.
Then work with a partner and make up more dialogues of your own.

Homestudy
H3

Companion:
Grammar 2.6.3, 2.7.6

C2c   Work together and change some of the examples
of *will* in the text in C1b to *may* or *might*.
How does that affect what Dave is saying?
Example: This trend *may/might* continue.

Exploring learning   p. 76

TIP 2 Experiment with written texts by changing some of the words.

C2d   Dave says that we could slow down these changes.
We could all do something to save energy and reduce CO_2 emissions.
Collect some ideas on the board.
Examples: I switch off the lights when I leave a room.
I'd buy a car with much lower fuel consumption.
We use LED products for lighting.

C2e   What is the most useful, realistic idea? Take a class vote.

D   Back to the basics

D1a   If you could keep only one outfit or set of clothes and had to wear it for a whole year,
which outfit would that be? Talk to a partner.
Examples: I have a favourite dress. I'd wear that.
I'd wear my jeans and a blue shirt.

Remember
What **would you wear** if **you had**
to choose one outfit for a year?

D1b   Look at the first paragraph of the text in D1c.
What do you think the word *sustainable* means? Tick.

☐ using methods that protect the environment

☐ wearing things for a long time without washing them

D1c   Now read this text about Sheena Matheiken's Uniform Project.
Fill in the word wheel on the next page with all the words and phrases from the
text that have to do with sustainable fashion.

Blog + News   **About**   *Dress For Sale*   *Donate*   *Accessories*

SHEENA MATHEIKEN *is a young Indian woman who lives in New York
City. She promised to wear one dress for a whole year as an exercise in
sustainable fashion. How does that work?*

*There are actually seven identical dresses, one for each day of the week. Every
day she wears the dress differently, with layers and second-hand accessories
that she buys on eBay, in charity shops, or at flea markets. Her friend, who
is a designer, took one of Sheena's favourite dresses and improved on the fit.
It can be worn both ways, buttoning in front or at the back, and also like an*

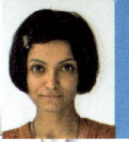

open jacket. It's made of good breathable cotton, which is good for New York summers and for layering in cooler seasons, and it's easy to wash. There are also some big pockets because Sheena hates carrying things.

If you have any old accessories that you don't need anymore, you can donate them to Sheena.

She's using The Uniform Project to support a school project in India and to help children living in Indian slums. It lasts one year and at the end, all the money will go to this project for school uniforms, books, computers, teacher training, etc.

Exploring learning p. 76

TIP 3 When you read a text use a word wheel for a main idea and add related words.

sustainable fashion

D1d Decide together how you could wear the outfit you chose in D1a in different seasons and for different occasions. Draw a simple sketch with your partner.

Example: I'd wear my black jeans and a grey shirt. In the summer I could roll up the sleeves. I have a pullover that I'd wear with it in the winter.

Homestudy
4

Companion:
Grammar 2.6.2

D1e Make plans to support your local charity shop. Tell the class about it.

Example: There's an Oxfam shop just around the corner from my house. I'm going to take some stuff there next week.

Focus on grammar
I'm **going to** take some stuff there next week.

D2a Throw away or use? Look at the pictures and match the statements.

1. ☐ I used to be a yoghurt container but now I freeze soup.
2. ☐ I used to be an oil drum but now I'm part of a cello.
3. ☐ I used to hold a candle but now I'm an egg cup.
4. ☐ I used to be a pullover but now I'm a scarf.

b.

a.

c.

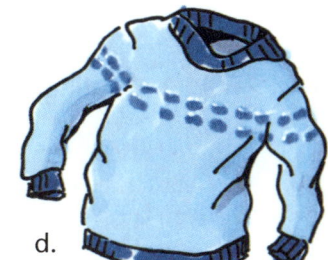

d.

D2b What do you have at home that could be turned into something else instead of throwing it away? Work in groups and collect some ideas. The group with the best idea is *Recycler of the Week*.

Exploring my progress

At the end of this unit I can …

… talk about how things used to be and compare that with today. (People used to buy milk from the milkman; today they go to a shop.)	☐	☐	A1a, A2, H1
… read and understand a longer text by guessing unknown words from the context. (I think "herd" must mean a large group of animals of the same type.)	☐	☐	A1d, A1e
… talk about possible changes and imagine what the effects of these changes would be. (If I rode my bike more, I'd be healthier.)	☐	☐	B1c, H2
… talk about what I think is certain in the future and what I think is possible. (Experts say that islands will be destroyed, but they may not.)	☐	☐	C2a, C2c, H3
… talk about and share ideas for a different lifestyle. (I'd get a car with better petrol consumption.)	☐	☐	C2d, D1d
… talk in a simple way about ideas for recycling.	☐	☐	B2f, D2b, H2

Online-Übungen ▶ S. 128

Exploring learning – reading

A1d TIP 1 **When you read try to guess words and phrases**

Very often it's possible to guess the meaning of unknown words and phrases from the context. You can always look in a dictionary, but try to get into the habit of trusting yourself and guessing.

C2c TIP 2 **Experiment with written texts by changing some of the words**

A good way to practise English is to take a reading text that you like and change something. You can change the verbs or the verb forms, you can use different nouns or you can add something. This way you get a better feel for the language.

D1c TIP 3 **When you read a text use a word wheel for a main idea and add related words**

This is a good way to understand and structure more difficult texts and work on vocabulary at the same time.

 Reading

It can also be helpful to put away an English text after reading it and to note down all the words and phrases you can remember. The interesting thing is that you will not always write down exactly what was in the text, but something similar. This shows that you have understood the text because you are using other language that you know.

 Learning outside the classroom

If you read something in English, try and retell in English what you understood to yourself – or to someone else. Remember to use simple language. You may easily discover that you have understood more than you think.

Good health

What language does your heart speak?

Would you like an appointment at a spa?

Have you ever had health problems or
an accident on holiday?

9

A Your body

Homestudy
H1

A1a Work in pairs. How many different parts of the body can you label?

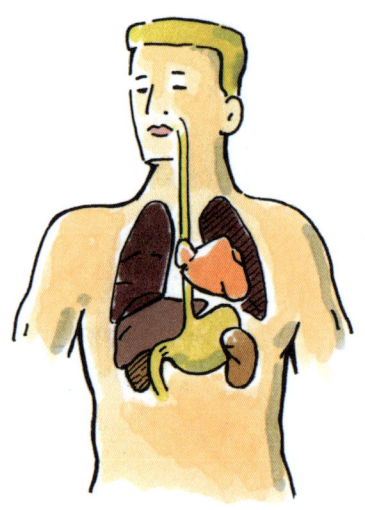

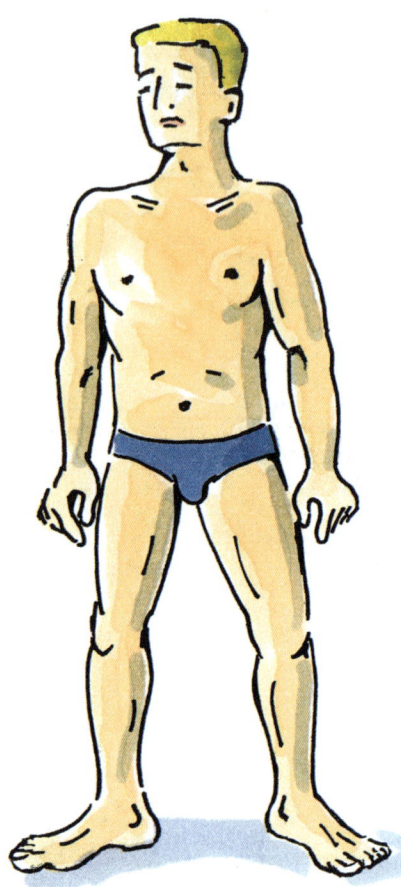

A1b Compare your labels with other students in the class.

 A2a In an English class for migrants in England, the teacher asked the students a question (see below). Listen and make notes of the students' answers.

The teacher's question: Think about the languages that you know.
Imagine that different languages "live" in different parts of your body.
Which languages go with which parts of your body?

Name	Part of the body / Language
Hassan from Iran	heart / Farsi
Ximena from Colombia	
Rolf from Germany	

A2b What about you? What parts of your body "speak" different languages? Write down your ideas with a partner and then tell the rest of the class.

A3a What do you think the following expressions mean? Match them with the explanations.

1. Use your head.
2. Have a heart.
3. Oh dear, I put my foot in it.
4. Give us a hand, please.
5. You've got green fingers (UK) / a green thumb (US).

a. Please help us.
b. Think. Don't be stupid.
c. You're very good at gardening.
d. Be kind, be nice.
e. I said the wrong thing, something embarrassing.

A3b Do you have the same expressions in your language(s) or similar expressions?

Homestudy
H2 – H4

A4 What medical problems do you know? Match a word from a box on the left with a word or phrase from the box on the right. There's more than one solution.

| cut \| cut \| break \| get \| sprain |
| get \| get \| get |

bitten by a snake | your finger | your leg
hit on the head | sunburnt | your ankle
yourself | stung by a wasp

Example: cut yourself

Exploring learning p. 84 **TIP 1** Learn expressions and words that go together.

B Looking after your body

B1a Work with a partner. Read the adverts for treatments and exercise at the Utopia Spa. Find a good programme for the situations below. (More than one answer is possible!)

1. You have dry skin and you think you're looking old. _____
2. You often have headaches after sitting at your computer all day. _____
3. You don't get enough exercise and you sit all day. _____
4. You work very hard and you're feeling generally tired and stressed. _____

Utopia Spa and Health Salon

Trilling Farm, Chanley, Wiltshire, BA38 6BY — 01227 682 4592 www.utopia-trilling.com

Indian head massage

This is the ideal treatment if your neck or shoulders are stiff and aching. It's also excellent if you're suffering from a head-ache. The massage includes a neck and shoulder massage, followed by a massage of the head. This improves your blood circu-lation. The treatment finishes with a face massage to really relax you.

You sit in a chair for this treatment and the therapist uses a range of different move-ments, both strong and gentle massage. It lasts from twenty to forty-five minutes, but it's a good idea to sit quietly for ten or twenty minutes after the massage is over.

Abhyangam

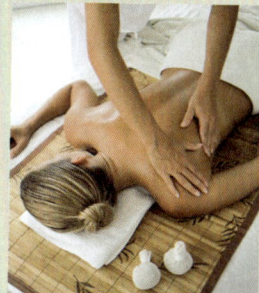

This is a tradi-tional Ayurvedic de-stress mas-sage. It'll relax you and help to decrease your blood pressure. It'll make you feel well.

The therapist in this treatment uses special oils. The oils are warmed and poured over the body. The therapist then waits some minutes before she starts with the massage. She massages the whole body using rhyth-mic, gentle strokes of the palm of her hand. This massage is different from a lot of Western massage techniques: it's not strong and deep, it's gentle. The oils are massaged into the skin. After the treatment, you should take a warm shower and relax.

Facial

We have a range of luxurious facials. Do you want skin that's healthy and soft? Do you want to look young and relaxed? We have treatments for tired skin, for dry skin, for oily skin, for every kind of skin. After one of our facials you'll leave us feeling better and looking great.

Each facial treatment begins with a fifteen-minute skincare consultation which allows you and your therapist to discuss your needs, and for your therapist to analyze your skin before beginning the treatment. To continue the benefits of your facial treat-ments at home, we offer a full range of skincare products to keep you looking and feeling fantastic for the weeks to come.

Pilates

Do you have back problems? Stiffness in your hips and legs or your shoulders and arms? Do you feel unfit? Pilates is an exer-cise method to strengthen and balance your body. Your Pilates teacher will develop a full and personal exercise programme for you. Pilates is a form of exercise that's good for everyone. It doesn't matter what your age or what your fitness level is, Pilates can help you restore your body's strength and balance. Pilates is a gentle, non-aerobic form of exercise that will strengthen your muscles and help your posture when standing, sitting or moving. It can help stop back pain. It can relax your muscles and help you sleep better. It can reduce stress.

9

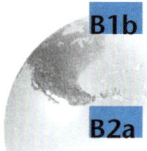

B1b Which programme would you like to have yourself?
Are these programmes popular in the area where you live?

B2a Work in pairs. Prepare the following phone call.

Doris Speich from Bochum has an old friend from England who lives near the Utopia Spa.
Her friend's name is Samantha Stone and it's her fortieth birthday next week. Doris thinks
she'll buy her a treatment at the Utopia Spa. She telephones the spa to ask about the treatments
that she's seen on their website and to book one for her friend, Samantha.

What questions will she need to ask? What information will she need to give?

Exploring learning p. 84

TIP 2 Prepare if you can.

2 12 **B2b** Listen to Doris calling the spa. The first part of the conversation is about choosing
a treatment. Is the telephone conversation like the one you prepared in B2a?

2 12 **B2c** Listen again and tick the problems that Doris had.
What did she do when she had these problems?

Problem	Yes	No	What Doris did
1. She wasn't sure if she had the right number.	[X]	☐	_She asked a checking question._
2. She didn't know how to pronounce a word.	☐	☐	_____
3. She didn't expect a question from the spa.	☐	☐	_____
4. She had trouble with the names of the days.	☐	☐	_____

Exploring learning p. 84

TIP 3 Prepare for when things go wrong.

2 13 **B2d** Listen to the second part of the conversation about paying for the treatment.
Is this part of the telephone conversation like the one you prepared in B2a?

Homestudy
H5

B3a Now try the phone call with your partner.

Student A (Doris) asks about the different treatments, asks about the prices, chooses a
treatment, gives the necessary information to book the treatment and pay for it.
Student B (Utopia Spa) answers questions, says when the spa is full, asks for the names
of the people and the credit card details. Look at page 99 for more information.

B3b Change roles and try it again.

C Holiday problems

C1 What's the most common health problem that
tourists have?

- sunburn
- upset stomach and diarrhoea
- alcohol poisoning
- flu
- broken leg
- …

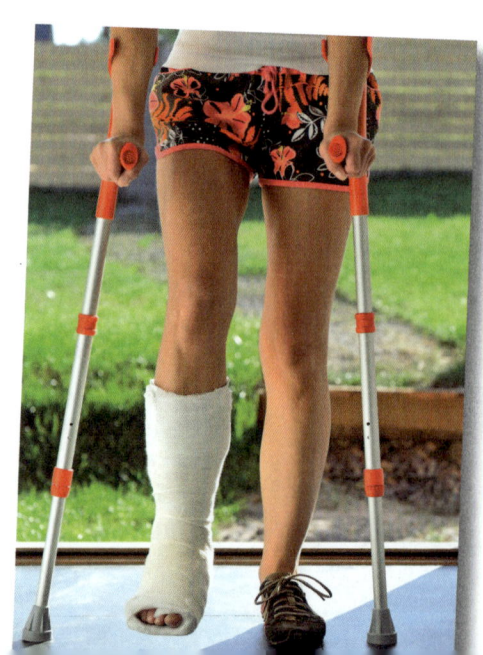

C2a Fergal Connor is a family doctor in a village in the west of Ireland.
Tourists come to see him when they're ill. Listen to Dr Connor talk to three patients.
What are the problems and what does Dr Connor tell them?

a. What's the problem?

Michael: He has _____.

Teija: She _____.

Pierre: He _____.

b. What's the treatment and advice?

Michael: He needs to _____.

He should _____.

Teija: She needs to _____.

She should _____.

Pierre: The doctor needs to _____.

Pierre should _____.

mpanion:
ammar 2.9.2

mpanion:
ammar 3.18

Focus on grammar
Teija **got sunburnt** yesterday.

Focus on grammar
Pierre **cut himself** yesterday.

C2b Listen to Pierre again.
What does he do when he has a problem understanding the doctor?

C3a What can the following things protect you against?

- vaccination
- hat
- sun cream / sunblock
- bottled water
- pills / tablets
- good shoes or boots

Example: A vaccination protects you against an illness.

mestudy

C3b What advice can you give to holidaymakers to avoid illness and accidents?
Work in pairs and make a list of pieces of advice for the following situations.

a. when you go to the beach
b. when you go walking in the mountains
c. when you travel in very hot countries in Asia or Africa
d. when you travel by air

mpanion:
ammar 2.7.3

Remember
You **should** wear good shoes. / You **ought to** wear good shoes.
You **need to** put on sunblock. / You **need** sunblock.

C3c Compare your ideas with the rest of the class.
Make a "top ten" list of advice for travellers.

9

D The worst holiday

D1a Work in twos or threes and discuss the following situation.

When people get married, they often spend a lot of money on their honeymoon. But sometimes things can go wrong. What can go wrong on a holiday? Make a list of your ideas and compare them with the rest of the class.

D1b Ross and Lara's honeymoon went wrong. Read the beginning of the report in their local newspaper. Can you find any of your ideas from D1a?

Local couple has unexpected guests on honeymoon

Ross (29) and Lara (32) Jenkins from Little Basset planned the perfect honeymoon, but their romantic dreams went terribly wrong. Lara booked for them to stay in a special resort on an island in Malaysia. In this resort they had a little cabin in the jungle by the sea. The cabin was about 500 metres from the town of Tengukan where there was a normal hotel and a couple of restaurants. On their first day they walked along the beach to the little town and had some lunch in the restaurant. When they got back, they found monkeys in their cabin! This is our artist's impression of what Lara and Ross saw when they came back.

D2 The holiday got worse.
When Lara got home from the holiday, she wrote the whole story in an email to the travel company. Read part of her email to find out what happened next. Can you guess the missing words? Work with a partner and complete the sentences.

To: admin@honeymoon...
From: Lara.jenkins@fmail.co.uk
Date: 25 June

My husband, Ross, tried to get the monkeys out of the cabin. He went in and shouted at them but then they _____ (1) him. One of the monkeys _____ (2) him on the hand. Then when Ross ran out of the cabin, he fell and _____ (3) his _____ (4). We were on the beach then but Ross couldn't _____ (5) so I stayed there with him. One of the monkeys came and took my hat. Somebody went to get help but we had to wait for over an hour. It was very hot and the sun was very strong and I got _____ (6). In the end, the ambulance people came and they took us to the _____ (7) in the main town. We had to spend 24 hours there.

2 16

D3a There was a representative of the travel company on the island.
His name was Mr Johnson. Lara asked him to come to the hospital.
What did he say? Listen and fill in the gaps.

Mr Johnson: "Oh, I _____ (1) so sorry, but I'm afraid I _____ (2) very busy at the moment
but I _____ (3) come as soon as I _____ (4). I _____ (5) sure the people in
the hospital _____ (6) look after you well."

D3b Mr Johnson didn't come for three
hours. Here is what Lara wrote
about Mr Johnson in her email to the
travel company. As you can see the
words you filled in under D3a change.
Compare and underline them.

> When I first called Mr Johnson, he said that he <u>was</u> sorry but he was busy. He told us that he would come as soon as he could. He said he was sure the people in the hospital would look after us well. In fact, we had to wait three hours before he came.

D3c When Mr Johnson came to the hospital
he still did not do anything to help
Lara and Ross. Instead he made a lot
of excuses and promises. Read them first and then
read the next part of Lara's email. Fill in the gaps.

> "I'll get you some more clothes." ▌ "I can't move you to the hotel because it's full."
> "I'll make sure that the monkeys don't come into the cabin again." ▌ "I'll send somebody
> to sleep in the cabin with you." ▌ "I can't stay. I'm sorry but I'll see you tomorrow."

> When Mr Johnson came to the hospital he said that he _____ (1) us some more
> clothes. We explained that we wanted to move to a hotel. He explained that he _____ (2)
> us to the hotel because it _____ (3) full. He promised he _____ (4)
> that the monkeys _____ (5) into the cabin again. We said that we were afraid
> to sleep in the cabin. Mr Johnson replied that he _____ (6) somebody to sleep in
> the cabin with us. But this person never arrived. We were alone in the hospital and we needed help,
> but Mr Johnson said that he _____ (7). He said he _____ (8) sorry but
> that he _____ (9) us the next day.

Companion:
Grammar 1.7.2

Focus on grammar

"The hotel's full."
He said (that) the hotel **was** full.
"I'll come as soon as I **can**."
He said (that) he **would** come as soon as he **could**.

Homestudy

D4 Has a travel company ever promised you something that it didn't do?
Or were you ever ill or did you ever have an accident on holiday?
What did people say that they would do? And did they do it?
Share your stories with the rest of the class.

Examples: The company said that the hotel **was** near the beach
but it was two kilometres away from the sea.
The company said that they **would** organize activities for the children, but they didn't.

9

Exploring my progress

At the end of this unit I can ...			
... talk about some basic medical problems or accidents. (I've cut myself.)	☐	☐	A4, C1, C2, D3, H2–H4
... read short texts, for example advertisements, to locate specific information.	☐	☐	B1a
... make a phone call to make a reservation, for example at a health spa.	☐	☐	B3, H5
... give somebody advice, for example to avoid illness or accidents. (You should wear good shoes.)	☐	☐	C3, H6
... report what somebody said. (He told us he would come as soon as he could.)	☐	☐	D4, H7

Online-Übungen ▶ S. 131

Exploring learning – strategies and techniques for better communication

A4 TIP 1 **Learn expressions and words that go together**

Don't forget to notice expressions and groups of words that go together. Learn them and then use them when you're writing or speaking.

B2a TIP 2 **Prepare if you can**

Before you make a phone call or before you go into a shop to buy something, you can think about what you're going to say, and guess what the other people are going to say. Imagine the conversation and prepare it.

B2c TIP 3 **Prepare for when things go wrong**

If you don't understand something or you don't know how to say something, there are lots of different things you can do. Don't panic! Doris in B2b and Pierre in C2b show you a few ways to deal with such problems.

The secret of good communication

Good communication is like a good dance with a partner. One partner can lead but the other person has to work hard, too. Your English isn't perfect but you can now communicate in English. You just need some strategies and some techniques to help you when there are problems. The learning tips in this unit are ideas for you to use.

Learning outside the classroom

If you know that you are going on holiday soon, you can get your suitcase ready but you can also prepare your English. Think about what words and phrases you will need. Try to learn them or make some lists to take with you and look at when you're travelling. If you have an English-speaking person who is coming to visit you, you can also prepare things that you will need to say. Remember the motto of the scouts: Be prepared!

C1 If you had to live and work in another country for two years, which country would you choose? Why? Discuss this with your partner.
Example: I'd love to go to Brazil. What about you?
– I think I'd prefer Spain.

C2a You get an email from a friend of yours, Kira. Read the first part of her email. Where is she going to live? Why? Who is Dustin?

Dear friends,

Guess what? Last week my boss called me into his office and asked me if I wanted to work abroad for two years! At first I thought he meant the USA or Great Britain but no, it's China! I had to think about it for a day or two and didn't tell anyone except Dustin, but now I've decided. It's a great chance and I must take it. I'll miss Dustin of course, but I think we'll stay together and he can come and see me in China. I'm leaving at the end of next month …

C2b What questions do you want to ask Kira?
In groups, decide on three questions you would ask her.
Example: How much will you earn?

C2c Now read the rest of Kira's email. Can you find the answers?

I'm going to live in Shanghai. I'll have a small flat which belongs to the company. It's smaller than the flat I have now but fully furnished. I also have a maid to clean the flat for me. Luxury! I will earn a lot more than here so that Dustin and I can get a big flat together when I come back. I will also have a car and a driver so my life will be quite different. I'll tell you more soon.
Love Kira

C3a What do you know about China? Can you answer these questions?

1. How many people live in China?
2. What are the three biggest cities?
3. What are the two main languages?
4. Which countries have borders with China?

C3b Do you think this information will be useful for Kira?

C3c After you get the email you hear a radio programme about China and want to give Kira the information. Make notes and compare your answers in groups.

What information will she need about …

1. … food?   4. … business?
2. … language?   5. … festivals?
3. … transport?

C4   **Here is some information about Kira.**
What will change for her when she lives in China?
Examples: She often eats currywurst. – She won't eat currywurst very often.
          She cleans her flat once a week. – She won't have to clean her flat.
          She'll have a maid to work for her.

1. She goes skiing and snowboarding in the winter.
2. She often goes to the cinema.
3. She takes the underground to go to work.
4. She watches German films.
5. She takes the car to the garage to get it repaired.
6. She does the dishes when she gets home after work.
7. She often goes to an Italian restaurant to have dinner.

C5a   **Kira invites her friends to a clutter party.**
What's a clutter party?

a) a party where you give things away
b) a goodbye party
c) a party only for girls and women

C5b   **Now read her invitation. Were you right?**

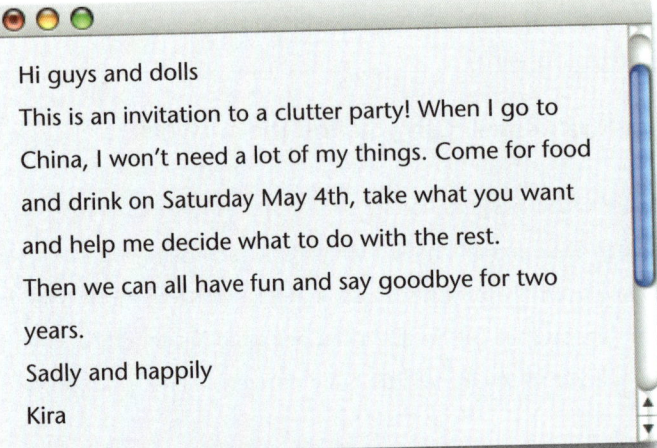

Hi guys and dolls

This is an invitation to a clutter party! When I go to China, I won't need a lot of my things. Come for food and drink on Saturday May 4th, take what you want and help me decide what to do with the rest.
Then we can all have fun and say goodbye for two years.
Sadly and happily
Kira

C6a   **Here's a list of things Kira doesn't want.**
What can she do with them? Decide what you would do with some of the things on her list.
Examples: She can throw them away.
          She can give them to me /
          to somebody / to an Oxfam shop …
          She can sell them on eBay …

an old cassette player
novels in German and English
a wok
an exercise bicycle
garden chairs
a lamp
files
a Teach-Yourself-Spanish course
a ballgown
a computer and printer

C6b   **Discuss your answers with a partner.**

C7   **You and your friends write a goodbye letter to Kira.**
Write the letter. Include the following points.

- say how you feel about her leaving
- say something about China
- thank her for the things she gave you
- wish her good luck

 # Party time

Is there anything that you don't eat or drink?

What kind of party food do you prefer?

What have you learnt on this course?

10

A   What don't you eat?

A1a Work with a partner. Find two or three examples of these types of food.
Then compare your answers with the rest of the class. How many examples did you find?

meat

vegetables

salad

fruit

A1b Can you match the following types of food with their examples?

> cod **|** crab **|** lobster **|** prawns **|** salmon **|** herring **|** sea bass
> shrimp **|** trout **|** perch **|** oysters **|** mussels **|** clams

freshwater fish _____

sea fish _____

other seafood _____

Homestudy H1

A1c Now match the animals with their meat.

1. beef
2. game
3. lamb
4. mutton
5. pork
6. veal
7. venison

a. any kind of wild animal or bird
b. calf (young cow)
c. cow
d. deer
e. lamb (young sheep)
f. pig
g. sheep

2 ⊙ 23

Homestudy H2

A2a A local radio station recently asked people in London about what they don't eat.
Match the people with what they say.

1. Sally
2. Neil
3. Sanjiv
4. Shakira
5. Kee Loo
6. Kelly
7. Bruce
8. Branwen
9. Mike

a. no horse meat
b. no meat, fish, cheese, milk, eggs, etc.
c. no green vegetables
d. no bread
e. no meat or fish
f. no pork
g. no cheap eggs
h. no alcohol
i. no beef

A2b Work in small groups. Talk about what you eat or don't eat. What about other people in your area? Are there some things that nobody eats in your country or region?

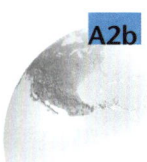

Is there any food that …
- you can't eat because it makes you ill?
- you don't eat for moral, cultural or religious reasons?
- you don't eat because you just don't like it?
- you don't eat for health reasons?

Exploring learning p. 94 **TIP 1** Make sure that you can give important information about yourself.

B Organizing the party

Homestudy
H3

B1 In pairs, write an email.

Step 1: Read about the situation.

Amy Black works for the Phoenix Foundation, an international organization that supports networks of young business people from all over the world. It's near the end of a course in England with thirty international participants and Amy has to organize a final dinner for all the participants. She writes to them to get some information.

Step 2: Which expressions do you think Amy will choose for her email to the participants? Tick.

1. ☐ a. Your course finished after two weeks.
   ☐ b. Your course finishes in two weeks.

2. ☐ a. I'd like to organize a dinner for you on the Friday after next.
   ☐ b. I'd like to organize a dinner for you on the Friday before last.

3. ☐ a. I need to decide on the menu, so it would be very helpful if you could tell me about what you like or don't like to eat.
   ☐ b. I need to decide what we're going to eat, so is there anything that you refuse to eat?

4. ☐ a. Please let me know tomorrow morning because I'm meeting the catering company at 9:00.
   ☐ b. Please let me know by tomorrow morning because I'm meeting the catering company at 9:00.

Step 3: Read a copy of Amy's email text in the key at the end of the book.

Step 4: Write a message like this to your class.
Tell them

Companion:
Grammar 5.4.1, 5.4.2

- that you are organizing a meal or a party.
- when and ask them what they'd like to eat and drink.
- when to send you their answer.

> **Focus on grammar**
> Friday **after next**
> **by** 9:00 tomorrow morning

Step 5: Exchange messages with another pair.
Write a short answer to the message that you get.
Can you go to the meal/party? What can you eat and drink?

B2a   **What kind of meal would be best? Match the words with the photos.**

1. ☐ finger food

2. ☐ a sit-down meal

3. ☐ a buffet

c.

a.

b.

B2b   **Work with a partner. Amy has a meeting with Rob from the catering company that wants to do the meal and the entertainment for her party. Listen for the following information.**

1. Does Amy prefer finger food, a buffet or a sit-down meal?
2. What food does she not want at the party?
3. What two kinds of entertainment does Rob suggest?

B3a   **Listen again. What do the following sentences mean? Tick.**

1. "I'll get that organized."

☐   a. Amy's going to make the tea herself.

☐   b. Amy's going to ask somebody else to make the tea for her
(but we don't know who at this point).

2. "They can get the people to sing and to dance."

☐   a. They can somehow encourage or persuade the guests at the party to sing and dance.

☐   b. They can sing and dance for the guests at the party.

B3b   **With your partner, organize a party for your class. Decide who can do the work to prepare the party! You don't want to have to do anything: you just want to organize the party! Here are some ideas of the jobs that have to be done.**

> send out the invitations **|** prepare food **|** book the room
> go shopping for the drinks **|** choose the music **|** sing **|** dance

Homestudy
H4

Companion:
Grammar 2.9.2

B3c   **Report your "decisions" to the class. What do the others think about your ideas?**
Examples: We'd like to get Michael to prepare
the food because we know he likes cooking.
We think that we'll get Sandra to choose
the music.

> **Focus on grammar**
> I'll **get** that **organized**.
> They can **get** the people **to sing**.

C Changing the arrangements

C1a Rob sends Amy two quotes for the catering: one for the buffet with karaoke and one for the Greek evening. With a partner, think about the following questions.

a. Which quote do you think Amy will choose?
b. What sort of changes do you think Amy needs to make?

C1b Now listen to the phone conversation between Amy and Rob and check your answers from C1a.

C2a Listen to the beginning of the conversation again. What question does Rob ask Amy?

"… Did you get my quotes? I gave you a choice between the mixed buffet with karaoke and the Greek evening. _____ _____ _____ _____ prefer?"

C2b Work in pairs. Practise asking your partner what he or she would prefer.
Example: What kind of wine have you got?
   – I've got red, white or rosé. Which one would you prefer?

wine	red, white, rosé	**pizza**	salami, tuna, mushroom
meat	beef, lamb, pork	**soft drinks**	mineral water, Coke, orange juice
music	pop, jazz, classical	**coffee**	espresso, latte, americano

> **Focus on grammar**
>
> **What** kind of meat have you got?
> – I've got beef, lamb or pork. **Which** (one) would you prefer?

C3a Discuss in groups.

Imagine that the English classes in your school have won some money and you have decided to have a party and hire a catering company. Divide into two groups. Discuss the points below. Everybody has to make notes of what you decide.

Group A You represent the English classes. You have to decide:
- how many people are coming to the party
- how much money you can spend (e.g. twenty euros per person)
- if any people are vegetarian or if they can't eat certain types of food
- the time and date for the party
- what kind of food and entertainment you want

Group B You represent the catering company. You have to decide:
- what sort of food your company can offer
- what sort of entertainment your company can offer
- how much things cost (for example a buffet with a DJ)

C3b Role-play the situation in the following way.

- One person from Group A and Group B play the situation and try to decide what sort of party it's going to be. You don't have to decide everything. The caterer can agree to send a quote later.
- The others listen and give some feedback afterwards. Was the meeting successful? Was the information clear? Did they agree at the end about anything?
- Then change roles. The first two people now listen to the others and give some feedback.

xploring learning p. 94   **TIP 2** Learn from the other students.

10

C3c If you enjoyed C3b and you have time for more practice, continue. Have new conversations. There are more changes.

1. A has to tell B about some changes to the party plans. Look at p. 97 for some ideas. B has to react.

or

2. B has to tell A about some changes to the quote two days before the party. Look at p. 99 for some ideas. A has to react.

D At the party

D1a The end-of-course party is taking place. Listen to these little extracts from different conversations. With a partner, guess the situation. What's happening?
Example: I think he's going to get his food from the buffet.

Homestudy H6

D1b What could you say in the following situations?
Match the expressions.

1. You are offering somebody a drink.
2. You've just spilt a glass of wine on the table.
3. You're looking for somewhere to sit down.
4. You want to get food from the buffet.

a. Is anybody sitting here?
b. Are you in a queue?
c. Oh, I'm so sorry. How clumsy of me!
d. Is this a line?
e. Can I get you something to drink?
f. Is this seat free?
g. Oh, how stupid of me! Please excuse me.
h. Would you like a glass of wine?

D2 Role-play the party, using as many expressions from D1 as possible. Mime the different situations.

Imagine that the party is taking place in your classroom.
There are different things happening at the same time.
- Set up a barbecue (teacher's desk) with your teacher in charge of it. Now take turns and ask him/her for food.
- Arrange a table with some chairs where some people are already sitting. Take turns and ask politely if you can sit with them.
- Make small talk about the weather, their families, their jobs, etc.

D3a Bharat, a participant on the course from India, gives a little speech at the end of the party. Listen.

a. Is it a personal speech or does he speak for the whole group?
b. He thanks three people or groups of people. Who are they? Who is the main person he thanks?
c. What does he thank the different people for?
d. Is he positive about the course? In what way?

27 **D3b** **Listen again.**

1. How does Bharat explain that he's speaking for the whole group?

2. Tick what Bharat says.

   ☐ a. We learnt that we all have the same problems.

   ☐ b. We've learnt that we all have the same problems.

ompanion:
rammar 2.3.1

Focus on grammar

We**'ve learnt** lots of new things so now we **can** do our job better.

3. What do you think Bharat means by using *we've*? Tick.

   ☐ a. He wants to say: we now "have" what we learnt and so we now have new ideas for our work.

   ☐ b. He wants to say: the course is now finished and perhaps we'll forget this when we get home.

4. How many times does Bharat say *we've* …?

D4a **Read the following extract from a learner's diary. Use this text as a model and talk with a partner about your English course. What have you learnt, and what can you do better now? Then compare your ideas with the rest of the class.**

Our course started about a year ago. At that time, some of us came from an earlier course and some were new in the group. A year ago I could only take part in very simple and very short conversations. I often had a lot of problems understanding the CDs when we heard something only once. But now we've learnt more English so we can have longer conversations and I can talk about everyday situations a lot better. We've had

a lot of practice listening to English so now I can often understand the main points from something on the CD when I hear it for the first time. I've learnt the most important verb tenses so I can now talk about things in the past, the present and the future. I don't always remember to use the right form at the right time, but it's getting better slowly. I've learnt a lot of words but there are still lots more words that I'll have to learn.

D4b **Find the right form of the verb for the following sentences from the text in D4a.**

a. Our course _____ (start) about a year ago. … I often _____ (have) a lot of problems understanding the CDs when we heard something only once.

b. But now we _____ (learn) more English so we can have longer conversations and we can talk about everyday situations a lot better. We _____ (have) a lot of practice listening to English so now we can often understand the main points … when we hear it for the first time.

ompanion:
rammar 2.3.2

D4c **Highlight the verb forms in the text in D4a.**

Focus on grammar

Our course **started** a year ago.
Now **we've learnt** more English so we can have longer conversations.

omestudy
7

D5 **Write a short text about what you've learnt on the course and what you can do better now.**
Then compare with what other people on the course have written.

Exploring learning p. 94 **TIP 3** It's good to look back.

D6 **With a partner, prepare a short speech for the end of your course.**
Then you can all give your speeches to the class!

Exploring my progress

At the end of this unit I can …			
… tell people what I do not or cannot eat. (I don't eat any meat or fish. I'm a vegetarian.)	☐	☐	A2, H2
… write a short email to organize a party.	☐	☐	B1, H3
… listen to a conversation and understand important information from it, for example information about the food for a party.	☐	☐	B2b
… ask people to choose between a number of possibilities. (Which one would you prefer?)	☐	☐	C2, H5
… hold a short meeting with someone, e.g. to organize a party.	☐	☐	C3b, C3c
… deal with situations at a party. (Is anybody sitting here? / Can I get you a glass of wine? etc.)	☐	☐	D2, H6
… explain what I've learnt on the course.	☐	☐	D5, H7
… give a short speech at the end of something, e.g. a course.	☐	☐	D6

Online-Übungen ▶ S. 132

Exploring learning – making progress

A2b TIP 1 Make sure that you can give important information about yourself
One of the main aims for you at this level of English is to give important information about yourself. When you think about what you've learnt, make sure that you can explain, for example, about dietary requirements, but also about your family, your job and other important parts of your life.

C3b TIP 2 Learn from the other students
Have you noticed that you can often learn a lot from the other students in your class? It's because they are at about the same level as you, so you can easily copy them. When you give feedback to other people, give the sort of feed-back that you would like to have. Was it clear? Did you understand? Did the other person use some good words or expressions?

D5 TIP 3 It's good to look back
It's important to look back at the end of a semester or at the end of a course. When you're learning English, you sometimes think that you are not getting better because you get better too slowly. But remember what you could do at the beginning of the course and then compare that with what you can do now. You can then usually see a difference. Now you need to think about your next course! What do you want to learn next?

How good am I now?
When you get to the end of the course, it's a good moment to think about how good your English is now. You've finished the B1/1 book. At the end of the B1/2 book you should be at the B1 level.

Companion → Look in Your link to the Portfolio for more information about the B1 level and how to measure how good you are now.

Learning outside the classroom
For most people at your level now, the biggest challenge is to learn more and more vocabulary. There are so many words and expressions to learn. A good way to learn words and to remember them is to read and listen to lots of English. Ask your teacher about easy things to read (for example the "readers"). Try to watch more TV in English if you have the chance. Use the Internet.

What can you say in English?

Play a game and find out!

Rules
1. Play the game on page 96 in groups of three or four.
2. Each player uses a different small object as a marker (for example a coin).
3. Put your marker on START and throw the dice.
4. Move the number of squares on the dice.
5. Read the sentence on the square you land on. Give an example or role-play the situation with a partner.
6. The other players decide whether your example is correct or not.
   If they are not sure, they can turn to the key on page 146.
   There's a reference to the unit and an example to check.
7. If your answer is correct, you can stay on the square until your next turn.
8. If your answer is not correct, you must go back to your original position.
9. The first player to reach FINISH is the winner.

Have fun!

I can ...

START	2 ... ask what someone enjoys doing.	3 ... say what I find difficult about learning English.	4 Miss a turn.	5 ... say what I ought to practise in English.	6 ... give my opinion in a discussion.
7 ... report something someone said.	8 Go back three squares.	9 ... complain about something in a hotel.	10 ... describe a good job or a bad job.	11 ... describe my recent life using *since* or *for*.	12 Have another turn.
13 ... describe a person's character.	14 ... answer a question about myself in an interview.	15 Go ahead two squares.	16 ... tell a short story about something that happened to me.	17 ... talk about which films I like to watch at the cinema.	18 ... talk about your reading habits.
19 Go back seven squares.	20 ... say something about my taste in music.	21 ... give some details about my family.	22 ... ask someone for their opinion.	23 Have another turn.	24 ... disagree with someone politely.
25 ... compare life in two different countries.	26 ... say what I would do if won a lot of money.	27 Go back five squares.	28 ... talk about how things have changed.	29 ... say how things will change in the future.	30 Miss a turn.
31 ... talk about how things used to be.	32 ... say that something may or may not happen.	33 ... describe a basic medical problem.	34 Go back four squares.	35 ... make a reservation on the phone.	36 ... report an accident.
37 ... report what somebody said.	38 Go back two squares.	39 ... say what I don't or can't eat.	40 ... give someone a choice of two things.	41 ... explain something I've learnt in this course.	**FINISH**

Unit 2

C2a **Group 1**

Here's what some soap opera fans say.

- I watch soap operas to escape from reality; it's a break from my real life.
- I can imagine myself as one of the characters in one of those real life situations on the show. It's a mirror on everyday life.
- I like to watch drama. I can sit back, relax and watch how other people can deal with problems.
- It gives me a way to shut the world out for an hour or so. We all need a break every now and then.
- The best soap today is one that provides not only entertainment, but also updates in areas like fashion, food, sociology, health, childcare, etc. in a most practical way.
- *Coronation Street* is quite definitely the best soap, because it's funny.
- I like *Doctors* (a daytime soap opera). It's when I have a nice cup of tea and a rest while my son is asleep. I love the stories with the doctors and their patients and how every-thing is OK in the end.

Unit 2

E2a **Text for Group 2**

The Internet is the key

The government is worried about people who don't have Internet access. "These people pay a price", said a spokeswoman. "You can often get cheaper prices if you shop online and pay electronically, for example." "I bought a new telephone", one man reported. "I wanted to find out how to record an answer-phone message, but I could only get the full instructions online. What happens if you don't have an Internet connection?" Another woman was angry about one of the budget airlines: "It's cheaper if you check in online. What about people who can't? Why should they pay more?" And there are other problems. At a community centre in the Midlands, Tina and Brian Whitehouse are work-ing hard at their computer skills after both losing jobs in the recession. "A lot of the jobs now, you can only apply for online", says Tina. "If you don't have an Internet connection and if you don't know how to use a computer, how can you apply online?" At this centre, the people who come for help are also not all older people. "We have people of all ages who come here with no computer experience", says John Payne, who works at the centre. He's in his late twenties and only recently started using the Internet because his parents couldn't afford to be online at home. The government wants to move more and more services online: they say that online services can be better and cost less to deliver. But if millions of people stay offline, it will be difficult and expensive to reach them. The government spokeswoman says, "I don't think you can be a full citi-zen of our society in the future if you aren't online." But she worries about the people who choose not to join the digital world. "We need to talk to these people", she says, "but the question is: How will they communicate?"

Unit 10

C3c **Notes for student A**

Choose one or two of the following or use your own ideas:
- a change in the number of people coming
- a person with a very special dietary requirement (for example an allergy or intolerance)
- a change to the date and / or time
- a change to the budget: you have less money than you thought!

Unit 2

E2a Text for Group 1

The Internet refuseniks

The Internet "have-nots" aren't just people who can't go online, there's also a big group of people who don't want to. It's estimated that as many as seventeen million people in Britain aged over fifteen aren't using the Internet and this number isn't falling fast any more. Non-users are "becoming less and less likely to want to be engaging with technology such as the Internet", says Ellen Helsper, who has carried out a survey for the Oxford Internet Institute. There's a rise in the number of people who say they are just not interested in being online. But why do people want to stay outside the online world?

The refuseniks are mostly over fifty and several say that they have no time for the Internet: they need their time for other activities that they think are more important. "I know a lot of friends, they're hooked on the damn thing", says one woman. She knew a "marvelous artist" who stopped painting in order to spend time computing. "It's destroyed a lot of family life", says another woman.

Others think the Internet is too impersonal. "We tried emailing but we're now writing letters again", was one answer in the survey. Privacy is another worry. "The whole world's on computers", says one woman. "You just have to say your postcode and they know everything about you. I'm just not interested." "If you hit the wrong key", says her neighbour, "what about privacy?"

And then there are complaints about computer design. "I'm bad with fingers, and I make mistakes", one woman said. Alan Newell, professor at the Dundee University School of Computing, points out computers are usually "designed by young male computer scientists". They often don't understand the needs of other people. Most people think that the Internet is important because there's so much information on it, but for other people that's a problem. "You get so much junk you have to clear out", one man complained. "I just don't feel I'm going to get any pleasure out of it."

Unit 2

C2a Group 2

Here's what some people say who do not like soap operas.

- Soap operas are so popular in Britain because people have very sad lives.
- I hate the whole idea of soaps. If I watch something on TV, I want it to start and finish in one viewing.
- How can people like *EastEnders*? It's the most miserable, boring and depressing soap on the TV and its story lines are so unreal.
- Soaps are based on schadenfreude; "I'm glad it's not happening to me!"
- They are a waste of time.
- Nothing real ever happens.

Unit 9

B3a Student B

treatments, exercise, prices

Indian head massage:	45 minutes	£50
Abhyangam:	65 minutes	£65
Facial:	1 hour 15 minutes	£55
Pilates, special offer, individual introductory course:	45 minutes	£45

When "Doris" says the day that she wants for the treatment, explain that you are fully booked and offer another day or another time.

You need
1. the name of the person who is having the treatment
2. the credit card details of the person who is paying:
- the type of card: Visa / Mastercard …
- the number of the card
- the name of the card holder
- the expiry date

Unit 10

C3c Notes for student B

Choose one or two of the following or use your own ideas:
- A special person in your company is not available for the party so you need to change the date, if possible.
- You can't get the ingredients to cook something that you promised, so you have to change the menu.
- You'd like to change the time of the party.

Student B

E   How smart are you?

E1   "There are at least seven different ways of being smart" is what a famous American psychologist says. Work in pairs. Match the words with the photos. Who do you think is/was the most intelligent?

☐ a. music smart   ☐ c. body smart   ☐ e. self smart   ☐ g. picture smart
☐ b. word smart   ☐ d. number smart   ☐ f. people smart

E2a   Everybody is unique and has a mixture of different kinds of intelligences. What about you? What are you good at? Rank from 1 (strongest) to 7 (weakest).

☐ number smart   ☐ word smart   ☐ music smart   ☐ self smart
☐ people smart   ☐ picture smart   ☐ body smart

E2b   What's your intelligence profile? Tick each statement that's true for you and then look at the key at the end of this activity.

	YOUR PERSONAL INTELLIGENCE PROFILE			
1	I like reading books, newspapers and magazines.	☐	11	I like working with my hands. ☐
2	I enjoy word games.	☐	12	I'm hopeless at sitting quietly for a long time. ☐
3	I like telling stories.	☐	13	In my free time I enjoy listening to music. ☐
4	I'm good at chess.	☐	14	I play an instrument or sing in a choir. ☐
5	I enjoy doing sudokus.	☐	15	I often tap to sounds or sing melodies while working or studying. ☐
6	I'm good at doing maths in my head.	☐	16	I enjoy talking to my friends. ☐
7	I'm good at reading maps.	☐	17	I like helping people. ☐
8	I love drawing.	☐	18	I have a lot of friends. ☐
9	I can remember faces better than names.	☐	19	I like to spend time alone. ☐
10	I'm good at sports.	☐	20	I learn from my mistakes. ☐
			21	I write a personal diary. ☐

E2c   Are you surprised by the results? Tell your partner. How is your partner different from you? Which type(s) of intelligence have you used in unit one?

Examples: I'm really surprised, I didn't know I was "people smart". How about you?
     Well, I knew I was good at maths. But it surprises me that I'm "self smart".

Key to your intelligence profile

Type of intelligence	word smart	number smart	picture smart	body smart	music smart	people smart	self smart
numbers	1, 2, 3	4, 5, 6	7, 8, 9	10, 11, 12	13, 14, 15	16, 17, 18	19, 20, 21

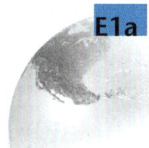

E   To surf or not to surf?

E1a   Think about possible answers to the following questions about people in your area.

a. What percentage of people have an Internet connection at home?
b. How much time on average do people spend online at home every day?
c. What percentage of people use text messaging every day?
d. Do people use mobile phones more than fixed-line phones?

E1b   Talk about your ideas with two other people.

E1c   Compare your answers with information from the UK. Look in the key for the official UK figures for 2009.

Focus on spoken English
I think that most people have an Internet connection, perhaps 70%.
I don't think it's so many.
I read that only 50% have a connection at home.
I'm not sure. I guess 50%.
I've got no idea.

E2a   Form two groups.

Group 1 is going to read about why some people don't go online and don't want an Internet connection.
Group 2 is going to read about the reasons why it's necessary today for everybody to have an Internet connection.

Instructions
Group 1
1. Discuss in your group the possible reasons why people don't like the Internet.
2. Take time to read the article on page 98 and see if you find the same reasons there.
3. Prepare to tell Group 2 about what you read.

Group 2
1. Discuss in your group the possible reasons why people need to have an Internet connection.
2. Take time to read the article on page 97 and see if you find the same reasons there.
3. Prepare to tell Group 1 about what you read.

E2b   Form new, small groups with a mixture of people from Group 1 and Group 2. Exchange your ideas about the Internet and new technology. Do you want to be in the new digital world or do you want to be outside it?

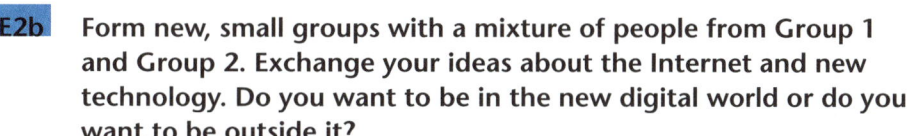

E   Have you ever been bumped?

 13

E1a   Paulette spent her last holiday in the States. After spending some days in New England she flew from Boston to San Francisco. Listen to the announcement she heard at the airport in Boston and choose one word to describe the problem.

E1b   What do you think Paulette will do? What would you do?

E1c   How does overbooking happen? Work with a partner and try to give a short explanation using the phrases below.

airlines **|** seats available **|** passengers **|** no-shows **|** flights with empty seats **|** sell more seats give up their seats **|** seat on a later flight **|** money voucher **|** meal voucher **|** hotel voucher

E1d   Has this ever happened to you? If so, tell the class what you did.

Examples: I got on a later flight and got a meal voucher.
I didn't give up my seat.

E2a   Paulette didn't give up her seat, but some people had to. In the plane she sat next to an interesting woman with a cello. Work with a partner, look at the picture and guess what happened.

 14

E2b   After Paulette got to San Francisco she phoned a friend in London. The connection was bad, so her friend had trouble understanding everything. Listen several times to their conversation and take notes.

woman and her cello
flight overbooked
refused to put cello in the hold
...

E2c   Compare your list with your partner's list. In pairs, retell Paulette's story using your notes to help you.

E Dictionaries

E1a Answer the following questions with a partner.

1. Is a dictionary important when you are learning a language?
2. Is a big dictionary better than a small one?
3. Is an electronic dictionary better than a book?
4. Is an English-English dictionary better than a dictionary that translates English into your language?

E1b Daniela and Martin are German students in an English class. Their teacher asked the class to talk about the questions in E1a. Listen and compare their answers with your answers.

E2a Work with a partner. Look at this section from an English-English dictionary (*Macmillan Essential Dictionary for Learners of English*). Match the numbers with the explanations.

a. ☐ help with how to pronounce the word

b. ☐ examples of how to use the word

c. ☐ different meanings

d. ☐ information about how often English speakers use this word

e. ☐ words in the same word family

f. ☐ words that you often find with the word "challenge"

g. ☐ information about grammar

h. ☐ the opposite of the word

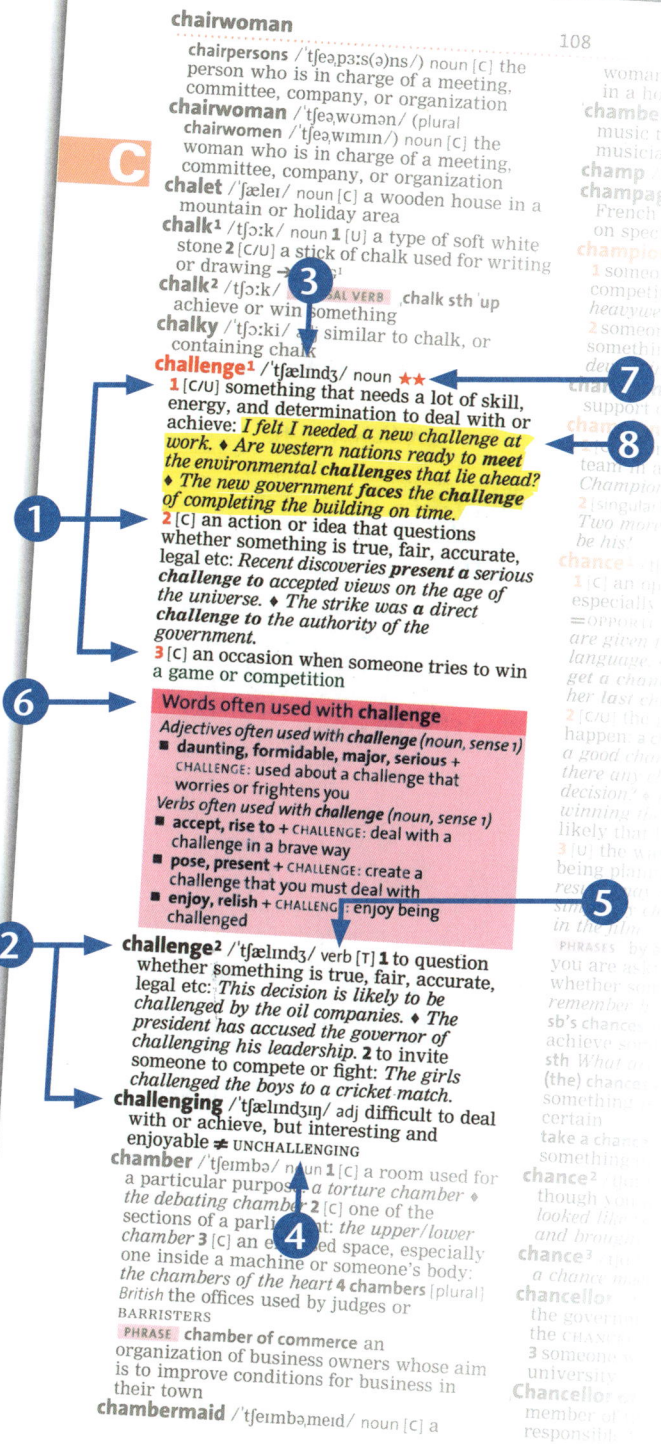

E2b Look at the dictionary or dictionaries that you and the rest of the class have. Do they have the same information? Do they have different information? Which dictionaries (English-English or with translation) do you like best?

5 Plus

E What's in a name?

E1a Tick which answer you think is correct.

1. El Sistema is …

a. ☐ … a criminal operation run by the Mafia.

b. ☐ … a network of children's and youth
orchestras in Venezuela.

c. ☐ … a new computer game.

2. The West-Eastern Divan Orchestra is …

a. ☐ … the name of a heavy metal rock group.

b. ☐ … the title of a painting by Picasso.

c. ☐ … an orchestra of young musicians
from the Middle East and Germany.

E1b Compare your answers with a partner.

E1c Now listen to part of a radio programme to find out if you were right.

E1d Listen again and sort the phrases into the right group. Can you add anything?

> social work and classical music | founded in 1999 | playing together
> young musicians from … | played in … | based in Seville because …
> started in 1975 with children from slums | over 300,000 children

El Sistema	West-Eastern Divan Orchestra
_____	_____
_____	_____
_____	_____
_____	_____

E2a In groups, discuss whether you agree or disagree with these statements.

a. If more people played a musical instrument, the world would be a better place.
b. If more people made music together, the world would be a better place.
c. Music is only for the very gifted.

E2b Now imagine that your group has 10,000 euros to set up a music project in your town.
Work in groups and make decisions.

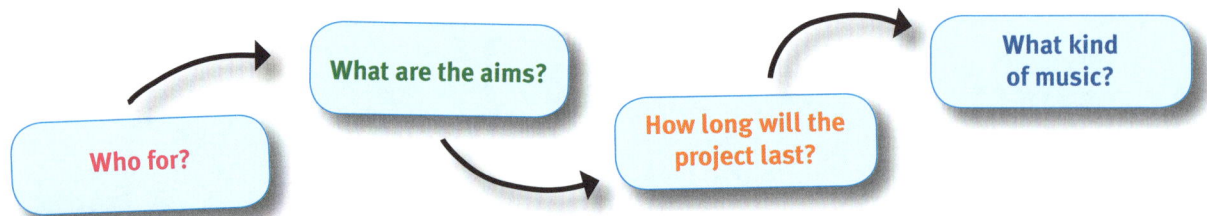

Who for? → What are the aims? → How long will the project last? → What kind of music?

E2c Present your project to the class. Who has the most interesting project?

E Feelings

E1a Which of these feelings are positive and which are negative? Divide the words into two groups.

disappointed | excited
angry | relieved

+ happy _____ _____

- sad _____ _____

E1b Jasmin writes to Petra about some things that have happened in her life. Here are three pieces of news about Jasmin. How do you think she feels about them?

    a. She's going on holiday next week.
    b. Her husband has a new job.
    c. Her dog died last week.

E1c Read her email. Were you right about Jasmin's feelings? Fill in the missing words in the email. Use the words from E1a.

From: Jasmin   To: Petra

Hi Petra,
How are things? I haven't heard from you for ages and just want to get in touch before we go on holiday next week. The children are really (1) _____ about it. We're going to Greece for two weeks and are all looking forward to it. We had to cancel our holiday last year because Jim's boss didn't give him any time off work. We were very tired so this holiday will be a real treat! Jim was very (2) _____ about the holiday cancellation and so (3) _____ with his boss that he changed jobs not long after that. He's quite (4) _____ in his new job so things are looking good. The only (5) _____ news is that our dog died last week. In a way I was (6) _____ because he was ill and suffering.
See you soon I hope.

Love,
Jasmin

E2a Work in pairs. Answer the following questions and think of another two.

How do you feel when …
    a. … your English class is cancelled?
    b. … you plan a picnic and then it starts to rain?
    c. … your holiday starts tomorrow?
    d. … a good friend tells you she's getting married?

E2b Ask another pair the questions and report back to the group.
Example: Luis feels sad when it rains.

E3a Listen to these three people talking about last week. Who had a good week and who had a bad week?

    a. Andy ☐ good week ☐ bad week
    b. Claire ☐ good week ☐ bad week
    c. Tim ☐ good week ☐ bad week

E3b Listen again. What happened? Fill in the gaps

    a. Andy _____ He felt _____
    b. Claire _____ She felt _____
    c. Tim _____ He felt _____

E3c Think of one good thing and one bad thing which happened to you last week. Write two sentences.

A good/bad thing that happened to me last week was that …

E3d Now talk to a partner about what happened to you last week and how you felt.

What was your week like?
I had a … week. One thing that happened was …

How did you feel?
I felt …

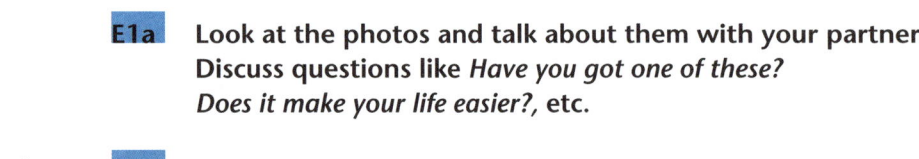

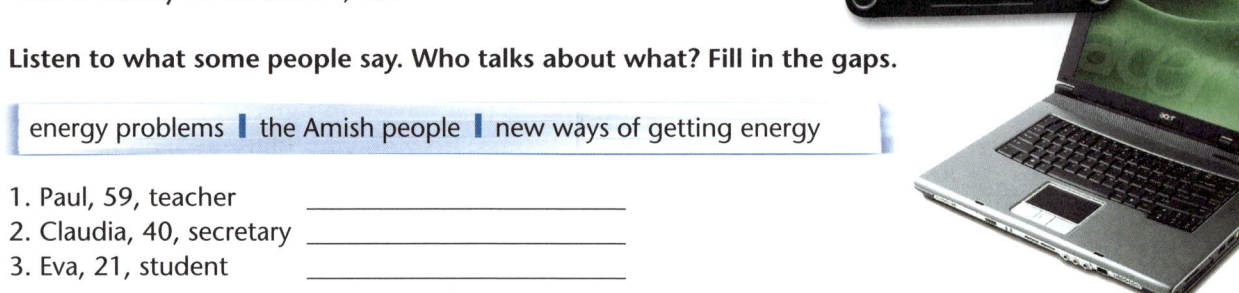

E More or less technology?

E1a Look at the photos and talk about them with your partner.
Discuss questions like *Have you got one of these?*
Does it make your life easier?, etc.

E1b Listen to what some people say. Who talks about what? Fill in the gaps.

> energy problems | the Amish people | new ways of getting energy

1. Paul, 59, teacher _____
2. Claudia, 40, secretary _____
3. Eva, 21, student _____

E2a Work in pairs. Have you ever heard of the Amish people? What do you know about them?

E2b Read this text about the Amish people. What do you think about their way of life?

Most Amish people do not have a car or a tractor. However, they will ride in cars when needed. They do not use electricity, or have radios, TV sets, personal computers, computer games, etc. Telephones are not normally allowed at home. Some families have a phone outside the house. They do not take photographs or have photographs of themselves. Electricity is used in some situations when it can be produced without outside power. Batteries are sometimes okay. Some Amish families have non-electric machines, such as kerosene-powered refrigerators. Some Amish are allowed to use solar panels. Petrol-powered farm machines may be pushed by a person or pulled by a horse.

E3a There are new ways of getting energy. But can you produce energy from the following?
What do you think? Discuss this with a partner.

	Yes	No			Yes	No
1. an exercise bicycle	☐	☐		4. the floor of a disco	☐	☐
2. walking boots	☐	☐		5. your knees	☐	☐
3. a rucksack	☐	☐				

E3b Read the texts. Were you right?

The **movement of dancers** on the floor is used to produce energy to **work the lights**. This is done in Club Watt in Rotterdam. The more you dance the wilder the lights are!

In a gym in Hong Kong, the **movements you make** when doing exercises are used to work the machines themselves and to **power the televisions** you watch while keeping fit!

In Canada scientists have developed a **knee dynamo** which uses the movement of your knees when you are walking. This energy goes to a generator in your rucksack and you can use it to **make a cup of tea** when you have a rest!

E4 What do you think? Does modern technology make our lives better?
Form two groups and think of reasons for YES and NO. Then discuss the question in class.

E The most beautiful place on earth

E1a If you could choose, is there some special place you'd
like to live or at least spend a lot of time?
Use the words in the box to make some phrases about
a beautiful place.

> mountain **|** Dakota **|** plains **|** long, rolling **|** high
> hills **|** bottom of **|** prairies **|** northern **|** an ocean

long, rolling hills

...

E1b Read the following text about somebody's special place
and check the expressions from E1a.

> My special place is a mixture. On the one side I have the mountains and rocks of Norway. With
> this go the magical extremes of light and darkness that you have there. I sometimes see myself
> walking up a high mountain with many wild flowers. When I get to the top there's a trail down the
> other side to the Dakota prairies in North America. Many people think that these northern plains
> are flat, but they aren't. They're more like very long, rolling hills that go on for miles and miles.
> It reminds you of the bottom of an ocean. There was actually an ocean here millions of years ago.
> I imagine this place when I'm tired or sad and it makes me feel better.

E1c Close your book and write down all the
words and phrases that you remember
from the text. Compare with a partner
and then look at the text.

E2a Now tell your partner about your special place.
Your partner makes a simple sketch of your
description. Then draw your partner's special
place. Don't look at each other's drawings.
Example: My special place is by the ocean.
There's a long sandy beach and lots
of seagulls …

E2b Put all the drawings on the wall.
Can you find the drawing of your special place?
Choose your favourite drawing.

9 Plus

E Water

E1a Look at the photos of different kinds of water. Work with a partner. What can you see? What feelings or memories do you have when you see the different pictures?

> **Focus on vocabulary**
>
> This picture **reminds me of** holidays by the North Sea.
> We went there every summer when I was a child. I remember …

E1b Compare what you see and what you feel with the rest of the class.

E2a Listen to a sound collage of different kinds of water. What can you hear? What memories do the sounds make you think of? Make notes.

Sound	What is it?	my memories
1	waves on a beach	holidays by the North Sea
2	…	…

E2b Compare your notes with another person. Choose one memory each to share with the rest of the class.
Example: I'd like to talk about the water going into a glass. That reminds me of the best glass of water I had in my life. I was very, very thirsty because …

E3 We played part of the sound collage to Oliver and asked him to talk about what he heard. Are any of his memories the same as yours?

E4 Water can sometimes be something good, and sometimes it's something bad. Can you think of some more examples of the good and bad sides of water?

E Games

E1 Things to eat

- Form groups of three. Person A has the numbers 1 and 6, B has 2 and 5, C has 3 and 4.
- Throw a dice. If it's one of your numbers, you have to think of something to eat or drink starting with the first letter in the row of letters below.
- If you can think of a word, you get a point. If you can't, the next player has a chance to answer.
- When you have been through all the letters, the winner is the person with the most points. (You can also play the game with another group of words, for example things in the house, or holiday words.)

A	G	N	V	F	O	B	J	T	I	W	M	E	C	S	D	L	H	R	P

E2 Tell a story word by word.

In this game you have to write a story on the board.
You go round the class. Each person has to add one word.
Carry on until your story comes to an end!

Example: person A: One ...
person B: One day ...
person C: One day a ...
...

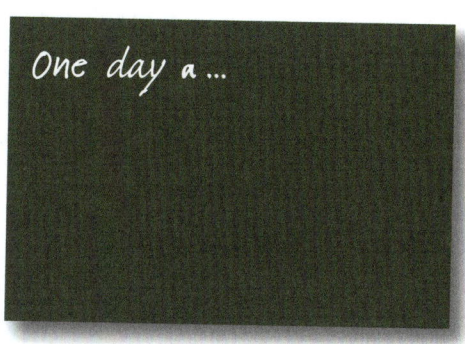

E3 Twenty questions

Your teacher gives person A in the group a card with the name of a job on it.
The other people have to guess the job. They can ask questions, but A can only answer *yes* or *no*. If A can answer *no* twenty times, he or she wins the game.

Example: Do you work in an office? – No.
Do you work on your own? - ...

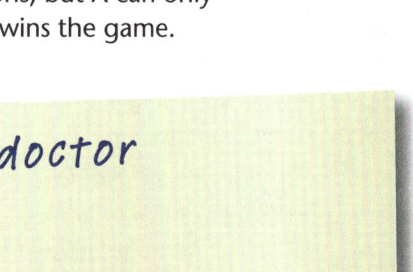

E4 The drawing game

- Divide the class into two teams. Each team sits round a table in different corners of the room. You need paper and pens or pencils.
- One person from each team goes to the teacher. The teacher whispers a word from the B1/1 book. The people have to go back to their teams and draw the word. The team has to guess the word. The "artist" can only say *yes* or *no*. When somebody in the team guesses the word, that person goes to the teacher and gets the next word.
- The winners are the team that gets to the end of the teacher's list first.

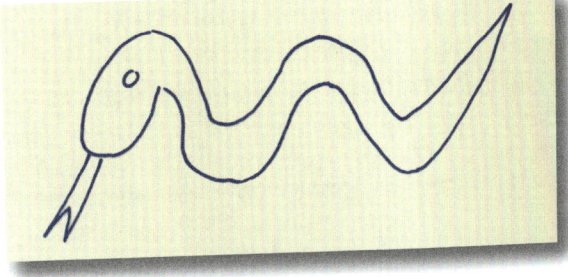

Unit 1

Native speakers of English
Why they are a problem in the modern world

Most native speakers are happy about so many people wanting to learn English all over the world. There's a big market for English books, English music and English classes.

British and American speakers of English are often very lazy about learning foreign languages because so many people speak English. Until recently native speakers were seen as "the gold standard", as David Graddol, an expert on the future of English says in one of his books, *English Next*. Native speakers knew all the answers and spoke the language well.

But is this really true? Native speakers sometimes use words that other people around the world don't know and don't understand. These words may be very trendy, very technical or may just be used in a particular region or by a particular group of people, e. g. kids. And because of their pronunciation and how fast they speak native speakers are often more difficult to understand than non-native speakers.

And there are not as many native speakers as one may think. It's a fact that there are non-native speakers in most of the conversations in English all over the world. The sort of English that people speak in business meetings around the world is "International English" or "English as a lingua franca" or "Global English" and this is a language which everybody speaks and understands. Some people say the best teachers nowadays are not native speakers but others who have learnt the language and so know more about it: the Chinese in China, Germans in Germany and so on.

Unit 2

My Favourite Soap Opera
It's Winter Love Song, a soap opera from Korea

Soap operas are so basic and universal that you can understand them without knowing the language. Subtitles help, but the basic forms are always there and everybody can recognize them. The Korean soap opera Winter Love Song has English at the bottom of the screen so it is even easier to understand.

The main female character is Yujin. She's beautiful in a sad way and she really has a lot of problems. She's engaged to Sang-hyuk but she doesn't really love him. She stays with him because if she leaves him, he'll stop eating and die. Also his mother will be so sad that she'll become ill and perhaps have to go to hospital.

Yujin has already tried to leave Sang-hyuk because she met and became interested in another guy. His name's Min-hyung and he's got red hair and wears glasses and a scarf. He's very quiet and Yujin doesn't know much about him, but she loves him because he looks like Joon-sang, her dead childhood sweetheart. Yujin and Min-Hyung fell in love and then Sang-hyuk stopped eating. So Yujin had to go back to Sang-hyuk and they planned the wedding to save his life.

But Min-hyung doesn't understand what's going on. Why has Yujin left him? He knows she loves him. He has heard about Joon-sang – the dead man he looks like and who Yujin loved. Are they twins? Or is he Joon-sang ... with another name and personality?

Winter Love Song has everything from a traditional soap opera: love, death and strange people. And it's very Asian because of topics like family and respect, the importance of marriage and life after death.

Unit 3

Pilots' strike leaves many passengers on the ground

Pilots have a good job, are well-respected and earn quite a lot of money. But they want more. That's one of the reasons for the recent pilots' strike which spoiled the plans of many passengers. We talked to some people at one of Germany's biggest airports. Julia, a busy teacher, wanted to go to her mother's eightieth birthday. She took time off work and asked her colleagues to teach for her so she could travel to the UK for three days. But she had to turn around and go home when her flight was cancelled. She says: "Actually I think pilots earn enough. And they can do a job they really like. I love my work but I earn much less than most pilots! When I was young I would have loved to be a pilot, but girls couldn't." The pilots' answer is that it's not just a question of money. We didn't find a pilot to talk to us but we know they like their work and usually love the travelling and the days off. What do you think? Do pilots do the same thing as lorry drivers just better paid? Let us know.

Unit 4

The Bird Man

This week we look at people who do unusual jobs. Today we speak to the man who looks after the famous ravens* at the Tower of London.

Derrick Coyle's working day starts early when he greets each of his ravens by name, letting them out of the cages where they spend the night. As he opens each door, the birds half fly, half hurry out, moving to their places on the Tower of London's greens, hours before the first visitors arrive.

Derrick spends the next hour or so checking on the ravens, feeding them and giving them water, and cleaning their cages. And all before his own breakfast. As the Tower of London's Yeoman Warder Ravenmaster, Derrick is responsible for the birds, making sure the royal order of Charles II – that there are always six ravens at the Tower – is obeyed. According to legend the birds must not leave the Tower of London, otherwise the Kingdom of England will fall.

Derrick has to cut raw meat to feed the birds, fill their water bowls, and look after them while he does his other work as a beefeater, one of the traditional guards. It can be a long day. The ravens are out in the grounds from morning till evening, when Derrick locks them up to protect them from foxes or cats. In summer, this means his day can end as late as 9.30 pm, and he gets up at 4.30 am for a shower and shave before starting again.

"Getting up in the morning is the worst part," Derrick, 61, admits. "And I don't have a social life in the summer, because if I go anywhere I always have to get back to put the ravens to bed. You can't really have a drink either, as you have to know what they're doing at all times."

But he really loves his job. "The best thing is looking after the birds, the working relationship I have with them. It's a lot of fun," he says. "I wouldn't do any other job. The ravens all have their own characters – they're very intelligent and playful."

* raven = Rabe

Unit 5

The Pink Panther 2
AN INTERVIEW WITH FILM CRITIC JEREMY WHITE

Q: What makes this film special?

JW: This was the most well-known film with Peter Sellers, a famous actor. Peter Sellers died in 1980 and many people think he was the greatest comedian of all time. He played Inspector Clouseau in the first *Pink Panther* film.

Q: Were there other *Pink Panther* films?

JW: Yes, there were about six with different actors in the main part.

Q: And who plays the main part this time?

JW: Steve Martin who made the film *Pink Panther 1* in 2006.

Q: Is he good?

JW: Not bad, but Peter Sellers was better.

Q: What's the story?

JW: The story isn't really important in any of these films. They're all about a police inspector who tries to catch a criminal. But the policeman is fairly stupid and things go wrong.

Q: Is Steve Martin funny as the police inspector?

JW: No, not really.

Q: Who are the other actors?

JW: Other parts are played by John Cleese. He tries a funny accent sometimes. Andy Garcia and Emily Mortimer are in the film too. But they just stand around and wait for something to happen. And nothing happens. It's not a thriller or a fantasy film and not even a comedy.

Q: So why go and see the film?

JW: I really don't know. Maybe if you like *Pink Panther* films. Or Steve Martin. But there are many better films to see. I think the earlier *Pink Panther* films were much better and that it's time for a new idea.

Unit 6

TWO SCANDALOUS FAMILIES

The Garlands/Minnellis
Judy Garland was a child film star (*The Wizard of Oz*). When she grew up, she started drinking and took drugs. She was married five times and divorced four times and died when she was forty-seven from a drug overdose. Her daughter is the famous singer Liza Minnelli, who starred in the film *Cabaret*. Liza's father was the film director Vincente Minnelli. Liza, like her mother, had problems with drink and drugs.

The Onassises
Aristotle Onassis was a millionaire when he was twenty-five but had to pay seven million dollars for breaking the law. He had an affair with the opera star, Maria Callas who was married. After President John F. Kennedy was killed, Aristotle Onassis married his widow, Jackie Kennedy. Aristotle's son died in a plane crash in 1973 and his daughter Christina died from a drug overdose in 1988.

Unit 7

What is the right way to greet someone?

This question is impossible to answer. Sometimes it depends on culture or nationality. Germans like to shake hands when they meet, the Japanese bow, the French like to kiss and the British often do nothing. But the British kiss more now than they did thirty years ago. So things are changing all the time and as the world gets smaller, unusual ways of greeting, like rubbing noses like the Eskimos or holding your hands together like people in India, may change or die out. A recent survey showed which forms of greeting were most popular among British business people. Here are the results:

Shake hands **83%**   Kiss **4%**   Hug **5%**   Bow **2%**   Do nothing, just say hello **6%**

The results are not surprising and perhaps shaking hands will become the most popular way of greeting for business people.

Unit 8

Have you read about an interesting person recently? We asked some people in the street.

Melanie, 23, student

I recently heard the word "freeconomist", which means somebody who lives without spending money, and yesterday I read about Mark Boyle, who has lived for one year without using money. He wears shorts in the middle of winter, brushes his teeth with cuttlefish bones and gets food which supermarkets throw away. He doesn't spend any money, doesn't waste anything, is always busy (finding things which don't cost money!) and loves his life. I can't really believe you can live without money but he does. He gets the electricity for his computer from the sun. Before he started the year without money, he made some plans of course, he bought a caravan and solar panels and some things he needed. But for fourteen months now, he has not spent any money and says he is very happy. He sometimes writes for *The Guardian* and is writing a book. He decided to live like this because he heard about the life of Mahatma Gandhi and liked one thing which Gandhi said: "Be the change you want to see in the world". Would the world be better if we didn't spend so much money?

Unit 9

What is a spa?

The name comes from the name of the town of Spa, Belgium, which is perhaps connected with the Latin word "spargere" meaning to make something wet.

In England in the 1700s, towns like Bath became spas and used water as medicine and for bathing. This was the first time the word spa was used, which at first meant a place for drinking water only, but this soon changed. Travelling to a place where the water was good started long before 1700. There were hot springs and spas in France, the Czech Republic and in Great Britain; and legend says that early Celtic kings found the hot springs at Bath in England.

Sometimes people also drank the water at spas. The first bath was in the morning, the second in the afternoon and bathers drank mineral water in the bath. At this time people did not bathe very much to get clean but rich people went to spas to drink and "take" the waters. So social activities started, with dances, concerts, playing cards, lectures, and walking down the street. A typical day at Bath was an early morning bath with other people, then a private breakfast party. After this, people drank water at the pump room (a building on the thermal water source) or went to a fashion show. The next hours of the day were for shopping, visiting the library, attending concerts, or stopping at one of the coffee houses. In the afternoon, the rich and famous dressed up in their finery and promenaded down the streets. Next came dinner, more promenading, and an evening of dancing or gambling. A nice way to spend your time and get healthy and you can do all these things in Bath today!

Unit 10

Lisa's World Trip

Well, folks, Singapore is certainly a gourmet's paradise. There is really everything to eat here and after some of my food experiences on this trip, I'm finally beginning to put on weight, although as you can see, I'm not fat yet. This is my last stop before I go on to Australia, which everybody says is just like home for us Brits. I wonder what the food will be like there. I'm looking forward to kangaroo and crocodile but I'm sure I can find them here in Singapore somewhere if I look. After three months in India, I can't spend a day without a curry. In the last three days, I have eaten Indian, Chinese and Vietnamese food and seen German, Austrian and Irish restaurants as well as many more. Singaporeans love to eat, it's really their favourite hobby and that's what they do best. I've had the best Italian ice-cream ever and the best Turkish coffee ever. I'm amazed at this place and so happy that I came here. It's the most modern city I've ever seen and so clean. As you know, my first plan was to go straight from India to Australia and I decided not to because I thought it would be a big culture shock, but I think this culture shock is bigger. Anyway, next stop Sydney on Thursday! I'll keep you informed …

H Language and learning

H1a **Complete the sentences.**

1. I'm not very _good at learning_ languages. (good / learn)

2. We're really _____ out more about how people live in India. (interested / find)

3. He's _____. (hopeless / ski)

4. I _____ you. (look forward / see)

5. Vanessa is _____ sudokus. (keen / solve)

6. I often _____ to the moon. (dream / fly)

H1b **Match the phrases to make as many sentences as possible that are true for you.**

1. I enjoy	a. playing the guitar.
2. I like	b. playing football.
3. I don't enjoy	c. fixing my car.
4. I don't like	d. going for long walks.
5. I'm interested in	e. cooking.
6. I'm good at	f. going to the cinema.
7. I'm hopeless at	g. running.

H1c **Use the phrases on the left in H1b and the words below to make at least five more sentences that are true for you. Add some information if you can.**

1. listen to music _I enjoy listening to classical music._

2. go to rock concerts _____

3. learn a language _____

4. read crime novels _____

5. swim in the sea _____

6. surf the Internet _____

H1d **Add three more sentences about other things you enjoy or don't enjoy doing.**

_____
_____
_____

H2a **Unjumble the sentences.**

1. find / I / practise / don't / time / enough / to
   I don't find enough time to practise.

2. school / liked / I / never / at / grammar
   _____

3. really / I / like / would / to / more / speak
   _____

4. say / if / you / never / won't / you / mistakes / make / anything
   _____

5. anything / learn / if / never / you / mistakes / you / make / won't
   _____

6. helps / to / really / it / lot / read / a
   _____

H2b   Now underline phrases in H2a that you find useful to learn and use them
to write five sentences that are true for you.
Example: find enough time (to do something) – I don't find enough time to exercise.

H3   Some things are *hard* to learn and others are *easy*, depending on the person.
You find *hard* and *easy* in many useful phrases in English. Look these two words up in
your dictionary or at www.macmillandictionary.com and note down as many different
expressions as possible. Is there one that you especially like? Try using it this week.
Examples: that's a hard one, hard times, (not) easy to get along with

hard: _____

easy: _____

H4a   Complete the sentences. Use *ought to, need to*
and *don't need to* and one of the following verbs.

| go (2) ∎ clean ∎ talk ∎ work ∎ buy |

1. The windows are fine. You *don't need to clean* them this week.
2. We've got to finish the project. So we _____ late tonight.
3. You _____ to the bank today. We've got enough cash.
4. It's a very good play. You _____ to the theatre and see it.
5. I think Maria's shoes are awful. She _____ some new ones.
6. Socializing is very important in this company, so you _____ to
people during your lunch break.

H4b   Is there something you *ought to* do this week? Are there some things you *don't
need to* do? Practise talking to yourself for a minute or two and complete the lists.
Here are some ideas to help you get started.

I ought to   get rid of that jacket. I never wear it.
phone my sister and find out how she is.
practise my English.
clean out the cupboard.

_____

_____

…

Spezielle can-do Übungen
zu dieser Unit finden Sie
online unter:

www.hueber.de/next
Code: XB1101

I don't need to   cut the grass this week.
go to the fitness centre today. I went yesterday.
get any eggs. We have enough.

_____

_____

…

H5   Fill in the gaps with these words: *myself, yourself, himself, themselves, ourselves.*

Families are interesting. I really like having time for (1) _____ once in a while and my husband

also enjoys time for (2) _____ too. However, some of our friends hate being alone, so they do

almost everything together. Otherwise they don't enjoy (3) _____. One of my relatives can

only read a book when she's alone. Once, my husband and I and her husband were sitting in

the same room quietly reading and really enjoying (4) _____. She thought we were being

unsociable, so we had to stop! Do you enjoy having time for (5) _____ now and again?

H Right, let's write

H1a Fill in the gaps with the correct form of the verb to talk about trends.

1. More and more young men aged twenty to thirty _are living_ (live) with their parents.
2. People _____ (spend) more money on leisure activities.
3. A lot of people _____ (become) more interested in what they eat.
4. People _____ (live) longer.
5. Global temperatures _____ (rise).
6. More and more people _____ (shop) online.

H1b Write on a piece of paper about what most people usually do and what the trend is.

Example: watch television channels /
         watch things on the Internet

Most people watch television channels,
but these days more and more people are
watching things on the Internet.

1. use a paper dictionary / use online dictionaries
2. buy CDs / download music
3. go to the shops / shop online
4. go shopping to buy something / go shopping as a leisure activity
5. live with their families / live alone

H2 Guess the meanings of the words in italics.

1. One of this restaurant's specialities is *kedgeree*. This makes a nice change from the traditional bacon and eggs, but I have a lot of friends from other European countries who really don't think fish is the best thing to eat for breakfast.

2. I was in the town centre yesterday. I was *dawdling* because I was free and I didn't have anything to do. It was a nice day and I was just *dawdling* along, looking in the shop windows, enjoying the sunshine. Suddenly my phone rang. It was my sister. "Where are you?" she said. "You should be here to look after the children. You promised!" That was the end of my relaxed afternoon!

H3 Read the following profile from the Internet.

I'm happy, positive, warm, easygoing, straightforward, and diplomatic. I'm calm. I'm not emotional, but I'm sensitive. I'm just not dramatic. I'm adventurous and spontaneous. I can pack a little travel bag and take off to go abroad at any time. I'm creative, innovative and highly energetic. I get on well with people who think like me. I have a lot of interests. They are a part of my life. I don't expect my partner to always share my interests, but I want to continue doing those things either with or without him. I'm looking for an independent partner.

Now read our expert's opinion about the profile. Can you guess what was in the gaps?

This person sounds quite complicated and her profile will probably not attract a lot of men. There's nothing in the profile about the sort of man that she's looking for. It's all about her. In the first line, she describes her character but at least two of the adjectives seem to be opposites, for example *straightforward* and (1) _____. And I'm not sure how easygoing she is, because later in the text she doesn't sound very tolerant: she says (2) _____. She says that she doesn't expect her partner to share all her interests.

That's fair enough, but why doesn't she explain what (3) _____?
She likes to think that she's not complicated. For example she says that she
can (4) _____. But when she says that
she's looking for an independent partner, I wonder if this means that she wants
a partner that she just sees when she feels like it!

H4 **Unjumble the following discussion.**
Fill in the gaps with the words in the
box and put it in the right order.

agree **|** disagree **|** don't think **|** sorry
think **|** think **|** think about

☐ A   I (1) _____ but I (2) _____ that's good. It's nice to watch
something that's not real. You can escape from your normal life.

☐ B   I'm (3) _____, but I (4) _____.
You see the same characters every week,
but I (5) _____ they're interesting.
They're not real.

☐ C   I (6) _____ soap operas are
great because it's interesting to see
the same characters every week.

☐ D   What do you (7) _____ soap operas?

H5 **Answer the questions.**

1. Which half of the following sentence describes the
   background scene? Which half describes the action?

   a Steve leaves the house
   b just when the sun's rising.

2. Which half of the sentence describes something
   that happens in the middle of the other half?

   a Steve's driving into town
   b when his telephone rings.

3. Which action is unfinished?

   a Steve's mobile phone battery runs out
   b while he's talking to his colleague.

H6 **Fill in the gaps in this soap opera story with the correct form of the verb.**

Ross is in love with Keira and they are a couple. But one day Ross (1) _is walking_ (walk) down the
street when he (2) _sees_ (see) Keira in a café with Nathan, his best friend. They (3) _____ (sit)
very close together and Keira (4) _____ (smile) at Nathan. Ross is shocked.
Later Ross (5) _____ (ask) Keira about Nathan and she (6) _____ (say) she's sorry, but Nathan
gave her money last month to buy new clothes. Then she (7) _____ (tell) Ross that she slept with
Nathan. Ross (8) _____ (run) out of the room.
He (9) _____ (go) to his parents' house. When Ross (10) _____ (come in), Irene and Mike
(11) _____ (have) dinner. They (12) _____ (talk) about Ross and Keira. They're happy.
Irene says, "Perhaps you'll get married soon." But then Ross (13) _____ (tell) them about Nathan.
"It's finished with Keira," he says. Irene looks shocked.
The next day both Ross and Keira are very sad. First, Keira (14) _____ (go) to talk with her best
friend Jenny. Then Jenny (15) _____ (go) to see Ross. "Don't give up," she tells him. "Keira loves
you." While Jenny (16) _____ (talk) with Ross, Nathan (17) _____ (find) Keira at her work.
Keira tells him that she told Ross about everything. Nathan
is very angry. He (18) _____ (start) shouting at Keira.
They (19) _____ (have) a big argument when Ross
(20) _____ (come) in. He (21) _____ (hit) Nathan
and Keira's very pleased.

Spezielle can-do Übungen
zu dieser Unit finden Sie
online unter:

www.hueber.de/next
Code: XB1102

3 Homestudy

H Changing places

Spezielle can-do Übungen zu dieser Unit finden Sie online unter:

www.hueber.de/next
Code: XB1103

H1a Unjumble the words.

1. sunssieb   _____
2. ferntefdi   _____
3. alidy   _____
4. tintreseing   _____
5. prit   _____
6. meti   _____
7. netiour   _____
8. traprens   _____
9. opleep   _____
10. fof   _____

H1b Match the words.
Sometimes there's more than one possibility.

1. business	a. places
2. different	b. trip
3. daily	c. languages
4. interesting	d. off
5. time	e. routine
	f. people
	g. partners

H1c Now add one of these verbs to the words in H1b to make a longer phrase.
Example: go on a business trip

> speak I get away from I meet I see I take I go

H1d Make four new sentences out of the sentence in the box by using each word as the sentence starter.
Examples: I may go on a business trip next week.   Don't you need a vaccination?

> I don't enjoy travel.

H2a Bill and his wife Janet travel a lot. Bill's writing to his friend John about their travel plans for the coming year. Fill in *going to* or *may*.

Dear John,

Next year we're (1) _____ be travelling a lot for all kinds of reasons. In January Janet's (2) _____ spend two weeks in Delhi working on a project and I (3) _____ go along. I wanted to stay home and paint the kitchen, but we (4) _____ just wait and do that together after the trip. If we feel like it! Then in May, if we have time, we (5) _____ drive to the South of France to visit a cousin who lives there. No business, just pleasure. Then, in September, it's my turn to have a business trip. I'm (6) _____ be in Central Asia for three weeks and Janet really wants to come with me. She (7) _____ have problems getting that much time off work but she's (8) _____ talk to her colleagues and see if they can work something out. They (9) _____ agree if she promises to work longer hours in the summer. It's such a great opportunity to see that part of the world. If we stay home this summer we're definitely (10) _____ paint the kitchen. How are things with you? Any plans to come and see us? You can help us paint!

All the best to you and Sally,
Bill

H2b Listen to what John tells Sally about Bill's letter. Fill in the missing words.

John: Hey Sally, I finally got a letter from Bill today. Sounds like they're really (1) _____ be travelling a lot next year. Wow!

Sally: So, what does he (2) _____?

John: Well, let's see ... He (3) _____ that he (4) _____ go along with Janet to Delhi. She's going there on business in January. He (5) _____ he doesn't want to stay at home and paint the kitchen.

Sally: Yeah, Delhi sounds much more exciting. And then?

John: Let me look. Then he (6) _____ that they (7) _____ go to France in May.

Sally: So what about the summer?

John: I guess they're painting the kitchen. He (8) _____ that, too. Let's see, where is it? Oh yes, he (9) _____ here that he's going to Central Asia in September. Janet really wants to go along.

Sally: Oh yes! What a great idea!

John: First she's got to see if she can get off work for three weeks. She (10) _____ have to (11) _____ to work more in the summer.

Sally: In the office and at home!

John: Well, he (12) _____ when we're coming to visit. He (13) _____ we can help with the painting.

H3 **Look at the following sentences and decide whether they are formal or less formal. Then fill in *due to/owing to, because of*.**

1. a. _Due to_ heavy snowfall in Austria, many drivers spent last night in their cars.
   b. _Because of_ the snow it took us twelve hours to get home.
2. a. _____ the economic crisis, unemployment figures rose steeply compared to the same period last year.
   b. _____ the economic crisis a lot of our friends have lost their jobs.
3. a. _____ advances in technology, videoconferencing is becoming commonplace in large companies.
   b. I used to travel a lot on business, but now _____ videoconferencing I stay home more often.
4. a. _____ a flu epidemic, some schools have closed for a week.
   b. Our kids are home this week _____ the flu scare.
5. a. There'll be delays on the M25 Saturday _____ several road construction sites.
   b. We need to plan in an extra hour to Central London _____ all the roadworks.

H4 **Here are some phrases that people use when asking for and giving directions. Fill in the missing vowels and sort the phrases into two groups: *asking for directions* and *giving directions*.**
Example: asking for directions: Excuse me, I'm afraid I'm completely lost.
    giving directions: That road takes you straight into the centre of Reutlingen.

1. _xc_s_ m_, _'m _fr__d _'m c_mpl_t_ly l_st. 2. Th_t r__d t_k_s y__ str__ght _nt_ th_ c_ntr_ _f Reutlingen. 3. _ w_nt t_ g_ t_ th_ r__lw_y st_t__n. 4. Dr_v_ _n t_ th_ n_xt tr_ff_c l_ghts. 5. T_rn l_ft _nd c_rry _n t_ th_ r__nd_b__t. 6. C_rry _n t_ll y__ s__ _ sm_ll c_f_ _n th_ l_ft. 7. T_rn r_ght th_r_ _nd dr_v_ _n t_ll y__ s__ th_ s_gn t_ th_ st_t__n. 8. H_w d_ _ g_t t_ C_ty H_ll fr_m h_r_? 9. C_n y__ h_lp m_? 10. Dr_v_ _n d_wn th_s r__d t_ll y__ g_t t_ th_ m_t_rw_y. 11. H_, _xc_s_ m_. 12. T_rn r_ght _nd th_r_ y__ _r_. 13. _ n__d t_ g_t t_ Reutlingen. 14. Y__ t_rn r_ght _t th_ c_rn_r h_r_. 15. W_lk thr__ bl_cks _nd t_rn r_ght _g__n _t th_ b_g ch_rch. 16. F_ll_w th_ s_gns f_r Reutlingen. 17. Th_n _t's _b__t t_n k_l_m_tr_s. 18. T_k_ th_ s_c_nd _x_t f_r Reutlingen.

H5 **What do you say in the following situations?**

1. You're on a flight and the light over your seat doesn't work. 2. You ordered a vegetarian meal and got chicken instead. 3. You're organizing a business meeting in a hotel and the presentation equipment doesn't work properly. 4. There's no toilet paper in the bathroom of your hotel room. 5. The airline has damaged your suitcase. 6. You're very disappointed that your hotel room has no view.

4 Homestudy

H I'm fed up with my job

Spezielle can-do Übungen zu dieser Unit finden Sie online unter: www.hueber.de/next Code: XB1104

H1 Find the correct form of the words.

1. It was very nois_y_ in the factory. There was a lot of nois_e_ there.
2. I don't like my job. It's too stress__ and I get very tir__
3. I didn't like the film. It wasn't excit__ – it was very bor__
4. We had to clean the kitchen because it was very dirt__
5. I'm so bor__ in my job. I'd like to do something that's more stimulat__
6. I'd like a job that's comfort__ and well-pa__

H2a Look at the two photos.
Which person is a safety officer and which is a security officer?

 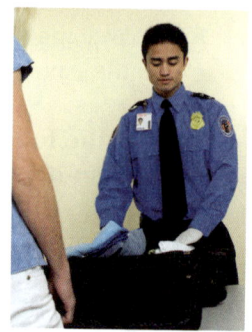

1. _____

2. _____

H2b Fill in the gaps with the words from the box.

safe | safety | secure | security

1. If you work for the government you usually have a _____ job.
2. Don't drive so fast! It's not _____ on this road.
3. Before you start work, read the _____ rules. We don't want any accidents.
4. Airports have more _____ checks now than before.

H3 Fill in the missing letters and match the words with their meanings.

1. m__n__t__nous
2. ch__ll__ng__ng
3. v__r__ed
4. r__w__rding
5. exh__ust__ng

a. giving you satisfaction, pleasure or profit
b. very tiring
c. difficult to do but interesting and enjoyable
d. including a wide range of things, not all the same
e. boring because you have to continue repeating the same thing(s), always the same

H4a Match the word with the phonetic transcription and underline the main stress in the word.
Example: interesting /ˈɪntrəstɪŋ/

1. dangerous
2. exciting
3. comfortable
4. secure
5. exhausted
6. quiet
7. rewarding
8. healthy

a. /ˈkʌmftəb(ə)l/
b. /ɪgˈzɔːstɪd/
c. /ˈkwaɪət/
d. /ˈdeɪndʒərəs/
e. /rɪˈwɔː(r)dɪŋ/
f. /ɪkˈsaɪtɪŋ/
g. /ˈhelθi/
h. /sɪˈkjʊə(r)/

 24 **H4b Listen to the CD to check the pronunciation.**

H5 Complete the following email enquiry to an employment company that finds people temporary jobs. You have to write the second half of the word.

Dear Ms Rowlands,

My name's Paul Miller. I'm a ch_ef_ in a veget_____ restaurant. I'_____ worked i__ this resta_____ for th____ years. I en____ working he____ but I thi___ I co____ do a more chall_____ job. Co____ you l____ me kn____ about a____ jobs th____ you ha____ that I co____ do? I a__ sending y___ my C__ to gi____ you mo____ information ab____ my edu_____, training and profess_____ experience. I lo____ forward t__ hearing fr____ you.

Best wishes,
Paul Miller

H6a Fill in the gaps with *since* or *for*.

1. I've worked here _____ six months.
2. Jane's lived in Germany _____ 1998.
3. Sven's been in the class _____ two years.
4. I've been married _____ fifteen years.
5. Tina has worked as a mechanic _____ last April.
6. I've lived in this flat _____ the beginning of the year.

H6b Write questions for 1 to 6 in H6a.

1. *How long have you worked here?*
2. _____
3. _____
4. _____
5. _____
6. _____

H7 Fill in the missing letters in these words for describing people. Then check the pronunciation on the CD.

1. __unc__ual
2. de__en__ab__e
3. __rea__iv__
4. o__t__o__ng
5. __en__i__ive
6. c__n__id__nt

H8 Fill in the gaps in the following email letter of application for a job. Find the correct form of the words in the box.

hear from | apply for | attach
let me know

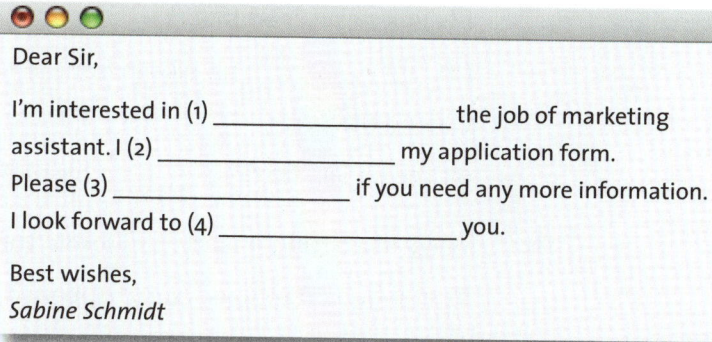

Dear Sir,

I'm interested in (1) _____ the job of marketing assistant. I (2) _____ my application form.
Please (3) _____ if you need any more information.
I look forward to (4) _____ you.

Best wishes,
Sabine Schmidt

H9a Look at the following information about Vicky. Write sentences about her.
Examples: She likes doing aerobics. / She likes to do aerobics. *(things she already does)*
She'd like to go climbing. *(one of her dreams)*

This is me, Vicky.
My hobbies: doing aerobics, playing volleyball, dancing, going to the cinema
My dreams: go climbing, speak Spanish, dance the tango, sail round the world

H9b What about you?
Write three things that you like doing and three things that you'd like to do.

H10 Write a longer letter to Grace Perkins (see D2b).
In your letter try to answer all the questions in D3.

H Imagine

H1a **Connect the phrases to make at least ten full sentences.**

1. I was having a lovely dream
2. I was having a shower
3. I was making breakfast
4. He was trying to lift the box
5. We were sitting down to supper
6. I was just going out the door

a. when the lights went out.
b. when I remembered it was a holiday.
c. when the alarm went off.
d. when I heard a crash.
e. when the doorbell rang.
f. when it slipped and fell on his foot.

H1b **Complete Ms Jones' and Bill's version of what happened.**

> slipped **|** was driving **|** fell off **|** was … cycling **|** lost

Bill said goodbye to his mother and went off to school.
Half an hour later he came back with a broken arm and a lady called Ms Jones.

Bill's version: I (1) _____ just _____ around the corner when my feet (2) _____

off the pedals. I (3) _____ my balance, fell and hit my arm and shoulder on

the street.

Ms Jones' version: I (4) _____ down the street when your son (5) _____ his bike in front

of my car.

H1c **Imagine you're Bill's mother or father. Tell the story.**

Ms Jones explained that (1) ____ _____ _____ down the street, when (2) _____ son

(3) _____ _____ his bike in front of her car.

Bill said (4) _____ _____ _____ around the corner when (5) _____ feet (6) _____

off the pedals. He (7) _____ his balance, fell and hit his arm and shoulder on the street.

H2a **Ways of starting a story. Unjumble the following phrases.**

1. strangest / The / thing / me / happened / to / last / week.

   _____

2. that / of / things / ever / One / the / was / happened / to / funniest / me / when …

   _____

3. week. / funny / A / happened / thing / last

   _____

4. believe / won't / this. / You

   _____

H2b **Use one of the sentences in H2a and continue a short story about something that happened to you.**

H3a Research shows that if the first and last letters of a word are in the right place, people can still read it even if the other letters are mixed up. See how fast you can read the following text.

I ruelgraly raed the naewpespr and one of my fauvotire socteins is the one wtih the book and flim rivewes. Praoblby mnay otehr plepoe pfeerr to raed the storps steiocn. I sedolm do taht, I jsut look tuhorgh it vrey qikculy. I aslo lvoe to raed books, ulsauly nevlos. I use the Intreent, but I sedolm raed bgols or Intreent furoms. Nadoways I olny osaiocncally raed miagazens and cimocs. Wehn I was yuengor I vrey oeftn septn huros raednig coobkooks.

H3b Now write a text about your reading habits or the reading habits of a friend, a colleague or someone in your family.

H4 Find out what films are on at the cinema in your area this week and report some of these things in the next lesson.

1. If there are any foreign films on, find out the original title.

2. Look at the following list and find out what kind of films are on.
   - adventure films
   - thrillers and suspense
   - fantasy films
   - romantic comedies
   - love stories
   - films based on novels
   - biopics
   - animated film

3. Choose one film and look it up on an English-language website. Find out the following:
   a. When was it made?
   b. Who's the director?
   c. Who are the actors and what characters do they play?
   d. What's it about? – No more than five sentences.

H5a Complete the following pairs so that they rhyme. Try saying them in rhythm.

> music (x2) **I** next **I** groovy **I** text **I** kick **I** sick **I** rap **I** movie (US for film) **I** clap

I've finished reading through the (1) _____
So what is going to happen (2) _____?

My friends thought last night's (3) _____
Was really pretty (4) _____

Hey, you wanna (5) _____?
You gotta move and (6) _____

Listening to my favourite (7) _____
Doesn't make me (8) _____

Listening to my favourite (9) _____
Gives me quite a (10) _____

 33

H5b Now listen to the rhymes and check your answers.

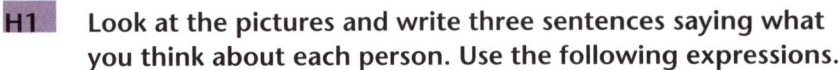

6 Homestudy

H All in the family

H1 Look at the pictures and write three sentences saying what you think about each person. Use the following expressions.

He / She must be …
I think he's / she's …
He's / she's probably …

H2 Complete the family tree using the sentences below.

Wendy's married to Jerry. They have two daughters and a son. Sophie's one of their daughters. James is Wendy's brother and Alicia is his wife. Katherine's one of their daughters. Helen, Katherine and Emily are Sophie's cousins. James is Chris's uncle. Brian is Wendy's father. Maybelle is Brian's wife. Brian and Maybelle are Dorothy's and Emily's grandparents.

Wendy ⚭

H3 Complete the second sentence so it means the same as the first.

1. She's one of my friends.	She's a friend of _mine_.
2. Bill's one of Anne's cousins.	He's a cousin of _____.
	She's a cousin of _____.
3. Is Andy one of your friends?	Is he a friend of _____?
4. Pam's one of my cousins.	She's a cousin of _____.

H4a Put these family members into two groups.

aunt ▎ brother ▎ father ▎ grandmother ▎ husband ▎ nephew ▎ niece ▎ sister ▎ uncle ▎ wife

men   _brother_ _____
women   _____

🔊 40 **H4b** Listen to Eve and Danny talking about Eve's family and complete the sentences.

1. Rosie and Jill are Eve's _cousins_.
2. Jill is one of Owen's _____.
3. Pam is Eve's father's _____.
4. Pam's married to _____.
5. Rosie's married to _____.

6. Lucy is one of Rosie's _____.
7. Craig is Jill's _____.
8. Harry and Louise are Eve's _____.
9. Bob is one of Harry's _____.
10. Sara is one of Eve's _____.

H5 **Fill in the missing words.**

> agree | all | more | nobody | opinion | right | so | some | think | true

1. _____ of us think it's nice to have children.
2. _____ people in the class think that mothers should stay at home.
3. _____ thinks that you should have a baby when you're thirteen.
4. I couldn't agree with you _____.
5. I don't _____ so.
6. I don't _____ with that at all.
7. I think _____, too.
8. I think you're _____.
9. In my _____, that's a good idea.
10. Yes, that's _____.

H6 **Complete the sentences with the right forms of the verbs.**

1. When did you _meet_ (meet)? – We _____ (meet) three years ago on holiday.
2. Have you ever _____ (have) an argument. – No, I don't _____ (think) we _____ (have).
3. How long have you _____ (be) married?
4. We _____ (get) married in 2008.
5. My parents _____ (be) married for ten years.
6. What _____ (do) you do when you feel happy?
7. Where _____ (do) you go on holiday last year? – We _____ (go) to Greece.

H7 **Match the words to their meanings.**

1. What's another word for child?
2. What's another word for good?
3. What's the word for how you feel when you're alone?
4. What's the word for not a child?
5. What's the word for not married any more?
6. What's the word for someone you work with?
7. What's the word for something you like best?
8. What's the word for somewhere you can find information?
9. What's another word for to fight or argue?
10. What's the word for what you think?

a. adult
b. colleague
c. divorced
d. encyclopaedia
e. fall out
f. favourite
g. kid
h. lonely
i. opinion
j. positive

H8a **Match the questions to the answers.**

1. Who's this?
2. How long have you known her?
3. Where did you meet?
4. Have you ever fallen out?
5. Have you ever been on holiday together?
6. Where did you go?

a. Yes, it was great.
b. At work when we shared an office.
c. It's Ellen, a good friend of mine.
d. For about ten years.
e. No, we get on really well.
f. We went to Greece together last year.

H8b **Choose someone you know and write your answers to the questions in H8a about that person.**

Spezielle can-do Übungen zu dieser Unit finden Sie online unter:

www.hueber.de/next
Code: XB1106

7 Homestudy

H Modern times

H1 Fill in the gaps with *more* or *less*.

1. _More_ people in India eat curry than in Germany.
2. The French drink _____ beer than the Germans.
3. Greeks spend _____ on heating than people in Sweden.
4. _____ people in Sweden drive Saabs than in Spain.
5. French men do _____ work in the house than Dutch men.
6. _____ people in Britain go to evening classes than in Austria.
7. There are _____ states in the USA than in Germany.

H2a Fill in the gaps with an *-ing* word.

1. I think _eating_ eggs for breakfast is nice.
2. I like _____ hands when I meet somebody.
3. I think _____ on the left is difficult.
4. I hate _____ to work.
5. _____ people is a nice way of greeting them.
6. I think _____ curry for breakfast is strange.

H2b Write sentences about yourself like the ones above.

H3 Write sentences about your class beginning with the following words.

Most people _____
Nobody _____
Everybody _____
Hardly anyone _____
Some people _____

H4a Fill in the gaps with the right form.

1. If I _____ (win) a lot of money, I _____ buy a big car.
2. If you _____ (lose) your job, how _____ your life change?
3. If I _____ (have) more time, I would _____ to Australia.
4. If I _____ (change) my job, I _____ become a teacher.
5. If I _____ (be) clever, I would go on "Who wants to be a Millionaire?"

H4b Write sentences about *yourself* like the ones above.

H5a Listen to the interview and fill in the table about Mo and Allie.

	Mo	Allie
came to Germany	ten years ago	
likes		
job		
doesn't like		
surprised him / her most		
finds strange	—————	

H5b Write sentences about Mo and Allie.

Example: Mo came to Germany ten years ago. He likes …

Allie came to Germany two years ago. She likes …

H6 Make a list of tips for someone who wants to live and work in a big city in Germany.

Always _____

Never _____

Be _____

Don't _____

H7a Complete the text with the right forms of the verbs.

A 50-year-old talks about the past, the present and the future:

When I (1) _____ (be) a child, we only (2) _____ (have) three television channels and no remote control so we (3) _____ (have) to get up and change the programme. Now life (4) _____ (be) more comfortable. You can watch cinema films at home and I think that soon there (5) _____ (be) no more cinemas at all. In ten years' time, everyone (6) _____ (choose) their own films from the Internet.

Listening to music (7) _____ (be) different now too. Thirty years ago we (8) _____ (listen) to cassettes. Then CDs (9) _____ (come) along and now all you need is a gadget with all your music on it. I don't know how that (10) _____ (change) in the future.

H7b Complete these sentences about the past, the present and the future.

1. Thirty years ago people _____ to cassettes. Then they _____ to CDs and now a lot of people _____ MP3 players. But nobody knows what people _____ in the future.
2. Thirty years ago nobody _____ a mobile phone. Now _____.
3. Thirty years ago we _____ maps to find our way. Now many people _____. In the future we _____.
4. Thirty years ago we all _____ the same television programmes. Now _____ _____.

H8 Put these words into four groups.

burglar | bus conductor | cheese | clock | curry | eggs | letter opener | lipstick noodles | nurse | pickpocket | postman | robber | shop assistant | mugger | toy

jobs	criminals	food	things

Spezielle can-do Übungen zu dieser Unit finden Sie online unter:

www.hueber.de/next

Code: XB1107

8 Homestudy

H Our world

H1a   Teresa is a retired schoolteacher from Leeds. She travelled a lot in the States. Here she's talking about a couple of things that have changed in the last forty years. Fill in *used to* or *didn't use to*.

People _____ (1) have mobile phones like they do today. So, whenever we went camping in the States we _____ (2) have to collect coins to use the public telephones. I _____ (3) like mobile phones when they first came on the market. Now I think they're OK and they're good to have when you're travelling and need to contact someone. You don't have to look for a public telephone like people _____ (4) do.
There's another thing that's different from what it _____ (5) be when driving in the States. If you stopped at a petrol station, someone _____ (6) come out and fill up the car for you. Nowadays you go in first and pay for the petrol you want. Then you go out and fill up the car yourself. Or, you just use a credit card.

H1b   Write five sentences about things that you *used to do* or *didn't use to do*.

H1c   In A1c you learned how the Lakota way of life has changed: what it used to be like and what it is like now. Make four sentences using *used to* and *didn't use to*.
Example: The Lakota used to live in tepees, but now they live in houses.

H2a   Complete the sentences with something that is true for you and then add two sentences of your own.

a. If I won a million dollars, I'd _____
b. If I could travel anywhere, _____
c. If we put in new windows, _____
d. _____ we'd have a big garden.
e. _____ I'd get one with lower fuel consumption.
f. _____ I'd learn how to cook better.
…

H2b   Tick what you recycle, reuse or throw away.

		recycle	reuse	throw away
a	plastic bottles			
b	jam jars			
c	plastic bags			
d	newspapers / advertisements			
e	tins / cans			
f	running shoes			

H2c   Now listen to Jan's experiences and compare your answers with what she says.

H3a   Match the words. You can use some words more than once.

1. heavy
2. polar
3. destructive
4. serious

a. ice caps
b. droughts
c. rainfall
d. storms
e. flooding

Spezielle can-do Übungen zu dieser Unit finden Sie online unter:

www.hueber.de/next
Code: XB1108

H3b **Use the words from H3a to match with the definitions below.**

1. when a lot of water falls from the sky _____
2. when there is no rain for a very long time _____
3. when a lot of water covers land, houses, cars, etc. _____
4. strong winds and a lot of rain that cause great damage _____
5. huge amounts of ice at the north and south tips of the earth _____

H3c **Now fill in the gaps in this recent letter to a news-paper with the expressions from H3b. In some cases you have to choose between *will* and *may / might*. Are you a "will" or a "may / might" person, or a bit of both?**

remember
The coastline **will** be destroyed. = you are quite certain about this The coastline **may / might** be destroyed. = you are less certain about this

Dear Sir or Madam,

Your paper often writes about how people living in foreign countries may have to move because of climate change. However, a lot is also happening closer to home. Where we live there has been a tremendous increase in (1) _____ and (2) _____ over the last ten years. There has been (3) _____ in some places and people have lost their homes, their cars, and, sometimes, their lives. Scientists say that if the Sahara continues to grow, people living in the region (4) _____ (will / may / might) have to leave their homes due to (5) _____. However, if the (6) _____ continue to melt at the present rate, some of us (7) _____ (will / may / might) have to move because there is too much water where we live. If the present trend continues, the coast-line near my home (8) _____ (will / may / might) be destroyed in the next fifty years.

Yours faithfully,
John and Mary Smith

H3d **Complete the following statements.**

died **I** would (x2) **I** may / might (x2) **I** will **I** rose **I** won't

a. Some people believe that Albert Einstein said: "If all the bees in the world (1) _____, man (2) _____ have only four years to live." However, the bees (3) _____ not die. And I don't think they (4) _____.

b. Some scientists say: "If water levels (5) _____, coastlines (6) _____ be destroyed." However, we (7) _____ be able to stop temperatures rising by reducing CO_2 emissions. So this (8) _____ happen.

H4a **Think about your local charity shop or the last flea market you visited. What do / did they sell there? Draw word wheels on a piece of paper and add what comes to your mind.**

charity shop   flea market

H4b **Now listen to Tom's description and add the things he mentions to your word wheel.**

H Good health

2 19

H1 Listen to the words on the CD and write them under the correct pictures.

1. _____   2. _____   3. _____   4. _____

5. _____   6. _____   7. _____   8. _____

H2 What happened to the people?

1. John _broke his arm._

2. Sue _____

3. Tim _____

4. Lucy _____

5. Ian _____

Tim

John

Sue

Lucy

Ian

H3 Fill in the gaps with the correct reflexive pronoun: *myself, yourself,* etc.

1. My wife cut _herself_ when she broke the glass.
2. Paul hurt _____ when he fell down.
3. We enjoyed _____ a lot at the party.
4. I was shocked when I saw _____ in the mirror.
5. The children cut _____ when they played with the knives.
6. You need to look after _____ when you're ill.

H4 What happened to poor Jim?

1. He _got bitten_ by a snake.
2. He _____ by a wasp.
3. He _____ (by the sun).
4. He _____ by a falling tree.
5. He _____ by a dog.

H5a Put the following phone call into the correct order. Number from 1 to 8.

a. ☐ And when would you like to come?

b. ☐ Yes, that'd be fine. Thanks.

c. ☐ Certainly. Could I have your name please?

d. ☐ Would 9 o'clock be OK for you, Mrs. Jones?

e. ☐ Good morning. Could I book a facial, please?

f. ☐ Utopia Spa. Can I help you?

g. ☐ What about next Thursday?

h. ☐ Yes, it's Nerys Jones.

2 20

H5b Listen to check your answer.

H5c **Fill in the gaps in the following phone conversation.**

- Hello.
- Oh, hello, _____ (1) Utopia Spa?
- Yes, it is. _____ (2) Lucy speaking.
- Oh, good morning. I _____ (3) book a massage, please.
- Yes. When _____ (4) come?
- _____ (5) an appointment on Friday afternoon?
- _____ (6) 2 o'clock be OK for you?
- Yes. That's fine.

H6 **Give these people advice for the following situations. Use the ideas in the box and**
should / shouldn't, need (to) **or** *ought to.*

> drink the local water ❙ get a vaccination (get vaccinated) ❙ go to the doctor
> put on some sunblock ❙ take warm and waterproof clothes

1. Diana's had diarrhoea for two days.
2. Alfred's 70 years old and they expect a lot of flu soon.
3. Daisy's going down to the beach for the day and it's very sunny.
4. Mark's going walking in the Scottish Highlands.
5. Sonia's going on holiday to India.

H7a **Match the present and past forms.**

1. am	a. could
2. will	b. had
3. can	c. thought
4. have	d. was
5. think	e. would

Spezielle can-do Übungen
zu dieser Unit finden Sie
online unter:

www.hueber.de/next
Code: XB1109

H7b **Listen to the CD and report what Mr. Smith said.**

Dear Sir

I'm writing to complain about our stay in one of your hotels: the Grand Hotel in Oxford. I had a meeting with the manager, Mr Smith, and this is what he told me:

He said he _____ (1) sorry about the situation but he _____ (2) afraid that he _____ (3) do anything about it immediately. He told us that he _____ (4) need to talk with his staff, but he promised that he _____ (5) call us the next day. He said that if what we told him _____ (6) true, we _____ (7), of course, have our money back. He also said that he _____ (8) the service in his hotel _____ (9) a problem. He said that he never _____ (10) any complaints normally. He hoped that we _____ (11) come back to the hotel another time, and he promised us that we _____ (12) have anything to complain about next time.

Mr Smith never called me, and I never want to go back to that hotel again. I am writing to ask you to pay back all the money we paid for our weekend. It was going to be a special celebration of our wedding anniversary, but it ended up as a complete disaster.

Best wishes
Margaret Tyler

H Party time

H1 What are the following kinds of meat?
Fill in the missing letters and write the name of the animal that the meat comes from.

1. b__ __f _____
2. l__m__ _____
3. __ea__ _____
4. __o__ __ _____

5. __a__e _____
6. v__n__s__n _____
7. __u__ __on _____

H2 Listen and complete the sentences with the missing words.

1. I don't eat meat or fish because I'm a _____.
2. I can't eat peanut butter because I'm _____ to peanuts.
3. I'm sorry, but I can't eat normal pasta because I have a gluten _____.
4. I'm sorry. I don't eat any animal products. I'm a _____, you see.
5. I won't have the starter, thank you. You see, I have a seafood _____.
6. I'm sorry, but I don't eat pork. It's against my _____.

H3 Fill in the gaps in the email with the words in the box.

after I ago I before I before I by I in I last / final I next I until / till

Dear colleagues

Our course finishes _____ (1) two weeks on the Friday after _____ (2). Do you think we should organize an end-of-course party? We had a nice evening together two weeks _____ (3) so I don't know if you'd like another party now. I spoke to some of the group the day _____ (4) yesterday, and they seemed to be interested in doing something. When would be best? I know we'll continue to have a lot of homework to do _____ (5) the end of the course, so the best evening for a last party might be on the _____ (6) Thursday evening, the evening _____ (7) the end of the course. We haven't got much time, so please let me know _____ (8) the day _____ (9) tomorrow (Thursday) if you'd like a party, so we'd have two weeks to organize something.

Best wishes
Miranda

H4 Where do you go to get things done?
Example: I go to my teacher to get my work corrected.

1. teacher – to correct my work
2. hairdresser – to cut my hair
3. garage – to service my car

4. Mr Price – to paint my flat
5. the jeweller's shop – to repair my watch
6. local travel agent – to book my flight

H5 Write pairs of sentences using the question word *which*.
Example: Which T-shirt would you prefer: red, blue or green?

1. T-shirt — red, blue, green
2. restaurant — Italian, Indian, Chinese
3. rental car — Volkswagen, Peugeot, Fiat
4. DVD — a romantic comedy, a fantasy film, a comedy
5. magazine — a woman's magazine, a nature magazine, a news magazine
6. prize — a bottle of wine, a box of chocolates, a bottle of perfume

Spezielle can-do Übungen
zu dieser Unit finden Sie
online unter:

www.hueber.de/next
Code: XB1110

H6   **Match the two halves of the dialogue, then listen and check your answers.**

1. Excuse me. Is this a line?

2. Is anybody sitting in these places?

3. Can I get you something to drink?

4. Oh, I'm so sorry. How clumsy of me!

5. Would you like a glass of wine?

6. Is this seat free?

a. No, I'm sorry. She's just gone to get something to eat.

b. No, thank you. That's very kind, but I'm driving.

c. No, they're free. Please take a seat. Do you know everybody here?

d. Oh, don't worry. It was only water. Most of it went on the table.

e. Oh, that's very nice. Thank you. I'll have a glass of red wine, please.

f. Yes, this is for the main course. The starters are over there.

H7a   **What have you learnt? What can you now do? Match the two halves of the sentences.**

1. I've learnt a bit of Japanese
2. I've had a meeting with the boss
3. My mother's had the vaccination
4. I've broken my leg
5. The children have eaten too much chocolate
6. I've made the coffee
7. The government has increased the tax
8. The cat's learnt to open the door
9. We've finished the book
10. It's stopped raining

a. so I can't walk.
b. so he now knows that I'm not happy in my job.
c. so I can now say a few words when I go to Tokyo.
d. so it can go out when it likes.
e. so we can go out now.
f. so now they feel ill.
g. so now we have to get a new one.
h. so she shouldn't get the flu now.
i. so whisky is now more expensive.
j. so you can have a cup if you like.

H7b   **Complete the sentence with the correct form of the verbs.**

1. When I _started_ (start) the cookery course, it _was_ (be) very difficult. But now I _'ve learnt_ (learn) to make some simple things.

2. I _____ (start) work here five years ago. At the beginning it _____ (be) very hard, but now I _____ (finish) my first project and I feel better.

3. When the restaurant _____ (open), nobody _____ (know) it. But now it _____ (win) a prize for the best restaurant in the town and it's full every evening.

4. The old factory _____ (lose) lots of money last year. Now the company _____ (decide) to close it. The employees are very worried about their future.

5. Our local football team _____ (play) very badly last year, but this year it _____ (win) every home game and it's near the top of the table.

6. My colleague _____ (want) to go on holiday next month but now she _____ (break) her ankle and she can't go.

7. My old computer _____ (be) so slow. But now I _____ (buy) a new one, and it's fantastic.

8. I used to stay in a little hotel by the sea, but now they _____ (increase) their prices and it's too expensive for me.

9. We _____ (plan) to go out for a walk this afternoon, but now it _____ (start) raining so I don't know if we'll go.

T

Tapescripts
Texte der Hörverständnis-Übungen

Unit 1

Language and learning

A1b

John: Hi, I see that your name's Vanessa. I'm John.

Vanessa: Nice to meet you, John. Where are you from?

John: I'm actually English, but right now I live in Prague.

Vanessa: That's interesting. I live in Nuremberg. That's not far from Prague. How do you like Estonia?

John: Very much. What do you do?

Vanessa: I'm still a student. I do European Studies. Do you have a job?

John: Yes, I work for a large European company. When do you finish university?

Vanessa: Next summer. Are you staying the full two weeks?

John: No, only till Monday. Do you speak a lot of languages?

Vanessa: Well, I guess my English is pretty good. German is my first language and I speak a bit of French. Last year I started to learn Russian.

John: Wow! You must be good at languages. Do you want to use languages in your future job?

Vanessa: Oh, absolutely! That's so important these days. But tell me, do you have any hobbies, things that you're interested in? And, do you speak Czech, since you're living in Prague?

John: Well, I enjoy playing football and tennis. I also like playing the clarinet. As for my Czech …

A2b

Speaker 1
J'aime jouer du piano et de la clarinette. Ma soeur aime beaucoup danser. Elle joue aussi au football.

Speaker 2
Я люблю играть на пианино и на кларнете. Моя сестра очень любит танцевать. Она также играет в футбол.

Speaker 3
Ben piyano ve klarnet çalmasını seviyorum. Kızkardeşim dans etmeyi çok seviyor. Futbol da oynuyor.

C1a

John: Asko, you've been learning English for some time now. What do you still find difficult?

Asko: I don't have enough time to practise.

John: What about you, Maria?

Maria: I think many English words are hard to pronounce.

Asko: Yes, because the spelling's difficult. So if you see a word you don't know how to pronounce it, and if you hear a word you don't know how to write it.

Maria: And another thing, people talk too fast, so it's hard to understand.

Asko: Yeah, that's right. Another problem that I have is that I'd really like to talk more but I'm afraid of speaking and making mistakes.

Maria: What about grammar? I think the grammar is hard to learn. The different verb forms and things like that. I never liked grammar at school. It's so theoretical.

D1a

John: OK, Vanessa, so what do you do?

Vanessa: Well, I have a special thing to help me with my Russian. I talk to myself - in Russian - when I'm working out at the gym. What about you Asko?

Asko: I read simple texts, things that I understand or know something about. I also look up information on the Internet. It's your turn, Maria. What do you do?

Maria: I enjoy watching DVDs of English films and reading the English subtitles. How about you, John?

John: Sometimes I write my shopping list in Czech – if it's not too long!

Unit 2

Right, let's write

B1b

Judy: How did I meet my husband? I've never forgotten. It was nearly forty years ago and it was in a pub. I saw this very sexy bloke and I asked my friend, Pam, to introduce us cos she said she knew him. On our first date we went to the cinema and then we talked all evening nonstop, and it felt really good. I think physical attraction and personal chemistry is very important. We didn't need a computer to match us! After forty years we're still happy together.

I think our secret was big sexual attraction, similar backgrounds and the same sense of humour.

Matt: I met my partner, Ali, through an Internet dating company three years ago. We used a company that says it's found ninety-nine factors that are important for successful relationships. It's a mathematical system and it's based on research with 10,000 married couples. We had to fill in a very complicated questionnaire, but it certainly worked for us. It was much better than meeting someone for an hour in a bar or club and then arranging to meet. The company says they're very successful at bringing the right people together. As I said, it worked for us. Ali and I like all the same things and I hope that we'll be together for a very long time.

B2c

NEXT: Well, thanks for talking to us about our three profiles today. What do you make of the first one?

Randy: Well, I thought I'd grade them for you out of ten and I'd give the first one five out of ten. There's nothing really wrong with it but it's not much fun to read. The first sentence is pretty boring and when he talks about his hobbies and interests, it's not very interesting.

NEXT: But he says he'd like to travel to Asia – that's quite exciting.

Randy: You're right – that's the best bit. That's something they could talk about on a first date.

NEXT: And what about profile number two?

Randy: Well, this is a lot better. We learn more about the person – who she is, what she's like. And she probably writes the way she is – she's lively and interesting.

NEXT: So what grade would you give her?

Randy: Seven out of ten maybe.

NEXT: Not more?

Randy: Well, she makes a mistake. She writes that she's looking for someone who's "financially secure". A guy reads that and he's like: "Uh-uh, she's after my money." But I really like it when she writes "mean what you say, and say what you mean". That's cute!

NEXT: OK, let's move on to profile number three.

Randy: Well, this is the winner for me. It's not perfect. It's maybe an eight out of ten, possibly a nine. It has a great start, a great opening sentence. It really makes you read more. She shows that she has a good personality. And the ending's good, also.

NEXT: Yes, it's good, but she sounds a bit serious to me, though. When she says that she doesn't like most guys, and that she thinks for days about a movie, that's a bit – I don't know – heavy, isn't it? A bit frightening perhaps?

Randy: Perhaps. But she could be good to talk with. She's just trying to get a date at the moment.

Unit 3

Changing places

A2a

Suzanne: Hi there, I'm Suzanne. Thank you all for coming here today and taking part in this interview. I'm doing a study on why people travel. Murat, why do you travel? Where do you go?

Murat: I work as a waiter in a hotel in Essen, but every summer I go to southern Turkey and work for three months in a big holiday hotel there. There are a lot of visitors from Germany. I speak German and Turkish – and some English, of course – so I can help them if they have any questions.

Suzanne: Do you enjoy working in both countries?

Murat: Yes. I like both countries a lot, but my dream is to have my own small hotel. I'm going to do a hotel management course here in Germany and one day I may have my own little hotel in Turkey. Who knows?

Suzanne: Irene, what about you? How much do you travel?

Irene: I work for an international company and I travel a lot for work. It's great because I can get away from the daily office routine and sometimes I meet really interesting people. Next week I'm going to meet the team in Istanbul. And next month I may go to China for the first time. But some trips are quite a challenge, so for my holiday I don't usually travel: I prefer to stay at home.

Suzanne: Sylvia, do you travel for business or pleasure?

Sylvia: Well, both, really. I'm going to work on an aid project in India. I want to get away from my daily routine and learn something new, so I'm going to give it a try. If it goes well, I may go again. Right now I'm applying for a visa.

Suzanne: David, do you travel every year?

David: Well, we wanted to do something different, so every year we take time off and hike for two or three weeks. This summer we're going to hike part of the trail from the North Sea to the Baltic. It's really beautiful and I think we'll see lots of interesting things. In fact, we're getting ready for this year's trip now and we just need to check our equipment.

Suzanne: Pierre, do you like to travel?

Pierre: I certainly hope so, because travelling is my job. I'm a flight attendant and I do a lot of long distance flights. We always get time off between flights, so I see a lot of interesting places. It's fun to meet people and speak different languages. But I have next week off and I'm just going to relax. It's hard work: I may stop in a few years and do something different.

A2b

Murat: Yes. I like both countries a lot, but my dream is to have my own small hotel. I'm going to do a hotel management course here in Germany and one day I may have my own little hotel in Turkey. Who knows?

A3

go to university
go on a business trip
speak different languages
get away from the daily routine
meet interesting people
see interesting places
go on holiday
find a job
take time off
do something different
visit family and friends
meet business partners

B2a

a.
We have an announcement for all passengers on Kuwait Airways flight number 208 from London-Stansted to Delhi. This flight will be delayed owing to bad weather. Departure time from London-Stansted is now twenty hundred hours. We apologize to passengers for the delay.

b.
Notice to all passengers travelling to Cambridge. Due to work on the railway line at Royston, all trains departing to Cambridge will be delayed approximately one hour. We repeat: Due to work on the railway line all trains departing to Cambridge will be delayed approximately one hour.

c.
Here's the latest update for you motorists out there. Owing to a serious accident on the M25 at Junction 7 southbound, the motorway will be completely closed for at least four hours. People travelling south from London to Gatwick and Brighton are advised to find alternative routes or to use public transport.

C3a

Donna

Donna: Excuse me, I'm afraid I'm completely lost. I need to go to the railway station.

Man: Don't worry. It's actually quite easy. Drive on to the next traffic lights. Turn left and carry on to the roundabout. Go straight on at the roundabout and carry on till you see a small café on the left. Turn right there and drive on till you see the sign to the station. Turn right and there you are.

Donna: So, left at the traffic lights. Straight on at the roundabout, straight on to the café, right and then left at the sign.

Man: No, right at the sign.

Donna: Great. Thanks a lot.

Man: You're welcome.

David

David: Excuse me, how do I get to City Hall from here?

Man: You turn right at the corner here. Walk three blocks and turn right again at the big church. Then you'll see a market down a street on your left. Walk through the market to the end of the street. Then you'll see a sign for the City Hall.

David: Thanks very much.

Man: No problem.

Lizzie

Lizzie: Hi, excuse me. Can you help me? I need to get to Reutlingen.

Woman: Oh, that's easy. Drive on down this road till you get to the motorway. Follow the signs for Reutlingen. Then it's about 10 km. Take the second exit for Reutlingen. That road takes you straight into the centre of Reutlingen.

Lizzie: Thanks a lot.

Woman: You're welcome.

D1a

1.
a. This room's a mess. It needs to be cleaned now.
b. This room's not very tidy. Could you please send someone to clean it?

2.
a. I'm sorry, but the shower in my room doesn't work. Are there any other rooms available?
b. The shower doesn't work. I want another room.

3.
a. The air conditioning in the conference room is far too noisy. Can't you switch it off?
b. The air conditioning in the conference room is a bit loud. Would you mind switching it off?

4.
a. Excuse me, I ordered a veggie burrito, not a beef burrito.
b. You've got my order wrong. I want a veggie burrito.

5.
a. My soup is cold. Bring me another one.
b. I'm afraid this soup is cold.

E1a

We have an announcement for all passengers on American Airlines flight 569 from Boston to San Francisco. This morning's flight is overbooked. We ask any passengers willing to accept a seat on a later flight to please come forward now.

E2b

Friend: Hi, Paulette, got there in one piece?
Paulette: Yes, I got here safely. I sat next to a woman and her cello.
Friend: The connection's really bad. I can't hear you. Did you say cello?
Paulette: The flight was overbooked. There weren't enough volunteers.
Friend: What did you say?
Paulette: She refused to put the cello in the hold.
Friend: What? She wanted to hold a cello?
Paulette: No, she refused to let the airline put the cello in the hold. So another passenger had to take a later flight to make room for the cello.
Friend: Huh?
Paulette: She's a very nice person. She studies music at the Boston School of Music. We …
Friend: Oh! Now the connection broke. Maybe she'll phone back. What's all this about a cello?

H2b

John: Hey Sally, I finally got a letter from Bill today. Sounds like they're really going to be travelling a lot next year. Wow!
Sally: So, what does he say?
John: Well, let's see … He writes that he may go along with Janet to Delhi. She's going there on business in January. He says he doesn't want to stay at home and paint the kitchen.
Sally: Yeah, Delhi sounds much more exciting. And then?
John: Let me look. Then he says that they may go to France in May.
Sally: So what about the summer?
John: I guess they're painting the kitchen. He explained that, too. Let's see, where is it? Oh yes, he writes here that he's going to Central Asia in September. Janet really wants to go along.
Sally: Oh yes! What a great idea!
John: First she's got to see if she can get off work for three weeks. She may have to promise to work more in the summer.
Sally: In the office and at home!
John: Well, he wants to know when we're coming to visit. He says we can help with the painting.

Consolidation 1

C2d

I don't have time to go to classes every week so I go to a club to practise my English. I can go when I want but I usually meet the other members about once a month. We go to the opera together and then meet and talk about it afterwards. The operas are not always in English but that doesn't matter very much. The members are from different countries and English and American people come to the club too. You just have to be interested in opera. It's nice because you can meet a lot of people with the same interest as you but the level of English is very high and sometimes I can't understand everything.

C4a

A: What about The English Club as a name? We're the first one in the town and so that would be the easiest. Everyone would know what it is about.
B: That's boring! It just sounds like a lesson, like The English Class. I think something like The Shakespeare Club would be better.
A: But that's confusing and wrong. We don't want to talk about Shakespeare. Everyone will get the wrong idea.
B: OK, what do we want to do, then? The name should say something about that. If we only want to talk then we can have a name like Speakeasy English but if we want to go to the cinema then something like Watch and Talk would be good.
A: Maybe we should first decide what we want to do.

Unit 4

I'm fed up with my job

A4a

Nigel
I work as a night porter in a London hotel. The job's badly paid but it's comfortable. It's usually very quiet so I can read and think about the book that I'm writing. I can even sleep a bit. My friends think it must be very boring but I like it because it's not tiring and so when I go home I'm not exhausted. I just want a job that's secure and that doesn't take too much energy. I like my routine.

Becky
I work for a small company that organizes weddings for people. It's very challenging because a wedding day is one of the most important days in a person's life and it can be very stressful. I like the work because it's quite varied and very rewarding: I meet lots of different people and they all have different ideas. It can also be exciting because we organize weddings in different parts of the world. But it's exhausting. I work very long hours and when I come home I'm very tired.

B1

Lauren: Hi Tina. How's things? You look a bit down!
Tina: Oh, hi, Lauren. Yeah, I'm fed up.
Lauren: Well, what's the matter?
Tina: I'm bored. The job's boring. Life's boring. Everything's boring.
Lauren: Well, that's not very nice.
Tina: Oh, sorry. I'm not talking about you and my friends – you're all great. It's me.
Lauren: But what's wrong with the job?
Tina: I can't stand it any more. It's so monotonous - always the same every day. I want something more varied, more challenging. I need something new.
Lauren: Well, why don't you talk to the HR people? Perhaps you could do some training for something different.

Tina: Yeah, perhaps I will. But that's enough about me. What about you? You went out with Darrell last night, didn't you?

Lauren: Oh, yeah. And …

B3b

Ed: Come in!

Tina: Oh, good morning. I'm Tina.

Ed: Hi, I'm Ed. Come and sit down, Tina.

…

Ed: Now, you came here from Germany, right?

Tina: Yes.

Ed: So how long have you lived here?

Tina: Oh, since 2003.

Ed: And why did you come to Britain?

Tina: Well, it's because I have an English boyfriend.

Ed: Oh, I see. And how long have you worked for the company?

Tina: For nearly five years.

Ed: That's quite a long time. What did you do before you came to Britain? What education did you have in Germany?

Tina: I did an apprenticeship as a florist.

Ed: A florist? That's a bit different to working in a factory. Why aren't you working as a florist here?

Tina: I tried to get a job when I came here but I couldn't. There aren't many flower shops in this area.

Ed: That's true. Most people buy flowers at the supermarket these days. And now you say you want to know about training for a new job. Why do you want to change your job?

Tina: I'd like a job that's more challenging. I think I can do a more responsible job.

Ed: Well, what sort of thing would you like to do?

Tina: Well, I think I'm good at talking to people, and I think I can learn new things quickly. I'd like to be a manager. I'd like to be responsible for a group of people. I'd like to be a team leader.

C2d

Hi babes. So what kind of girl are you? Bossy! Yeah, but sexy, too. No, I'm just kidding. Seriously, I think you could say that you're outgoing, cos you're good with people, you know. I mean, you made lots of friends when you came here. Then you're a good learner. Think about when you learnt English. I mean, when you came here you learnt really fast. And what about hard-working? When you came here, you worked all day in the factory and then you went to English classes every evening. Wow, that was hard work, you know. And I

think you can say that you're good at organizing things. Remember, you told me that you organized lots of activities at your school. As I said, you're bossy, but I love you! Oh, that's four things – sorry, you asked for three. See you this evening!

D1b

Sharon: Right, Tina, you've told me about your apprenticeship in Germany. Now, why do you want to do this team management course?

Tina: Well, I'd like to do something new. My job at the moment is a bit boring and I'd like something more challenging. I think that I'd like to be a team leader. I'd like to have more responsibility.

Sharon: OK. So what sort of person are you? How would you like to describe yourself?

Tina: Well, I like people. I'm friendly and outgoing. But I also like to organize things. Sometimes I'm a bit bossy at home! What else? Well, I like to learn new stuff. And I'm hard-working.

Sharon: Do you have the time to do this course? First you'll have to go away for two weeks and then you'll have to study in your free time – at weekends or in the evenings.

Tina: Oh, that's OK. I can do that. I learnt English in that way.

Sharon: That's good. Now let me tell you a bit about …

E1b

Daniela: What do you think? Is it important to have a dictionary?

Martin: Of course. There are so many words that I don't understand. A dictionary helps me. But I like to have a small dictionary that I can carry around with me easily. Some dictionaries are too big and heavy.

Daniela: Yeah, but the little dictionaries are not so helpful.

Martin: Why not?

Daniela: Well, if you look up a word you sometimes find two or three different possible words and you don't know which word to take. If you have a bigger dictionary, they usually give you some examples, so it's easier to find the word you need.

Martin: But what about electronic dictionaries? What do you think about them?

Daniela: There are some good online dictionaries.

Martin: That's right, but you need to be able to access the Internet. And when you're travelling or you're in class, that's not easy.

Daniela: Yeah, well new mobile phones can do that. Most dictionaries are on CD now, of course. And a lot of them have the pronunciation as well. You can hear how to say the words.

Martin: Yeah, that's good. I don't really like that "Phonetik".

Daniela: The phonetic alphabet?

Martin: Yeah, the thing that they have in dictionaries.

Daniela: What about an English-English dictionary? Do you like them? Or do you prefer English-German?

Martin: I don't know. I just use a German-English one, because my English isn't so good.

Daniela: OK, but I've got an English-English dictionary for learners and it's very interesting. I've got a German-English one, too. I use them both.

Martin: Isn't the English-English one too difficult?

Daniela: Well, not really. It's for learners. It explains the words in an easy way. And, of course, it gives you lots of examples. I sometimes like to just look at the dictionary and read about different words. It's good practice for my English.

Martin: But if you don't know a word in English, how can an English-English dictionary help you? You have to have a German-English one then.

Daniela: That's right.

H4b

1. dangerous, 2. exciting
3. comfortable, 4. secure, 5. exhausted,
6. quiet, 7. rewarding, 8. healthy

H7

1. punctual, 2. dependable, 3. creative;
4. outgoing, 5. sensitive, 6. confident

Unit 5

Imagine

A1b

I'm in the garden – I can't move – My foot's stuck – My foot hurts – I can hardly stand the pain – I can't get my shoe off – My toes are under the box – I can't get myself free – The box is too heavy – The box needs lifting – I need a tool – The tools are in the house – Nobody's home.

The box is too heavy – The box needs lifting – I need a tool – The tools are in the house – Nobody's home – I'm in the garden – I can't move – My foot's stuck – My foot hurts – I can hardly stand the pain – I can't get my shoe off – My toes are under the box – I can't get myself free.

The tools are in the house – Nobody's home – I'm in the garden – I can't move – My foot's stuck – My foot hurts – I can hardly stand the pain – I can't get my shoe off – My toes are under the box – I can't get myself free – The box is too heavy – The box needs lifting – I need a tool.

A2a

Woman: You know, last week I was just reading the paper in the garden when I heard someone. He was shouting for help.

Man: Uh huh.

Woman: Well, I couldn't see anything, so I didn't think anymore about it. Later, I was just making some coffee when I heard the shouting again.

Man: So …?

Woman: Well, I decided to have a look and you won't believe this but …

B2b

Now for some current news on the reading front. A recent survey of adult reading habits in the UK shows a number of interesting – and amusing – aspects. It seems that of 4,000 readers interviewed, ten percent of the men admitted to bluffing about reading a book in order to impress women and fifteen percent lied in the workplace to impress a new colleague. Out of ten titles, the top title for impressing people was *Lord of the Rings*. It appears that women generally read more than men, but in both groups you find serial shelvers and double bookers. About twelve percent of men and women are double bookers, that is, they often read more than one book at a time. A serial shelver is someone who regularly buys books but never reads them.

Bed is the most popular place to read, but twenty-five percent of those interviewed read in the bath and twelve percent, mostly men, read on the toilet.

Thrillers and crime novels are increasingly popular among women, but about twelve percent said they would sometimes like to change the ending of a book. Men seem to prefer more open endings.

And, one last interesting titbit: another survey of 1,500 mostly married, working women aged thirty-five to fifty-nine found that the majority would prefer to read a good book than have sex, shop or sleep. Now, how about that?

C1b

Ben: So, what did you see?

Sally: Well, it's ages since I've seen a Laurel and Hardy film, so I went to see some of their short films.

John: Oh, wow! Never mind, I'm not much better. I always really liked

Billy Wilder's stuff, so I went for *Kiss Me, Stupid*. As funny as ever.

Sally: What about you, Ben?

Ben: Well, you know how much I like Hitchcock, so I decided to go and see *North by Northwest* again. It's still a great film.

John: Yeah, that scene with Cary Grant climbing around on Mount Rushmore. Actually, I prefer *The Birds*.

Sally: Ooh that's so scary. After the Laurel and Hardy I went for something completely different and saw *Sense and Sensibility*. I missed it when it came out.

John: Well, the festival's over now, so what'll we go and see next week?

Ben: How about *Angels and Demons*? Makes a change.

John: Might be an idea.

Sally: Have you read the book?

D1b

music: 1. jazz, 2. rock 'n' roll, 3. rap, 4. reggae, 5. classical, 6. electro, 7. country, 8. tango, 9. musicals

D2a

I like adventure films with action, I like thrillers and suspense.
And I'll even take a romance if I can see it with my friends.
As for books I go for something I can understand with ease.
And I'll even read in English, so my teacher will be pleased.
I don't care much for novels, I think news reports are great.
And I'll watch a film on TV if it isn't on too late.

E1c

Welcome to our Wednesday evening programme about inspiring music projects that make a difference. Tonight we're presenting two projects that bring young people together to make music. In 1975 the conductor, composer and economist José Antonio Abreu started the first Venezuelan children's orchestra with twelve children who lived in the barrios or slums. His vision was to combine social work and classical music and give poor children an alternative to a life on the streets. Today El Sistema is a network of children's and youth orchestras in which over 300,000 children learn to play a musical instrument and the project continues to grow. The main idea is not perfection, but playing together, and the result is a community where children learn to listen to and respect one another. Older children help to teach the younger ones and the most gifted go on to study music. However, there are also choirs for children with disabilities and orchestras in juvenile prisons.

Children can already start playing from the age of two. At the moment there are 270 music schools for these children, right in the slums, where the children live.

Another inspiring project is the West-Eastern Divan Orchestra founded by Daniel Barenboim and Edward Said. It was founded in 1999 in Weimar and brings together young musicians between the ages of fourteen and twenty-five from Palestine, Israel, Syria, Jordan, Egypt, Lebanon, Tunisia, and Weimar. One young violinist says that when they play music together, there are no longer any walls. Music is the common language. Since the first concert in Weimar in 1999, the orchestra has played in Berlin, Seville, Geneva and Rabat. In 2005, they played in Ramallah. The orchestra is based in Seville, Spain, because in the Middle Ages Jews, Christians and Muslims lived there in peace.

So, this evening we'll be talking to …

H5b

I've finished reading through the text
So what is going to happen next?
My friends thought last night's movie
Was really pretty groovy.
Hey, you wanna rap?
You gotta move and clap.
Listening to my favourite music
Doesn't make me sick
Listening to my favourite music
Gives me quite a kick.

Unit 6

All in the family

A1c

It's a bit difficult to see on this photo as there are so many people, but let's start with the most important two, me and Philip. That's us in the middle with Benjy, our pageboy who is Philip's cousin. Then you can see Phil's uncle, Alec, in the light brown trousers on the right and his wife Jen. They're Benjy's parents. Jen is much younger than Alec as you can see. Philip's parents are a bit difficult to see, but his dad, Miles, is the one in the dark suit and his mum, Pam, is next to him, a bit hidden behind some others. Alec's Pam's brother. Their parents, Phil's grandparents are both dead but his grandma, Dorothy looked after Phil a lot when he was young cos his Mum was working.

Phil's brother, Adam, is the dark-haired guy on the left. He and Phil don't look like each other at all. Phil's sister, Lisa, is the one in the grey dress in the middle to the right and the two boys with their hands in the air are her kids, Sam and Sid. There are lots of boys in Phil's family as you can see. Lisa is divorced and her ex, Nick, didn't come to the wedding. My parents are at the side …

A4b
Nadine
My family's very traditional really. I have a father and a mother. My dad's eight years older than my mom and they've been married for twenty-five years. They've just had their silver wedding anniversary. It's their first marriage and they met at work. I think they're quite happy. I've got a brother who's still at school. I'm studying business administration at a university near my home so I live at home and really like it. I have my own apartment in our house so I'm quite independent.

Julian
I have a sort of patchwork family, I suppose. My mother and father were married for twenty years but they got divorced six years ago. I then lived with my mum and my younger sister for five years but now I'm at college and live in a flat with friends. I come home in the holidays. My mum's partner lives with my mum and my sister. His kids are grown-up but I've met them and get on with them. I really like him and I'm glad my mum is happy with him. My dad has a girlfriend but I don't know her very well.

Belinda
I'm an only child. At least, I was until last year. My mother died ten years ago and I lived on my own with my father and grandmother. My grandmother died three years ago and last year my father married again. His new wife, my stepmum, has two quite small children and they live with us too now. It's okay, I suppose, but I think I'd like to move out next year when I finish school.

B1a
"My Favorite Things"

Raindrops on roses and whiskers on kittens – Bright copper kettles and warm woolen mittens – Brown paper packages tied up with strings – These are a few of my favorite things

Cream colored ponies and crisp apple strudels – Doorbells and sleigh bells and schnitzel with noodles – Wild geese that fly with the moon on their wings – These are a few of my favorite things

Girls in white dresses with blue satin sashes – Snowflakes that stay on my nose and eyelashes – Silver white winters that melt into springs – These are a few of my favorite things

When the dog bites – When the bee stings – When I'm feeling sad – I simply remember my favorite things – And then I don't feel so bad

C1d
Janette: Hey, I've just read something in the paper about grandparents looking after children. It says it's not always a good idea.
Philip: I don't know really, I think my grandma did a pretty good job of it. I was quite happy with her especially as my mother never had time for me.
Janette: Yeah, but she didn't have any other interests except for you, did she? She gave you all her attention and did everything for you.
Philip: It wasn't that bad. I went to kindergarten and school and learned lots of things there.
Janette: Actually, I think I'd like to look after my children myself. What do you think about that, darling?
Philip: Mmm, sounds okay. Why are you asking?
Janette: No reason at all at the moment. I'm looking forward to having children, but I think I'll wait a few years.
Phil: What do you mean?
Janette: Well, I suppose I'll be the one to stop work and stay at home with the baby. Or do you want to?
Philip: I think it must be quite nice, lots of free time.
Janette: Huh! Free time with a baby around. I think you can forget that. But anyway, I think it's a good idea to have a good job first and a bit of money, so let's wait a year or two for the kids. OK?
Philip: OK, boss.

D2b
This is Robert. We're really good friends but actually he's my ex-husband. Not many people know that, but it's not a secret. We met twenty years ago when we were at school and got married when we were very young. We separated after three years and got divorced but stayed very good friends. We've known each other for twenty years now. This is one of our wedding photos so it's really old.

And this is Don. We write to each other so I suppose he's a pen friend. We got to know each other through an online discussion list but now we write to each other off list. He lives in Australia and we've never met. We write emails about the books we're reading. Of course, we've never fallen out! I don't think you can fall out with a pen friend, can you? He mailed me this photo last year.

This is my colleague Hans-Peter. He's German but he's lived in England for ages. He speaks really good English. I can speak a bit of German but we always speak English. We see each other every day at work. Another colleague took this photo at an office party last year.

E3a
Andy
Last week? Well, it was more or less OK, I suppose, nothing special. The train to work was really full so I had to stand all the way. I was looking forward to sleeping on the train so was quite relieved when someone got off and I could have his seat. Otherwise nothing exciting happened at all.

Claire
My last week was wonderful. I got a new job and I'm so excited about starting it next month. I have applied for lots of jobs recently and been disappointed so many times that this was great news.

Tim
I had an awful week because I got really cross with my colleague. I came back from my holiday and was even looking forward to going back to work. But on my first day back I was really angry and upset about my colleague for smoking in the office we share. He always does it when I'm not at work and I hate it.

H4b
Eve: You'll meet some more of my family tomorrow at the party, you know.
Danny: Oh dear, I hope I can remember who's who. I've met some of them so it shouldn't be too difficult. Rosie and Jill are two of your cousins aren't they?
Eve: That's right and Owen is their brother. Pam will be there, too, she's their mum, my aunt. She's my dad's sister. Alan, her husband won't be there as he's away on business.
Danny: Oh, I thought Owen was Rosie's husband, but he's her brother. OK. Then who's Craig?
Eve: Craig is Jill's husband and Sam's Rosie's husband. Lucy and Rachel are their children. Jill and Craig haven't got any children.
Danny: That's good, less to remember. Then there are your parents, Harry and Louise, that's easy. But who's Bob? Is he one of your uncles?
Eve: No, Bob's just a good friend of my dad's. He's like one of the family so he's always at our parties. But there are more cousins, Sara and Peter and …
Danny: That's enough for now, let's go shopping and you can tell me the rest later. I'm confused already!

Consolidation 2

C3c
1. I want a cook book by one of those television cooks, you know like Delia Smith and Jamie Oliver and so on, but I'd like something new. I've got all Jamie Oliver's books!
2. I want a romantic novel for my grandmother. That's all she reads nowadays. Detective stories are too exciting for her, she doesn't like murder and so on.
3. I really need a book for a friend. She likes books which help her organize her life better and she talks a lot about changing her job because she wants a more exciting one.
4. I want a book for my nephew, something for school, perhaps. He likes languages and is quite good at them so maybe something to do with languages.

Unit 7

Modern times

A3b
Noelle
My name's Noelle. I'm French and I travelled to lots of different European countries when I was young but although I learnt English in school we never went to Great Britain. When I started work I had to use English, but I still never actually went to Great Britain. I was twenty-five when I went to England for the first time. My company sent me there and I lived in London with my husband for five years. I found that England was so different from the school books and also very different from France. Of course we all know that the English drive on the left and drink tea with milk and so on, so that was not a surprise; but one little thing I found really strange was that for English people black cats are lucky! I am not superstitious but everywhere else in Europe, people think black cats are unlucky. I suppose that's another thing where the British just have to be different!

Johann
I'm Johann. I come from Frankfurt in Germany which is a very international city and I travel a lot for my job and on holiday and often stay in international hotels so I thought I knew quite a lot about other countries and food. For instance the British eat bacon and eggs for breakfast and the Italians and Spanish don't eat much breakfast and so on. Well, my son got engaged to a Japanese girl and so my wife and I decided to go

to Japan and meet her family and get to know her culture. Imagine our surprise when on the first morning we got noodles for breakfast! That was the strangest thing for me, but it's only in Europe that we have special food for breakfast. In Japan you can eat anything at any time.

Mikito
Hi, I'm Mikito. I'm Japanese and I went to Germany to study and then I met Florian and fell in love with him and we decided to stay in Germany. Germany and Japan are so different that it is difficult to say what I found strangest, but I think it's greeting people. In Japan we don't even shake hands very often but I learnt how to do that quite quickly and now I think shaking hands is a nice way of greeting someone. But I think kissing people I don't know very well is strange. In Japan we don't even kiss our parents very often!

B1c
Woman radio presenter: Last week as we all know somebody here in Dublin won a million euros. Perhaps that person's listening. If they are, good luck to them. But we wondered what you would do if you won a million? Would you stop working? We sent our Patrick to ask some of you what you would do, and here are some of your answers.
Patrick: Excuse me, I wonder if I could ask you, what would you do if you won a million euros. Would you stop working?
Jan: This is a question we all ask, isn't it? I love my work as a primary school teacher but I am not sure if I'd do it until I'm 65 if I had the money to stop now. I'd probably work for some more years and then see. Maybe I'd do something else. I'm sure my life would change if I had a lot of money. I'd buy a house or a big flat and a new car for a start and I'd love to travel to Australia, which I can't afford at the moment.
Patrick: What about you? Would you stop working if you won a million euros?
Melanie: Ooh, that would be nice and yes, of course I would. I quite like my job working in a shop, but not enough to do it if I was a millionaire. I want to stop working when I have children so I'd stop now if I had the money. And if I had enough money, I'd have three or four children and buy a house in the country. That's what I would do. That'd be nice.
Patrick: Can I ask you a question, please? If you won a million euros, would you stop working?

Helmut: Well, I'm an artist and sometimes I sell enough paintings to make quite a lot of money, but sometimes it's a bit difficult, so it would be nice to be rich. Then I could paint what I want. But of course I wouldn't stop working if I won a lot of money and I don't think I'd change my life. I like it as it is.
Patrick. Hi there. Would you stop working if you won a millions euros?
Ellen: Well, to tell the truth, I have my own catering business as a cook, you see, and it's doing quite well so I think I'd invest some more money in my business and have more people to work for me. So no, I wouldn't stop working completely but I wouldn't work so hard. I think I'd change my life a bit but actually, you know, I'm quite happy as I am.

C2a
Sinead: Welcome back. This is Sinead Long. Today we're talking about crime. Have you got any stories to tell us about things that happened to you? We'd love to hear from you. Call us on 01 500 62 62. And our first caller is Maeve. Hello Maeve. How are you?
Maeve: I'm fine. And how are you Sinead?
Sinead: Oh, I'm just great, thanks. Now, what's your story, Maeve?
Maeve: Well, I'm always very careful with my purse and things because you hear so much about crime in crowded places. But there was one time, just before Christmas, when I had so many things to carry that I just put my purse in my pocket and thought I'd put it in my handbag later.
Sinead: Right, because your handbag is safer. Is that not so?
Maeve: Yes, you're right. My handbag's always closed with a zip so it's not easy to steal something from it. Well now, the shop was awfully crowded and the thief must have seen where I put my purse. Because when I got to the car and wanted to put my purse in my handbag, it wasn't there. And I never felt a thing. I don't know when the thief took it. The good thing was that I didn't have much money in it and I always have my credit cards and papers in a separate place.
Sinead: Well, that's very sensible. Thanks, Maeve for that. Now our next caller is Diarmid. Hello there, Diarmid.
Diarmid: Good afternoon to you.
Sinead: Well, Diarmid, what's your story?
Diarmid: I'd like to talk about muggers.

Sinead: Oh, dear. Were you robbed, then?

Diarmid: No, not personally, but I did see three young men once start to attack an older man on the train. They didn't really do anything but they said terrible things to him and told him to give them his money. They were big fellows and they looked dangerous and I was certainly a bit scared, there. There were no other people nearby and I'm not very big or strong. But luckily another man came into the carriage and saw them. He shouted at them and they ran away and then he helped the old fellow so nothing really awful happened. But I was a bit frightened, I have to say. And I always choose a carriage on the train with other people in it now when I'm travelling.

Sinead: That's good, now, Diarmid. That's very sensible. Now our next caller is Sheila. Hello Sheila.

Sheila: Hi, Sinead.

Sinead: Now your story's about a holiday in Italy. Is that right?

Sheila: That's right. We were on holiday by the sea. And one day when we got back to our car from the beach, we found that all our things were gone! Everything was in the car, because we were going to a new hotel that night. It was awful. We had to call the police. It was all very difficult. But because our car was locked we got the money from the insurance in the end. We bought new things. But we didn't enjoy the holiday as much after that and, in fact, we went home early. I still miss some of my clothes and the children had some toys that they liked very much. I'm sure nobody else could use them and there was nothing that was valuable at all. There was no money in the car. We had all our money with us at the beach. It was really stupid.

D3c

Andy: So when they open the new rooms in our college, the three of us are going to present the director with this time capsule and he'll put it somewhere for people to open in a hundred years' time. Have I got that right?

Beatrice: Yeah, that's right, and we in this group have to decide what goes in it, what sort of box it should be and so on. What do you guys think? It should have no more than ten things in it and they should say something about our life today, not too personal and …

Charles: We must be careful that there's nothing which goes bad, no hamburgers or anything like that.

Andy: No, no food, but even photos are difficult. They can fade, can't they, you know so you can't recognize anything.

Beatrice: But a book might be OK because the cover will protect it. There'll probably be no paper books in a hundred years' time, only electronic ones

Charles: Yes, a book's a good idea, what about our English course book?

Andy: OK, that's one thing. And a pen? We write with pens now but in a hundred years …?

Beatrice: Yeah, and stamps, because in a hundred years' time nobody will write letters anymore. And then we could put in a letter opener, we could also write an explanation of what it is.

Andy: What do you mean exactly by letter opener?

Beatrice: You know, like a knife to open letters.

Andy: Oh, OK, then that's four things. We can't have food or drink but what about an empty lemonade can?

Charles: Yes, good idea and perhaps a train ticket and a newspaper. And I think something like clothes or make-up or jewellery would be a good idea. A lipstick?

Andy: OK let's think about what sort of box to use …

E1b

Paul

I've never really needed most of these things and I don't think they'd make my life any easier. Of course I have a mobile phone but I don't send text messages or take photos with it. I like listening to music so I have a CD player but there's no other way of listening to music these days. I like reading but I don't think we need electronic books. Does technology make our lives easier? Does it make us happier? I'm just teaching my pupils at school about the Amish people. They seem quite happy without all these things. I think we could do with less technology in our lives.

Claudia

I'm not against technology and of course in many ways it makes our lives easier, but there are problems like energy and the environment. I have a really big modern television because I love watching TV and the quality of the pictures is so good. I don't think I need an electronic calendar as I can still write things down. But my boss has everything you can think of like that. He says

you can't escape technology and it makes business life much easier.

Eva

I've grown up with all these things so of course I have a mobile and a notebook computer and a digicam and if I had a car I'd have a satnav. I think when I start work there'll be far more technology in our lives. I'm studying medicine, and technology will make doctors' work much easier but it won't mean that we don't have to talk to patients or think about things. But I'm sure we'll have more chance of fighting illness and helping people and that can only be a good thing. There'll also be new ways of getting energy, I'm sure.

H5a

Interviewer: And now as part of our programme "The English Abroad", we meet Mo and Allie, two English people living in Germany, and talk to them about what they like and don't like about living in another country. Mo …

Mo: Well to start with, I must say, I really like living here. I've lived in Frankfurt for ten years, my German's quite good and I have lots of German friends. I'm a singer in a band. What surprised me was that Germans are not as formal as I thought. They shake hands more than the British but I like greeting people like that. What don't I like? Well, it's hard to say but I don't like sauerkraut and I don't drink beer. But I love drinking German wine!

Allie: I agree with Mo, I like living here too, but I came only two years ago and live with my husband in a small village near Munich. He works for a big company in Munich and I'm a housewife. I like living in a village because I come from London, so it's quite different. I still think driving on the right is strange and I don't like eating cheese for breakfast. My German's not very good but I'm learning. What surprised me most was that so many Germans speak English.

Unit 8

Our world

B2c

Good evening ladies and gentlemen and welcome to our weekly feature about our changing world. What would we do these days without credit cards, plastic wrapping, waterproof clothing, umbrellas and toilet seats? How could we live without shampoo and other cosmetics or the medicines you need? You say, what's the problem? The problem is that all of these things are made with oil or out of oil and that within the next fifty years there'll be less and less oil in the world and eventually none at all. It'll also become so expensive that production costs for many things that we use in our daily lives will go sky high. We already know about the rising cost of heating oil, petrol, etc., but oil is more important to our daily lives than many of us realize. Look around your home. How many things contain oil? I started to make a list and came up with my mobile phone, my regular telephone, lots and lots of things in my kitchen, my sports clothing, most of what is in my car, my skis, my snowboard, a lot of my children's toys …

C2b

1. As Dave said, ice caps will continue to melt. – Well, we don't really know. They may stop melting and then things will be all right.
2. There'll be an increase in heavy rainfall. – I'm not sure. There may actually be droughts in some areas.
3. Dave believes that we'll have serious droughts in southern Europe. – Or there may be more flooding. Who knows?
4. I'm sure that this trend will continue. – But we may be able to slow things down if we reduce CO_2 emissions.

H2c

Both my husband and I seem to have grown up in families that didn't throw everything away. We don't buy drinks in plastic bottles very often, but when we do, we always save three or four to have when we go on trips. We just fill them with water and use them for a while. Then we recycle them.

My husband loves to make jam so we save lots of jars every year for that. They get used over and over again.

We really try not to have too many plastic bags, but they're also useful. When it rains it's good to have a plastic bag to put a book in, for example, and they're also useful for rubbish. That way we don't have to buy extra rubbish bags.

I've never thought of saving my old running shoes, but last year in Boston we walked past a house where someone had used all their old jogging shoes as flower pots. It looked kind of interesting, but we haven't started doing that.

You can of course use tins and cans in different ways, but we hardly ever save those.

A friend of mine saves old advertisements and uses them to wrap presents. They look really nice and colourful. I just recycle wrapping paper and also sometimes use newspaper.

H4b

My girlfriend and I really like going to the local charity shop now and then. Of course we take stuff there as well, but my girlfriend bought a really nice kilt there a couple of years ago and just recently she bought a winter coat. The kilt only cost six euros and the coat was ten euros. I found a jacket there last year. It's quite old, but it's really comfortable and I like it. When my girlfriend and I moved in together we found quite a few things at a local flea market. We bought a set of dishes, some chairs and quite a nice cupboard for the kitchen. And, we unexpectedly discovered a really cool painting for the living room. It's kind of fun giving these things a second life.

Unit 9

Good health

A2a

Hassan

My name's Hassan and I come from Iran. My heart speaks Farsi because that's the language of my family in Iran. My legs speak English because this is the language you need if you travel. My stomach speaks Italian because my girlfriend comes from Italy and I love the food she cooks. And my eyes speak Japanese because I love Manga comics.

Ximena

I'm Ximena and I'm from Colombia but I grew up in France. So my heart and my stomach speak Spanish, but my head speaks French because I went to school in Paris. My feet definitely speak Spanish because I love to dance salsa, but my ears and eyes also speak Portuguese because I love to listen to Brazilian music and watch Brazilian dancing. And perhaps my arms speak Chinese because I love t'ai chi!

Rolf

My name's Rolf and I'm from Cologne in Germany. Well, my heart speaks two languages: German because that's my mother tongue but also French because my partner's French. And my ears speak French, too, because I love the French language and, especially, French songs. My hands sometimes speak English because I have to use English at work. My liver probably speaks with a Scottish accent because I love Scotch whisky.

B2b

Linda: Utopia Spa and Health Salon. I'm Linda. Thank you for calling. How can I help you?

Doris: Sorry. Is that the Utopia Spa?

Linda: Yes, that's right. How can I help you?

Doris: My name's Speich. I would like to book a treatment for my friend.

Linda: Lovely. What treatment were you thinking of?

Doris: Well, I'm not sure. I looked at your website and I was interested in one treatment but I don't know how to say it: ab – high – anjum

Linda: Oh, you mean Abhyangam. Yes, that's very popular. The massage therapist covers your head and your body in special oils – it's really lovely.

Doris: Oh, I didn't know it was the head and the body. Perhaps my friend wouldn't like that. Maybe I'll book a facial.

Linda: Lovely. So when would you like the appointment?

Doris: Next week, please. Perhaps Thursday afternoon.

Linda: Has your friend been to us before?

Doris: Sorry, I don't understand.

Linda: Well, we like to analyze somebody's skin before we do the facial. If she's been to us before, we know what kind of skin she has.

Doris: Oh, I see. No I don't think she's been in your spa before.

Linda: Right, well, she needs an hour and a quarter. Oh dear, I don't think I can offer her an appointment that afternoon. What about the morning?

Doris: No, she works in the morning.

Linda: Would Wednesday be any good? If not, it'll have to be the following week.

Doris: OK. Wednesday's OK.

Linda: Now I need your friend's name and your details.

Doris: I'm sorry, could you tell me how much that will be first.

Linda: Yes, of course. A facial including the skin analysis will cost you £55.

Doris: That's fine. My friend's name is Samantha Stone and I'm Doris Speich.

Linda: You'll have to spell that for me, please.

Doris: Yes, that's s-p-e-i-c-h.

Linda: Great. And how would you like to pay, Doris?…

B2d

…

Linda: Great. And how would you like to pay, Doris?

Doris: Visa card, please.

Linda: Lovely, what's the number?

Doris: It's 4929 3452 1625 2455

H4

1. agree, 2. think, 3. sorry, 4. disagree, 5. don't think, 6. think, 7. think about
A. 4, B. 3, C. 2, D. 1

H5

1. *a* describes the action,
   b describes the background scene
2. *b* happens in the middle of *a*
3. *b* is unfinished

H6

3. are sitting / 're sitting, 4. is smiling / 's smiling, 5. asks, 6. says, 7. tells, 8. runs, 9. goes, 10. comes in, 11. are having, 12. are talking / 're talking, 13. tells, 14. goes, 15. goes, 16. is talking / 's talking, 17. finds, 18. starts, 19. are having / 're having. 20. comes, 21. hits

Unit 3

A1a *(possible answers)*
train, time of departure, Third World, railway, rental car, aeroplane, airline, adventure, visa, vaccination, emigrate, luggage, lost

A1b

a. go to, b. go on, c. speak, d. get away from, e. meet, f. see, g. go on, h. find, i. take, j. do, k. visit, l. meet

A2a

Irene: for work, to get away from the daily office routine, to meet interesting people

Sylvia: to work on an aid project in India, to get away from the daily routine and learn something new

David: to do something different, to go hiking

Pierre: it's his job, he's a flight attendant, to see a lot of interesting places, to meet people and speak different languages

A2b

going to, may

A2c

may have his own little hotel
going to meet the team in Istanbul
going to do a hotel management course
going to work on an aid project in India
going to hike part of the trail from the North Sea to the Baltic
may go to China
may stop working as a flight attendant
going to relax next week

A2d

A: Next week she's going to meet the team in Istanbul.
B: That's Irene.
A: He's going to do a management course.
B: That's Murat.
A: She's going to work on an aid project in India.
B: That's Sylvia.
A: This summer they're going to hike part of the trail from the North Sea to the Baltic.
B: That's David.
A: She may go to China. B: That's Irene.
A: He may stop working as a flight attendant.
B: That's Pierre.
A: He's going to relax next week.
B: That's Pierre.

A2e

3. explained, 4. is, 5. mentioned, 6. go, 7. explained, 8. enjoys, 9. is, 10. is, 11. said, 12. goes, 13. explained, 14. works

A3

a. go to uni<u>ver</u>sity, b. go on a <u>bus</u>iness <u>trip</u>, c. speak <u>dif</u>ferent <u>lan</u>guages, d. get a<u>way</u> from the daily rou<u>tine</u>, e. meet interesting <u>peo</u>ple, f. see <u>in</u>teresting pla<u>ces</u>, g. go on <u>hol</u>iday, h. find a <u>job</u>, i. take time <u>off</u>, j. do something <u>dif</u>ferent, k. visit <u>fam</u>ily and <u>friends</u>, l. meet <u>busi</u>ness partners

A4a *(possible answers)*
Why do you travel? Where do you go? How much do you travel? Do you travel a lot / often? Do you travel for business? Do you travel for pleasure? Do you travel every year? Do you like to travel?

B2a

a. owing to bad weather, b. due to work on the railway line, c. owing to a serious accident

B2b

a. because of bad weather, b. because of work on the railway line, c. because of an accident

B2c *(possible answers)*
No, we didn't. And it's raining again. So we're going shopping at the mall today instead of going to the beach. Sally may meet us there. Want to come along?

Yes, I do. But petrol is getting really expensive, so Jan and I are going to car-pool. Want to join? It would be cheaper for all of us.

C2

b. C, c. F, d. C, e. FC, f. C, g. FC, h. C, i. F

C3a

Donna: e, d, a;
David: g, i;
Lizzie: f

C3b

Donna: Excuse me, I'm afraid I'm completely lost. I need to go to the railway station.
David: Excuse me, how do I get to City Hall from here?
Lizzie: Hi, excuse me. Can you help me? I need to get to Reutlingen.

C4 *(possible answers)*
D: detour (US), diversion (UK); I: information, inn; R: remember, right, road sign, route (US), rest area, railway crossing, right up to, roundabout, restaurant, railway station; E: easy, exit, east; C: country road, cell phone, café, completely lost; T: train station, turn left, to the next …, tourist information, traffic lights, that's right, thanks a lot, two blocks, three blocks, (that) takes you, (to the next) town; I: international airport, intersection (US), it takes you …; O: on the left; N: north, newsagent, navigator, navigation problem, no problem; S: south, sign, straight ahead, stoplight (US), stop sign, shop, station (bus, train), satnav

D1a

2. hotel, a; 3. conference centre / hotel, b; 4. restaurant, a; 5. restaurant, b

D1b

1. b. This room's not very tidy. <u>Could you please</u> send someone to clean it?
2. a. <u>I'm sorry, but</u> the shower in my room doesn't work.
3. b. The air conditioning in the conference room is a bit loud. <u>Would you mind</u> switching it off?
4. a. <u>Excuse me</u>, I ordered a veggie burrito, not a beef burrito.
5. b. <u>I'm afraid</u> this soup is cold.

D2a *(possible answers)*
… <u>Checking in was difficult, because everybody spoke German or French, but no English. And the hotel staff weren't helpful at all.</u>
<u>The hotel room was really disappointing. We discovered that there was no sea view as promised in the brochure.</u>
<u>…, but we only received Greek and German channels.</u>
… <u>We couldn't get a pint and there wasn't even a full English breakfast.</u>

E1a
overbooked / overbooking

E1c *(possible answer)*
All major <u>airlines</u> <u>sell more seats</u> than they have <u>seats available</u>. This is because they expect some <u>passengers</u> to be <u>no-shows</u>, and there is a risk of having <u>flights with empty seats</u>. Unfortunately, sometimes all the <u>passengers</u> turn up and then the flight is overbooked. When this happens, the airline asks if any passengers will <u>give up their seats</u> in exchange for a <u>money voucher</u> and a <u>seat on a later flight.</u> If there are not enough volunteers, the airline will have to book some on another flight. If there is a very long wait, passengers will get a <u>meal voucher</u>, or, if there is no flight until the next day, a <u>hotel voucher.</u>

E2c *(possible answer)*
Paulette said that she got there safely. She said that she sat next to a woman and her cello and that the flight was overbooked. There weren't enough volunteers for a later flight. Vanessa explained that the woman refused to put the cello in the hold. So the airline had to book an extra passenger on a later flight to make room for the cello. Vanessa said she was a very nice person. She studies music at the Boston School of Music. They exchanged email addresses.

H1a
1. business, 2. different, 3. daily, 4. interesting, 5. trip, 6. time, 7. routine, 8. partners, 9. people, 10. off

H1b
1.b/e/f/g, 2.a/b/c/e/f/g, 3.b/e, 4.a/b/f/g, 5.d

H1c *(possible answers)*
speak different languages, get away from the daily routine, meet interesting people / business partners, see interesting places, take time off

H1d *(possible answers)*
I want to do something different so I am going to work in an aid project.
Don't forget your passport.
Enjoy your trip.
Travel books are always fun to read.

H2a
1. going to, 2. going to, 3. may, 4. may, 5. may, 6. going to, 7. may, 8. going to, 9. may, 10. going to

H2b
1. going to, 2. say, 3. writes, 4. may, 5. says, 6. says, 7. may, 8. explained,

9. writes, 10. may, 11. promise, 12. wants to know, 13. He says

H3
2–5 a: due to / owing to (more formal), 2–5 b: because of (less formal)

H4
Asking for directions: 1. Excuse me, I'm afraid I'm completely lost. 3. I want to go to the railway station. 8. How do I get to City Hall from here? 9. Can you help me? 11. Hi, excuse me. 13. I need to get to Reutlingen.
Giving directions: 2. That road takes you straight into the centre of Reutlingen. 4. Drive on to the next traffic lights. 5. Turn left and carry on to the roundabout. 6. Carry on till you see a small café on the left. 7. Turn right there and drive on till you see the sign to the station. 10. Drive on down this road till you get to the motorway. 12. Turn right and there you are. 14. You turn right at the corner here. 15. Walk three blocks and turn right again at the big church. 16. Follow the signs for Reutlingen. 17. Then it's about ten kilometres. 18. Take the second exit for Reutlingen.

H5 *(possible answers)*
1. Excuse me, the light over my seat doesn't seem to work. / I'm afraid the light over the seat isn't working. Could you give me another seat? 2. Excuse me, I actually ordered a vegetarian meal. I don't eat chicken. Please bring me a salad. 3. The meeting starts in twenty minutes and we can't get the equipment to work. Could you send someone to help? 4. There doesn't seem to be any toilet paper in the bathroom. Could you please send somebody to look after this? 5. Excuse me, but this suitcase is rather badly damaged. I'll need to fill out a form. 6. I actually asked to have a view of the mountains. Could I have a different room?

Consolidation 1

C2a
a. 3, b. 1, c. 2

C2d
She is talking about *Cosi fan tutte*.
good: she can go when he wants, she can meet a lot of people with the same interests
bad: the level of English is very high

C4a
The English Club, advantage: everyone knows what it is about, disadvantage: boring, sounds like a lesson; *Shakespeare Club*, advantage: ..., disadvantage: confusing, people will get the wrong idea; *Speakeasy English ...,* *Watch and Talk ...*

Unit 4

A1a *(possible answers)*
good job: stimulating, well-paid, exciting; *good or bad job:* comfortable, quiet; *bad job:* tiring, stressful, dangerous, noisy, boring, dirty, badly paid

A1b *(possible answers)*
stressful – stress; stimulating – stimulation; dangerous – danger; quiet – quietly; noisy – noise; comfortable – comfort; boring – bored; dirty – dirt

A2
A safe job is a job which is not dangerous. A secure job is a job which you are not worried about losing.

A3
b. <u>rew</u>arding; c. <u>chall</u>enging; d. <u>var</u>ied; e. mo<u>not</u>onous; f. ex<u>haus</u>ting

A4b
Nigel: badly paid, comfortable, quiet, (friends think it must be) boring, not tiring, not exhausted, secure
Becky: challenging, varied, rewarding, exciting, exhausting, tired

B1 *(possible answers)*
She can't stand her job any more: she's fed up.

B2
1. I've worked in the production department, 2. enjoy working for, 3. more challenging, 4. you let me know about, 5. if you need more information, 6. look forward to hearing

B3a
a. How long have you worked for the company? b. How long have you lived here? c. What education did you have in Germany? d. What sort of thing would you like to do? e. Why did you come to Britain? f. Why do you want to change your job?

B3b
b, e, a, c, f, d

B3c

Ed: So how long have you lived here?
Tina: Oh, since 2003.
Ed: And why did you come to Britain?
Tina: Well, it's because I have an English boyfriend.
Ed: And how long have you worked for the company?
Tina: For nearly five years.
Ed: What education did you have in Germany?
Tina: I did an apprenticeship as a florist.
Ed: Why do you want to change your job?
Tina: I'd like a job that's more challenging.
Ed: Well, what sort of thing would you like to do?
Tina: Well, I think I'm good at talking to people, and I think I can learn new things quickly. I'd like to be a manager. I'd like to be responsible for a group of people. I'd like to be a team leader.

B4a

since: 1998, June, 6 o'clock, my birthday
for: two days, 10 minutes, a long time, seven years, four weeks

B4b

1. b, 2. a

C1a

2. a, 3. b, 4. c, 5. i, 6. h, 7. d, 8. g, 9. f

C1b

1. am<u>b</u>itious, 2. <u>calm</u>, 3. <u>c</u>onfident,
4. cre<u>a</u>tive, 5. de<u>p</u>endable, 6. hard-
<u>work</u>ing, 7. out<u>g</u>oing, 8. <u>punc</u>tual,
9. <u>sen</u>sitive

C2a

1. coming to see, 2. are interested,
3. attaching, 4. apply for, 5. let me know

C2d

a. outgoing, b. a good learner,
c. hard-working, d. organizing things

D1b

Why do you want to do this team management course? What sort of person are you? How would you like to describe yourself? Do you have the time to do this course?

D1c

I'd like: to do something new, something more challenging, to have more responsibility, to be a team leader

I'm: friendly and outgoing, a bit bossy at home, hard-working
I like: people, to organize things, to learn new stuff.

E2a

a. 3, b. 8, c. 1, d. 7, e. 2, f. 6, g. 5, h. 4

H1

2. stressful, tired; 3. exciting, boring;
4. dirty; 5. bored, stimulating;
6. comfortable, well-paid

H2a

1. safety officer, 2. security officer

H2b

1. secure, 2. safe, 3. safety, 4. security

H3

1. monotonous, 2. challenging,
3. varied, 4. rewarding, 5. exhausting
1. e, 2. c, 3. d, 4. a, 5. b

H4a

1. d <u>dangerous</u>, 2. f ex<u>cit</u>ing, 3. a <u>com</u>-
fortable, 4. h se<u>cure</u>, 5. b ex<u>hau</u>sted,
6. c <u>quiet</u>, 7. e re<u>war</u>ding, 8. g <u>healthy</u>

H5

vegetarian, I've, in, restaurant, three, enjoy, here, think, could, challenging, Could, let, know, any, that, have, could, am, you, CV, give, more, about, education, professional, look, to, from

H6a

1. for, 2. since, 3. for, 4. for, 5. since, 6. since

H6b

2. How long has Jane lived in Germany?
3. How long has Sven been in the class?
4. How long have you been married?
5. How long has Tina worked as a mechanic?
6. How long have you lived in this flat?

H7

1. punctual, 2. dependable, 3. creative,
4. outgoing, 5. sensitive, 6. confident

H8

1. applying for, 2. 'm attaching / am attaching, 3. let me know, 4. hearing from

H9a

She likes to play volleyball. / She likes playing volleyball.
She likes to dance. / She likes dancing.
She likes to go to the cinema. / She likes going to the cinema.
She'd like to speak Spanish.
She'd like to dance the tango.
She'd like to sail round the world.

Unit 5

A1b

see tapescript

A2a

1. I <u>was</u> just <u>reading</u> the paper in the garden when I <u>heard</u> someone.
He <u>was</u> <u>shouting</u> for help.
2. I <u>was</u> just <u>making</u> some coffee when I <u>heard</u> the shouting again.

B2b

a. true, b. true, c. false, d. true, e. false, f. false, g. true

C1b

Dick und Doof (Laurel and Hardy), Küss mich, Dummkopf *(Kiss Me, Stupid)*, Der Unsichtbare Dritte *(North by Northwest)*, Sinn und Sinnlichkeit *(Sense and Sensibility)*, Illuminati *(Angels and Demons)*

D2b

see tapescript

E1a

1. b, 2. c

E1d

El Sistema: started in 1975 with children from slums, social work and classical music, over 300,000 children, playing together
East-Western Divan Orchestra: founded in 1999, young musicians from …, played in …, based in Seville because …

H1a *(possible answers)*

1. c, d, e; 2. a, d, e; 3. d, e; 4. a, e, f;
5. a, d, e; 6. a, b, d

H1b

1. was … cycling, 2. slipped, 3. lost,
4. was driving, 5. fell off

H1c

1. she was driving, 2. my, 3. fell off,
4. he was cycling, 5. his, 6. slipped,
7. lost

H2a

1. The strangest thing happened to me last week.
2. One of the funniest things that ever happened to me was when …
3. A funny thing happened last week.
4. You won't believe this.

H3a

I regularly read the newspaper and one of my favourite sections is the one with the book and film reviews. Probably many other people prefer to read the sports section. I seldom do that, I just

K Key

look through it very quickly. I also love to read books, usually novels. I use the Internet, but I never read blogs or Internet forums. Nowadays I only occasionally read magazines and comics. When I was younger I very often spent hours reading cookbooks.

H5a
(1) text, (2) next, (3) movie, (4) groovy, (5) rap, (6) clap, (7) music, (8) sick, (9) music, (10) kick

Unit 6

A1d
2. Miles, 3. Pam, 5. Jen, 8. Nick, 9. Lisa, 10. Adam, 11. Benjy, 12. Sam, 13. Sid

A3a
1. b, 2. c

A4a
1. c, 2. d, 3. b, 4. a

A4b
2. Julian, 3. Belinda, 4. Nadine

B1a
1. roses, 2. kittens, 3. kettle, 4. package, 5. dog, 6. bee

B1b
1. roses, 2. kittens, 3. kettles, 4. packages, 5. dog, 6. bee

C1b
a. Too young to be a father?
b. Are grandparents as good as parents?
c. What's the best age to have a baby?

C1c (possible answers)
Brian Sanderson says he feels proud that he's a father.
He's quite happy to be a grandfather but …
Some people say you should have kids when …
Others say it's not a good idea …
Experts believe that grandparents …
Most people feel very happy when they remember their grandparents.
… so I think I know the good and bad sides of both ages.
There are really good and bad sides about both ages …

C1d
a. text b, b. in a year or two

D1a
b

D2a
Robert: ex-husband, Don: pen friend, Hans-Peter: colleague

D2b
a. (1) 've known, (2) met, (3) separated / got divorced
b. (1) 've never met, (2) got, (3) 've never fallen, (4) mailed
c. (1)'s lived, (2) took

D2c
a. pen friend, b. colleague, c. husband / wife, d. ex-husband / ex-wife

D3a
a

D3b
a. father, b. partner / girlfriend, c. left, d. argument

E1a
happy: excited, relieved;
sad: disappointed, angry

E1b (possible answers)
a. excited, b. happy, c. sad

E1c (possible answers)
1. excited, 2. disappointed, 3. angry, 4. happy, 5. sad, 6. relieved

E3a
a. good week, b. good week, c. bad week

E3b (possible answers)
a. … was looking forward to sleeping on the train to work. But the train was really full so he had to stand all the way. … quite relieved when someone got off and he could have the seat.
b. … got a new job. … so excited about starting it.
c. … came back from his holiday and found his colleague smoking in the office they share. … really angry and upset about it.

H2

Brian + Maybelle

Wendy + Jerry   James + Alicia

Chris Dorothy Sophie Helen Katherine Emily

H3
2. hers, his; 3. yours; 4. mine

H4a
men: brother, father, husband, nephew, uncle
women: aunt, grandmother, niece, sister, wife

H4b
2. sisters, 3. sister, 4. Alan, 5. Sam, 6. children, 7. husband, 8. parents, 9. friends, 10. cousins

H5 (possible answers)
1. All, 2. Some, 3. Nobody, 4. more, 5. think, 6. agree, 7. so, 8. right, 9. opinion, 10. true

H6
1. met; 2. had, think, have; 3. been; 4. got; 5. have been; 6. do; 7. did, went

H7
2. j, 3. h, 4. a, 5. c, 6. b, 7. f, 8. d, 9. e, 10. i,

H8a
1. c, 2. d, 3. b, 4. e, 5. a, 6. f

Consolidation 2

C1b (possible answers)
interesting, challenging, rewarding, stimulating, varied

C3B (possible answers)
travel books: *Frommer's Alaska 2010*
history books: *The Decline and Fall of the British Empire*
language books: *Baxter's English-French Dictionary*
cook books: *A Chef's Kitchen*
detective stories: *The Dark Night*
self-help books: *Tips for Teams, My Job is Boring!*
romance novels: *Love Lasts Longest*

C3c
1. *A Chef's Kitchen*
2. *Love Lasts Longest*
3. *My Job is Boring!*
4. *Baxter's English-French Dictionary*

C5a
Tips for Teams

Unit 7

A1a
1. Spain; 2. Canberra; 3. Belarus, Czech Republic, Germany, Lithuania, Russia, Slovakia, Ukraine; 4. fifty; 5. Illinois; 6. Uluru, also called Ayers Rock, is a large sandstone rock formation in the southern part of the Northern Territory, central Australia; 7. China, Japan, Korea, Vietnam, etc.; 8. Hawaii; 9. India, Pakistan, etc.; 10. English Channel; 11. dark red-brown; 12. the Netherlands

A3b
1. France, England, drinking tea with milk; 2. Germany, Japan, eating noodles for breakfast; 3. Japan, Germany, kissing people she doesn't know very well

B1c
Jan: yes, probably; Melanie: yes;
Helmut: no; Ellen: no

B3b
win, garden, designer, millionaire,
famous, Prince Charles, psychotherapist

B3c
He won a million pounds in the South
Yorkshire prize draw.

B3d (possible answers)
Judith was the first person to win a million pounds on the famous television
show *Who Wants To Be A Millionaire?* –
Morris was the first person to win a
million pounds in the South Yorkshire
prize draw.

Judith is a trained psychotherapist
and garden designer. – Morris is a
trained teacher and guitar player.

Judith has just written a quiz book. –
Morris started writing novels.

Judith lives alone in London. –
Morris lives with his wife in Leeds.

Judith didn't stop working but
became a full-time garden designer. –
Morris stopped working as a teacher
and became a full-time writer.

Judith has been married twice and
has three children. – Morris has two children.

Judith bought a car and spent a lot
of money on her garden. – Morris
bought cars for his wife and his children
and spent a lot of money on his house.

C1a
1. b, 2. a, 3. c, 4. d

C1b
2. somebody who steals something,
3. somebody who takes money or prop-
erty illegally, often by using violence

C1c
criminals

C2a
Diarmid: muggers, attacked an older
man on the train, said terrible things to
him, told him to give them his money;
Sheila: thief stole all their things from
their car

C2b
1. Always, 2. Never, 3. Always, 4. Never

D1a
1. c, 2. a, 3. b

D1c
1. junk mail, 2. same-sex marriage,
3. cyber crime

D3a
a box of things to show people in the
future what life is like now

D3c
clothes, a newspaper, an English course
book, a letter opener, a lipstick, a train
ticket, an empty can, a pen, stamps,
jewellery

E1b
1. Amish people, 2. energy problems,
3. new ways of getting energy

E3a
Yes: 1, 4, 5

H1
2. less, 3. less, 4. More, 5. less, 6. More,
7. more

H2a (possible answers)
2. shaking, 3. driving, 4. commuting,
5. Kissing, 6. eating

H4a (possible answers)
1. won, would; 2. lost, would; 3. had,
travel; 4. changed, would; 5. was

H5a
came to Germany: 10 years ago (Mo),
    two years ago (Allie)
likes: living in Germany / shaking hands
    (Mo), living in Germany / living in a
    village (Allie)
job: singer (Mo), housewife (Allie)
doesn't like: sauerkraut, beer (Mo),
    cheese for breakfast (Allie)
surprised him/her most: Germans not
    formal (Mo), many people speak
    English (Allie)
finds strange: – (Mo), driving on the
    right (Allie)

H7a
1. was, 2. had, 3. had, 4. is, 5. will be,
6. will choose, 7. is, 8. listened, 9. came,
10. will change

H7b (possible answers)
1. listened, listened, have, will have;
2. had, most people use one; 3. used,
use satnavs in their cars, will have
cars that find their way on their own;
4. watched, we choose among hun-
dreds of programmes

H8
jobs: bus conductor, nurse, postman,
    shop assistant
criminals: burglar, pickpocket, robber,
    mugger
food: cheese, curry, eggs, noodles
things: clock, letter opener, lipstick, toy

Unit 8

A1a (possible answers)
b. My grandmother used to wash
clothes once a month and my
mother used to wash clothes once a
week. Now we use the washing
machine almost every day.
c. My grandparents used to sit in their
living room every night and listen to
the radio. They listened to the news,
to radio plays and classical music. I
switch on the radio occasionally
when I'm in the car on my way to
the office.
d. My grandparents used to wash the
dishes by hand. My parents always
had a dishwasher and, of course, we
use ours every day.
e. My grandparents never travelled. My
parents went on holiday once a year.
My partner and I do a lot of travelling, at least three times a year.

A1b (possible answers)
They used to go on foot or ride on
horses, but now they drive pickup
trucks. They used to hunt the buffalo,
but now they keep cattle. They used to
wear traditional costumes, but now they
wear jeans and T-shirts most of the time.

A1c
the Lakota used to live in tepees / There
used to be huge buffalo herds / They
used to take only as much as they
needed / They used to stop the trains /
like we used to do / some of the richness that used to be on the Plains

B1b (possible answers)
2. f, 3. a, 4. e, 5. d, 6. b

B2a
1. bottle of shampoo, 2. plastic bag,
4. toothbrush, 5. crash helmet,
6. mobile phone, 7. plastic bottle

B2c
They are all made with oil or out of oil.

B2d
plastic wrapping, waterproof clothing,
umbrella, toilet seat, cosmetics, medicine, heating oil, petrol, telephone, lots
of things in the kitchen, sports clothing,
most of what is in the car, skis, snowboard, toys

C2a
1. d, 2. c, 3. b, 4. a

C2c *(possible answers)*
sea levels *may / might* rise – land below sea level *may / might* be destroyed – people *may / might* have to leave these areas – this trend *may / might* continue – we *may / might* have more serious droughts in southern Europe

(By using *will* Dave is saying what he knows or thinks will happen. He is predicting the future. *May* and *might* are used to say that something is a possibility. So by changing *will* into *may / might* Dave sounds less certain when talking about the future.)

D1b
using methods that protect the environment

D1c *(possible answers)*
wear one dress for a whole year – seven identical dresses, one for each day of the week – every day she wears the dress differently – it can be worn both ways, buttoning in front or in back, and also like an open jacket – it's made of good breathable cotton – it's easy to wash.

D2a
1. b, 2. c, 3. a, 4. b

E1a *(possible answers)*
Dakota prairies, northern plains, bottom of an ocean, high mountain

H1a
1. didn't use to, 2. used to, 3. didn't use to, 4. used to, 5. used to, 6. used to

H1c *(possible answers)*
They didn't use to drive pickup trucks, but now they do.
They didn't use to attend university, but now they do.
There used to be huge buffalo herds on the Plains. Nowadays there aren't many buffaloes left.
There used to be rich plant and animal life, but now there isn't.

H3a *(possible answers)*
1. c, 2. a, 3. d, 4. b, e

H3b *(possible answers)*
1. heavy rainfall
2. serious drought
3. serious flooding
4. destructive storms
5. polar ice caps

H3c *(possible answers)*
1. heavy rainfall, 2. destructive storms, 3. serious flooding, 4. (your choice), 5. serious droughts, 6. polar ice caps, 7. (your choice), 8. (your choice)

H3d *(possible answers)*
1. died, 2. would, 3. may / might, 4. will, 5. rose, 6. would, 7. may / might, 8. won't

H4b *(possible answers)*
charity shop: kilt, winter coat, jacket
flea market: set of dishes, chairs, cupboard, painting

Unit 9

A1a *(possible answers)*
shoulders, elbows, wrists, fingers, thumbs, hips, knees, ankles, heel, toes throat, heart, lungs, kidneys, liver, stomach

A2a
Hassan: legs / English, stomach / Italian, eyes / Japanese
Ximena: heart and stomach / Spanish, head / French, feet / Spanish, ears and eyes / Portuguese, arms / Chinese
Rolf: heart / German and French, ears / French, hands / English, liver / Scottish

A3a
1. b, 2. d, 3. e, 4. a, 5. c

A4 *(possible answers)*
get bitten by a snake, cut your finger, break your leg, get hit on the head, get sunburnt, sprain your ankle, get stung by a wasp

B1a *(possible answers)*
1. Facial, 2. Indian head massage, 3. Pilates, 4. Abhyangam

B2c
2. Yes. She says that she finds it difficult to pronounce the word and tries to say it.
3. Yes. She says she doesn't understand.
4. No.

C1
According to the World Health Organization (WHO), traveller's diarrhoea is by far the most common risk (affecting 30 percent to 50 percent of international travellers).

C2a
a.
Michael: He has had diarrhoea for the last three days.
Teija: She got sunburnt.
Pierre: He cut himself.
b.
Michael: He needs to go and see his doctor and he needs some tests. He should drink a lot of water.
Teija: She needs to put cream on her back and shoulders. She should always put on some sunblock before she goes to the beach.
Pierre: The doctor needs to stitch the cut. Pierre should get a tetanus injection.

C2b
Pierre asks the doctor to repeat the word and then he asks him to spell it.

C3a *(possible answers)*
A hat protects you against the wind, rain and sun.
Sun cream / sunblock protects you against sunburn.
Bottled water protects you against dehydration.
Pills / tablets protect you against sea-sickness.
Good shoes or boots protect you against hurting your feet.

C3b *(possible answers)*
a. You ought to wear a hat and put sun cream on your shoulders.
b. You should wear good boots.
c. You need to get a vaccination.
d. You should drink a lot of water during the flight.

D2 *(possible answers)*
1. attacked, 2. bit, 3. broke, 4. leg, 5. move, 6. sunburnt, 7. hospital

D3a
1. 'm, 2. 'm, 3. 'll, 4. can, 5. 'm, 6. will

D3b
When I first called Mr Johnson, he said that he <u>was</u> sorry but he <u>was</u> busy. He told us that he <u>would</u> come as soon as he <u>could</u>. He said he <u>was</u> sure the people in the hospital <u>would</u> look after us well. In fact, we had to wait three hours before he came.

D3c
1. 'd get / would get, 2. couldn't move, 3. was, 4. 'd make sure / would make sure, 5. didn't come, 6. 'd send / would send, 7. couldn't stay, 8. was, 9. 'd see / would see

H1
1. ankle, 2. stomach, 3. knee, 4. elbow, 5. toes, 6. wrist, 7. shoulder, 8. throat

H2
2. got stung by a wasp, 3. got sunburnt, 4. broke her ankle, 5. sprained his ankle

H3
2. himself, 3. ourselves, 4. myself, 5. themselves, 6. yourself

H4

2. got stung, 3. got sunburnt,
4. got hit, 5. got bitten

H5a

a. 5, b. 8, c. 3, d. 7, e. 2, f. 1, g. 6, h. 4

H5c *(possible answers)*

1. is that, 2. This is, 3. 'd like to / would like to 4. would you like to, 5. Could I have, 6. Would

H6 *(possible answers)*

1. She ought to go to the doctor.
2. He needs to get a vaccination.
3. She should put on some sunblock.
4. He should take warm and water-proof clothes.
5. She shouldn't drink the local water.

H7a

1. d, 2. e, 3. a, 4. b, 5. c

H7b

1. was, 2. was, 3. couldn't, 4. would, 5. would, 6. was, 7. could, 8. didn't think, 9. was, 10. had, 11. would, 12. wouldn't

Consolidation 3

C2a

She's going to live in China for her job. Dustin is her boyfriend.

C3a

1. about 1.3 billion; 2. Shanghai, Beijing, Guangzhou; 3. Mandarin and Cantonese; 4. Afghanistan, Bhutan, Burma, India, Kazakhstan, North Korea, Krygyzstan, Laos, Mongolia, Nepal, Pakistan, Russia, Tajikistan, Vietnam

C4

1. She won't go skiing or snowboarding in Shanghai, because it doesn't snow there very often.
2. If she goes to the cinema, she'll probably have to watch the films in Chinese.
3. She won't have to take the underground. She'll have a car and driver.
4. She won't be able to see many German films. She'll have to watch Chinese films.
5. She won't have to get the car repaired. Her company will take care of the car.
6. She won't have to do the dishes. The maid will do them.
7. There won't be many Italian restaurants. She'll probably eat Chinese food.

C5a

a

Unit 10

A1b

freshwater fish: perch, trout (salmon)
sea fish: cod, salmon, herring, sea bass
other seafood: crab, lobster, prawns, shrimp, oysters, mussels, clams

A1c

1. c, 2. a, 3. e, 4. g, 5. f, 6. b, 7. d

A2a

1. e, 2. b, 3. i, 4. f, 5. h, 6. d, 7. c, 8. g, 9. a

B1

1. b, 2. a, 3. a, 4. b

Dear course participants
Your course finishes in two weeks and I'd like to organize a dinner for you on the Friday after next. I need to decide on the menu, so it would be very helpful if you could tell me about what you like or don't like to eat. Please let me know by tomorrow morning because I'm meeting the catering company at 9.00.
Best wishes
Amy

B2a

1. c, 2. a, 3. b

B2b

1. She prefers a buffet. 2. She doesn't want beef. 3. He suggests karaoke and Greek musicians.

B3a

1. b, 2. a

C1b

Quote: Amy chooses the Greek evening.
Changes: (1) Amy wants to start an hour earlier. (2) There'll be fewer people (only be twenty-eight).

C2a

Which one would you prefer?

D1a *(possible answers)*

b. I think she's looking for somewhere to sit down. c. I think he's offering somebody a drink. d. I think she broke a glass.

D1b

1. e, h; 2. c, g; 3. a, f; 4. b, d

D3a

a. He speaks for the whole group.
b. He thanks all the other people on the course. He thanks their teachers and, most of all, he thanks Amy.

c. He thanks all the other people on the course for being such great participants. He thanks their teachers for their great work. He thanks Amy for organizing everything so well and for helping them with all their problems.
d. Yes, he is positive about the course. He thinks that they've learnt a lot.

D3b

1. He starts his speech by saying the following: The others asked me to say a few words of thanks for this wonderful party and the course that finished today.
2. b
3. a
4. 4 times

D4b

a. started, had; b. 've learnt, 've had

D4c

Our course started about a year ago. At that time, some of us came from an earlier course and some were new in the group. A year ago I could only take part in very simple and very short conversations. I often had a lot of problems understanding the CDs when we heard something only once. But now we've learnt more English so we can have longer conversations and I can talk about everyday situations a lot better. We've had a lot of practice listening to English so now I can often understand the main points from something on the CD when I hear it for the first time. I've learnt the most important verb tenses so I can now talk about things in the past, the present and the future. I don't always remember to use the right form at the right time, but it's getting better slowly. I've learnt a lot of words but there are still lots more words that I'll have to learn.

H1

1. beef (cow), 2. lamb (lamb / young sheep), 3. veal (calf / young cow), 4. pork (pig), 5. game (any kind of wild animal or bird), 6. venison (deer), 7. mutton (sheep)

H2

1. vegetarian, 2. allergic, 3. intolerance, 4. vegan, 5. allergy, 6. religion

H3

1. in, 2. next, 3. ago, 4. before, 5. until/till, 6. last/final, 7. before, 8. by, 9. after

H4

2. I go to my hairdresser to get my hair cut.
3. I go to the garage to get my car serviced.
4. I go to Mr Price to get my flat painted.
5. I go to the jeweller's shop to get my watch repaired.
6. I go to the local travel agent to get my flight booked.

H5 *(possible answers)*

2. Which restaurant would you prefer: Italian, Indian, or Chinese?
3. Which rental car would you prefer: Volkswagen, Peugeot, or Fiat?
4. Which DVD would you prefer: a romantic comedy, a fantasy film, or a comedy?
5. Which magazine would you prefer: a woman's magazine, a nature magazine, or a news magazine?
6. Which prize would you prefer: a bottle of wine, a box of chocolates, or a bottle of perfume?

H6

1. f, 2. c, 3. e, 4. d, 5. b, 6. a

H7a

1. c, 2. b, 3. h, 4. a, 5. f, 6. j, 7. i, 8. d, 9. g, 10. e

H7b

2. started, was, 've finished; 3. opened, knew, 's won; 4. lost, 's decided;
5. played, 's won; 6. wanted, 's broken;
7. was, 've bought; 8. 've increased;
9. planned, 's started

Consolidation 4

(possible answers)

Unit 1 and 4
2. Do you enjoy cooking? 3. English is hard to spell. 5. I ought to practise speaking more.

Unit 2
6. I think soap operas are rubbish and I don't enjoy them at all.

Unit 3
7. She said she likes going to Spain on her holiday. 9. My room is dirty. Can you clean it, please?

Unit 4
10. A pilot is well-paid. Jobs in banks are boring. 11. I've lived in this town for ten years. 13. Jan is good at organizing things. 14. I want this job because I want to work in a team.

Unit 5 and 6
16. A strange thing happened to me at the weekend. I was going home from work when I met an old friend. 17. I like adventure films with lots of action.
18. I like to read in the garden.
20. I like classical music.

Unit 6 and 3
21. I've got two sisters and a stepmum.
22. When is the best time to have children? 24. I don't know if that is right, really.

Unit 7 and 4
25. It's cheaper to live in Greece than in Germany. 26. If I won a lot of money, I'd stop working. 28. There are more TV channels now. 29. In the future we will all have mobile phones with television.

Unit 8 and 3
31. There used to be only three television channels. 32. Islands may be destroyed if the climate changes.

Unit 9 and 4
33. I've had a headache for two days now. 35. I'd like to book a holiday at the spa. 36. There has been an accident.
37. He said the car was going very fast.

Unit 10 and 3
39. I can't eat onions. 40. Would you prefer orange or apple juice? 41. I've learnt to talk about modern technology.

Vocabulary: English–German

Alphabetischer Wortschatz Englisch–Deutsch

Im **Alphabetischen Wortschatz** können Sie die wichtigsten Wörter und Ausdrücke nachschlagen, die in diesem Band neu vorkommen. Sollten Sie ein Wort nicht finden, benutzen Sie bitte ein ein- oder zweisprachiges Wörterbuch. Nützliche Hinweise zum Umgang mit Wörterbüchern finden Sie in Unit 4 E.

- Farbige Sternchen kennzeichnen ein Wort als sehr häufig.
  Entsprechend der Einteilung des *Bloomsbury Corpus of World English* markieren
    drei Sternchen *** die **2500** häufigsten Wörter,
    zwei Sternchen ** die **2500–5000** häufigsten Wörter und
    ein Sternchen * die **5000–7500** häufigsten Wörter der englischen Sprache.

- Jeder deutschen Bedeutung des Worts folgen eine oder mehrere „Fundstellen", z.B.:
    2B4 Unit 2, Abschnitt B, Schritt 4
    5H3 Unit 5, Homestudy-Teil, Übung 3
    2D1/T Unit 2, Abschnitt D, Schritt 1 / Tonaufnahme
    Co1C4 Consolidation 1, Schritt 4
    RCU6 Reading Club Unit 6

- Englische Wörter und Wendungen, die *kursiv* gedruckt sind, kommen nur in PLUS-Abschnitten, Arbeitsanweisungen, Homestudy-Übungen, Consolidation Abschnitten, Hörtexten oder im Reading Club vor. Sie werden für Ihr weiteres Lernen nicht vorausgesetzt.

Die folgende Wortliste enthält auch die phonetische Lautschrift, die Ihnen die Aussprache verdeutlicht. Weitere Hinweise und einen "Phonetic table" finden Sie im Companion.

Folgend finden Sie eine Erklärung der im Wortschatz benutzten Zeichen und Abkürzungen.

Erklärung der verwendeten Zeichen und Abkürzungen

US amerikanisches Englisch
UK britisches Englisch
pl. Plural
adj adjective *(Adjektiv)*
interj interjection *(Ausrufewort)*
n noun *(Nomen)*
vb verb *(Verb)*

A

access ['ækses] Zugang 2A1

accessories [ək'sesəriz] Accessoires 8D1

aching * ['eɪkɪŋ] schmerzend 9B1

action *** ['ækʃn] hier: Action (in Film) 5C2

admit (to something) *** [əd'mɪt]
   (etwas) zugeben 5B2/T

advance ** [əd'vɑːns] Fortschritt, Weiterentwicklung 3H3

adventurous [əd'ventʃ(ə)rəs] abenteuerlustig 2H3

advise *** [əd'vaɪz] raten 3B2/T

affectionate [ə'fekʃnət] liebevoll 2B2

(can't) afford *** [,kɑːnt_ə'fɔːd]
   sich nicht leisten können 7B1/T

afraid *** [ə'freɪd] ängstlich 1C1

   (be) afraid of [ə'freɪd_əv] Angst haben 1C1

ages *** ['eɪdʒɪz] eine Ewigkeit, Ewigkeiten 5C1/T

aid project ** ['eɪd ,prɒdʒekt] Hilfsprojekt 3A2/T

all right *** [,ɔːl 'raɪt] in Ordnung 8C2

allow *** [ə'laʊ] erlauben, zulassen 7D1

alternative *** [ɔːl'tɜːnətɪv] alternativ 3B2/T, 5E1/T

although *** [ɔːl'ðəʊ] obwohl 7A3/T

ambulance ** ['æmbjʊləns]
   Unfallwagen, Rettungswagen 9D2

amount *** [ə'maʊnt] Summe 2A1

analytical * [,ænə'lɪtɪkl] analytisch 2B2

   analyze ** ['ænə,laɪz] analysieren, untersuchen 9B1

animal rights [,ænɪml 'raɪts] Tierrechte 10A2/T

ankle ** ['æŋkl] Knöchel 9A4

anytime ['eni,taɪm] jederzeit 1D2

anywhere *** ['eni,weə] überall 1D2

approximately ** [ə'prɒksɪmətli] ungefähr 1B1

argue *** ['ɑːgjuː] streiten 6D1

argument *** ['ɑːgjʊmənt] Streit, Argumente 1B2, 6D3

(be) asleep ** [ə'sliːp] schlafen 2D1

attach ** [ə'tætʃ] (an eine E-Mail) anhängen 4C2

attack *** [ə'tæk] Angriff, Attacke 7C2/T, 9D2

attraction ** [ə'trækʃn] Attraktion 2B1/T

avoid *** [ə'vɔɪd] vermeiden 2D1, 9C3

B

balance ***vb ['bæləns]
   ausgleichen, Ausgewogenheit bewahren 2B2

balance ***n ['bæləns] Gleichgewicht, Balance 9B1

ballgown ['bɔːl gaʊn] Ballkleid Co3C6

Baltic (Sea) ['bɔːltɪk] Ostsee 3A2/T

battery ** ['bæt(ə)ri] Batterie 7E2

bee ** [biː] Biene 6B1/T

beefeater ['biːf,iːtə] Beefeater (Bezeichnung für die
   Leibgarde der englischen Königin) RCU4

behave ** [bɪ'heɪv] verhalten 2B2

bite ** [baɪt] beißen 6B1/T, 9D2

blacksmith ['blæk,smɪθ] (Huf)Schmied/in 7B2

block *** [blɒk] Häuserblock, Wohnblock 3C2

blood *** [blʌd] Blut 9B1

   blood pressure ['blʌd ,preʃə] Blutdruck 9B1

bluff [blʌf] bluffen 5B2/T

bone *** [bəʊn] Knochen RCU8

bookbinder ['bʊk,baɪndə] Buchbinder/in 7B2

border on * ['bɔːdə ,ɒn] grenzen an 7A1

bossy ['bɒsi] herrisch 4C2/T

bow * [baʊ] sich verbeugen RCU7

bows and arrows [,bəʊz_ən_'ærəʊz] Pfeil und Bogen 8A1

box *** [bɒks] Kiste, Kasten 5A1

break into [,breɪk_'ɪntʊ] einbrechen 7C1

bride * [braɪd] Braut 6A1

bring up [,brɪŋ_'ʌp] aufziehen 2D1

Brussels sprouts [,brʌslz 'spraʊts] Rosenkohl 10A2/T

buffalo ['bʌfələʊ] Büffel 8A1

   buffalo skins ['bʌfələʊ ,skɪnz] Büffelfelle 8A1

buffet ['bʊfeɪ] Buffet 10B2

bump vb [bʌmp] hier: einen Passagier wegen
   Überbuchung auf einen späteren Flug verschieben 3E1

burglar * ['bɜːglə] Einbrecher/in 7C1

bus conductor * ['bʌs kən,dʌktə]
   Fahrkartenkontrolleur/in im Bus 7B2

business administration ['bɪznəs
   ədmɪnɪ,streɪʃn] Betriebswirtschaftslehre 6A4/T

C

cabin ** ['kæbɪn] Hütte 9D1

cage * [keɪdʒ] Käfig 10A2/T, RCU4

calm * [kɑːm] ruhig, gelassen 2H3

can *** [kæn] hier: Dose 7D3

cancel ['kænsl] streichen RCU3

car pool ['kɑː ,puːl] Fahrgemeinschaft 3B2

caravan ** ['kærə,væn] Wohnwagen 7A2, RCU8

care for *** ['keə fə] sich interessieren für 5D2/T

carry on [,kæri_'ɒn] weiterfahren/gehen 3C2

cash *** [kæʃ] Bargeld 8B2

caterer ['keɪtərə] Partyservice,
   Lieferfirma für Speisen und Getränke 10C3

   catering * ['keɪtərɪŋ] Bewirtung, Catering 10B1

cattle ** ['kætl] Vieh 8A1

cello ['tʃeləʊ] Cello 3E2, 8D2

challenge ***n ['tʃælɪndʒ] Herausforderung 4D2

   challenging adj ['tʃælɪndʒɪŋ]
   anspruchsvoll, reizvoll 4A3

characters *** ['kærɪktəz] Charaktere (in einem Film) 2D1

charity shop *** ['tʃærəti ʃɒp] Charity-Läden,
   Läden von Wohltätigkeitsorganisationen 8D1

check in [tʃek_'ɪn] einchecken 3D2

chef * [ʃef] Koch, Köchin 4H5

chopsticks ['tʃɒp,stɪks] (Ess)Stäbchen 7A1

chore [tʃɔː]   Hausarbeit, lästige Pflicht 6D3

circulation ** [ˌsɜːkjʊˈleɪʃn]   Kreislauf 9B1

citizen *** [ˈsɪtɪzn]   Bürger/in, Einwohner/in 2E2

clam [klæm]   Venusmuschel 10A1

clap * [klæp]   klatschen 5H5

class skills [klɑːs ˈskɪlz]   etwa: besondere Kenntnisse und Fähigkeiten der Kursteilnehmer 1A1

cliffhanger [ˈklɪfˌhæŋə]   Merkmal von Fernsehserien oder Fortsetzungsromanen: am Ende einer Folge bleibt eine wichtige Frage offen, damit man die nächste Folge unbedingt sehen will 2C1

clockwise [ˈklɒkˌwaɪz]   im Uhrzeigersinn 5A3

clumsy * [ˈklʌmzi]   ungeschickt 10D1

clutter [ˈklʌtə]   Durcheinander, Kram Co3C5

coastline [ˈkəʊstˌlaɪn]   Küste 8C1

cod [kɒd]   Kabeljau, Dorsch 10A1

comedian [kəˈmiːdiən]   Komiker RCU5

comic * [ˈkɒmɪk]   Comicheft 9A2/T

commit *** [kəˈmɪt]   begehen 7D1

common *** [ˈkɒmən]   häufig, üblich 6A3

commonplace [ˈkɒmənˌpleɪs]   alltäglich 3H3

community [kəˈmjuːnəti]   Gemeinde 5E1/T

complain ***vb [kəmˈpleɪn]   sich beschweren 3D

complaint ***n [kəmˈpleɪnt]   Beschwerde 3D1

complicated ** [ˈkɒmplɪˌkeɪtɪd]   kompliziert 2H3

conduct *** [kənˈdʌkt]   durchführen 2A1

conference room [ˈkɒnf(ə)rəns ruːm]   Konferenzraum 3D1/T

confident ** [ˈkɒnfɪd(ə)nt]   selbstbewusst 1C2

connection *** [kəˈnekʃn]   Verbindung 2E1, 3E2

consultation ** [ˌkɒnslˈteɪʃn]   Beratung 9B1

consumption ** [kənˈsʌmpʃn]   Verbrauch, Konsum 8B2

container ** [kənˈteɪnə]   Behälter 8D2

content ** adj [kənˈtent]   zufrieden 6D3

context *** [ˈkɒntekst]   Kontext, Zusammenhang 2B2

cos [kəz]   umgangsprachlich für *because*: weil 2B1/T

cosy * [ˈkəʊzi]   gemütlich 9E3/T

count *** [kaʊnt]   zählen 1D1

count off [ˌkaʊntˈɒf]   abzählen 5A3

cover ***n [ˈkʌvə]   Umschlag, Buchcover 7D3/T

cover ***vb [ˈkʌvə]   bedecken; hier: (rundherum) einreiben 9B2/T

crab [kræb]   Krebs 10A1

crime ***n [kraɪm]   Straftat, Kriminalität 7C

criminal ***adj [ˈkrɪmɪnl]   kriminell 5E1

crocodile [ˈkrɒkəˌdaɪl]   Krokodil RCU10

cross [krɒs]   hier: böse, sauer 6D

culture shock [ˈkʌltʃə ˌʃɒk]   Kulturschock RCU10

cupboard ** [ˈkʌbəd]   Schrank 1H4

curtain ** [ˈkɜːtn]   Vorhang 2D1

cut ***vb [kʌt]   schneiden 9C2/T

cuttlefish [ˈkʌtlˌfɪʃ]   Tintenfisch RCU8

cyber crime [ˈsaɪbə ˌkraɪm]   Internetkriminalität 7D1

D

dating website [ˈdeɪtɪŋ ˌwebsaɪt]   Partnervermittlung im Internet 2B2

dawdle [ˈdɔːdl]   bummeln 2H2

deal with [ˈdiːl wɪð]   umgehen mit L10

decrease ** [diːˈkriːs]   senken 9B1

deep *** [diːp]   tief 9B1

delay **vb [dɪˈleɪ]   verspäten 3B2/T

delay **n [dɪˈleɪ]   Verspätung 3B2/T

depart ** [dɪˈpɑːt]   abfahren 3B2/T

dependable [dɪˈpendəbl]   zuverlässig, verlässlich 4C1

develop [dɪˈveləp]   entwickeln 2D1, 7E3

dialect * [ˈdaɪəlekt]   Dialekt 1A2

diarrhoea [ˌdaɪəˈriːə]   Durchfall 9C1

dice [daɪs]   Würfel 10E1

diet *** [ˈdaɪət]   Ernährung 10B2/T

digicam [ˈdɪdʒɪˌkæm]   Digitalkamera 7E1/T

dirty joke [ˌdɜːti ˈdʒəʊk]   schmutziger Witz 2B2

disabilities ** [ˌdɪsəˈbɪlətiz]   Behinderungen 5E1/T

disappointing * [ˌdɪsəˈpɔɪntɪŋ]   enttäuschend 3D2

divorce ** [dɪˈvɔːs]   sich scheiden lassen 6C1

donate * [dəʊˈneɪt]   spenden 8D1

down *** [daʊn]   niedergeschlagen, fertig 4B1/T

draw *** [drɔː]   zeichnen 1A1

dress up [ˌdresˈʌp]   sich fein machen, sich schön anziehen RCU9

drive on [ˌdraɪvˈɒn]   weiterfahren 3C2

drought [draʊt]   Dürre, Trockenheit 8C1

drug overdose [ˈdrʌg ˌəʊvədəʊs]   Überdosis Drogen RCU6

due to *** [ˈdjuː tə]   wegen 3B2/T

(the) Dutch [dʌtʃ]   die Niederländer 7A2

dynamo [ˈdaɪnəˌməʊ]   Dynamo 7E3

E

each other [ˌiːtʃˈʌðər]   einander, sich 6A1/T

egg cup [ˈeg ˌkʌp]   Eierbecher 8D2

electricity *** [ɪˌlekˈtrɪsəti]   Elektrizität, Strom 7E2

electronic calendar [elekˌtrɒnɪk ˈkælɪndə]   elektronischer Kalender 7E1/T

elevator (US) [ˈeləveɪtə]   Aufzug 5D1

embarrassing * [ɪmˈbærəsɪŋ]   peinlich 9A3

emissions ** [ɪˈmɪʃnz]   Emissionen, Ausstoß 8C1

encourage *** [ɪnˈkʌrɪdʒ]   ermutigen, auffordern 10B3

engaged to ** [ɪnˈgeɪdʒd tə]   verlobt sein mit RCU2

episode [ˈepɪsəʊd]   Episode, Folge 2C1

erase * [ɪˈreɪz]   ausradieren 5D3

escape *** [ɪˈskeɪp]   fliehen, flüchten 2C2

eventually *** [ɪˈventʃuəli]   irgendwann 8B2/T

exhausting [ɪgˈzɔːstɪŋ]   anstrengend 4A3

exit * [ˈeksɪt]   Ausfahrt 3C2

experiment *** [ɪkˈsperɪmənt]   Experiment 2D1

explanation *** [ˌeksplə'neɪʃn]   Erklärung 6A3

extended family [ɪkˌstendɪd 'fæmli]   Großfamilie 6A3

extremely *** [ɪk'striːmli]   extrem 2C1

F

facial ['feɪʃl]   Gesichtsbehandlung 9B1

factors *** ['fæktəz]   Faktoren 2B1/T

fade ** [feɪd]   verblassen 7D3/T

fairly *** ['feəli]   ziemlich RCU5

fall *** [fɔːl]   sinken 2A1

far away *** [ˌfɑːr_ə'weɪ]   weit weg 2A1

Farsi ['fɑːsi]   Farsi (die persische Sprache) 9A2/T

feature *** ['fiːtʃə]   Beitrag 8B2/T

fed up * [ˌfed_'ʌp]   satt haben 4B1

feelings *** ['fiːlɪŋz]   Gefühle 6E

fellow ** ['feləʊ]   Kerl, Typ 7C2/T

feminist ** ['femənɪst]   Feministin 2B2

festival *** ['festɪvl]   Fest, Festival Co3C3

film critic ['fɪlm ˌkrɪtɪk]   Filmkritiker RCU5

finery ['faɪnəri]   hier: Staat, prachtvolle Kleidung RCU9

fixed-line phones [ˌfɪkstlaɪn 'fəʊnz]   Festnetz-Telefone 2E1

flavour ** ['fleɪvə]   Geschmack, Aroma 2B2

flea market ['fliː ˌmɑːkɪt]   Flohmarkt 8D1

flight attendant ['flaɪt_əˌtendənt]   Flugbegleiter/in 3A2/T

florist ['flɒrɪst]   Florist/in 4B3/T

flu * [fluː]   Grippe 9C1

    flu scare ['fluː skeə]   Grippehysterie, Angst vor Grippewelle 3H3

fly *** [flaɪ]   fliegen RCU4

follow *** ['fɒləʊ]   folgen, befolgen 3C2

foot, pl. feet *** [fʊt, fiːt]   Fuß 6C1

forgive * [fə'gɪv]   vergeben, verzeihen 2D2

form *** [fɔːm]   bilden 2A1

founded *** ['faʊndɪd]   gegründet 5E1/T

fox ** [fɒks]   Fuchs RCU4

freeconomist [friː'kɒnəmɪst]   Bezeichnung für jemanden, der komplett ohne Geld lebt RCU8

freshwater ['freʃˌwɔːtə]   Süßwasser 10A1

fridge * [frɪdʒ]   Kühlschrank 1D2

fun-loving ['fʌnˌlʌvɪŋ]   lebensfroh, lebenslustig 2B2

furious ** ['fjʊəriəs]   wütend, zornig 2D1

G

gamble *vb ['gæmbl]   (um Geld) spielen RCU9

game [geɪm]   Wild 10A1

    game *** [geɪm]   Spiel 10E

gang ** [gæŋ]   Gang, kriminelle Bande 7D1

get away [ˌget_ə'weɪ]   wegkommen, entkommen 3A1

get divorced [ˌget dɪ'vɔːst]   sich scheiden lassen 6A4/T

get engaged [ˌget_ɪn'geɪdʒd]   sich verloben 7A3/T

get off [ˌget_'ɒf]   ausziehen 5A1/T

get on with [ˌget_'ɒn wɪθ]   zurechtkommen mit 6A4/T

get rid of [get 'rɪd_əv]   loswerden 1H4

get-together n ['getəˌgeðə]   Treffen, Zusammenkunft 6A

gifted ['gɪftɪd]   begabt 5E1/T

gluten intolerance [ˌgluːtn_ɪn'tɒlərəns]   Glutenunverträglichkeit 10A2

go along [gəʊ_ə'lɒŋ]   mitfahren, mitkommen 3H2

go back [ˌgəʊ 'bæk]   zurückgehen Co4

go bad [ˌgəʊ 'bæd]   schlecht werden 7D3/T

go on [gəʊ_'ɒn]   weitermachen, weitergehen 3C2

go wrong [ˌgəʊ 'rɒŋ]   schiefgehen, schieflaufen 9D1

gourmet ['gʊəmeɪ]   Gourmet RCU10

grade [greɪd]   benoten, einstufen 2B2/T

grateful ** ['greɪtfl]   dankbar 6C1

greatest ['greɪtɪst]   tollste/größte 2B2

groovy ['gruːvi]   stark, klasse 5H5

grown-up * ['grəʊnˌʌp]   erwachsen 6C1

guess *** [ges]   glauben 1A1/T

H

half-hourly ['hɑːfˌaʊəli]   halbstündig 2C1

handlebars ['hændlˌbɑːz]   Lenker 5H1

hard *** [hɑːd]   hart 3A2/T

hardly *** ['hɑːdli]   kaum 5A1/T

heating oil ['hiːtɪŋ ˌɔɪl]   Heizöl 8B2/T

helmet * ['helmɪt]   Helm 8B2

herd * [hɜːd]   Herde 8A1

herring ['herɪŋ]   Hering 10A1

hide *** [haɪd]   verstecken 6A1/T

hips ** [hɪps]   Hüften 9B1

hold *** [həʊld]   Frachtraum 3E2

holidaymaker ['hɒlɪdeɪˌmeɪkə]   Urlauber 9C3

honest ** ['ɒnɪst]   ehrlich 2B2

horseshoe ['hɔːsˌʃuː]   hier: U-Form 5A3

HR department [eɪtʃ 'ɑː dɪ'pɑːtmənt]   Personalabteilung 4B2

hug * [hʌg]   umarmen RCU7

hunt ** [hʌnt]   jagen 8A1

hurry * ['hʌri]   eilen, sich beeilen RCU4

I

identical ** [aɪ'dentɪkl]   identisch, gleich 8D1

imagine *** [ɪ'mædʒɪn]   stellen Sie sich vor / stell dir vor 5A

impersonal * [ɪm'pɜːsn(ə)l]   unpersönlich 2E2

impress ** [ɪm'pres]   beeindrucken 5B2/T

increase *** [ɪn'kriːs]   steigen, anwachsen 2A1

individual *** [ˌɪndɪ'vɪdʒuəl]   Individuum 2B2

ingredient ** [ɪn'griːdiənt]   Zutat 10C3

injection ** [ɪnˈdʒekʃn]   Spritze 9C2/T
innovative * [ˈɪnəʊˌveɪtɪv]   innovativ 2H3
instrument *** [ˈɪnstrʊmənt]   Instrument 1E2
insurance *** [ɪnˈʃʊərəns]   Versicherung 7C2/T
interactive * [ˌɪntərˈæktɪv]   interaktiv 2D1
interpreting *** [ɪnˈtɜːprɪtɪŋ]   Dolmetschen 1B2
intolerance [ɪnˈtɒlərəns]   Unverträglichkeit, Intoleranz 10C3
invent ** [ɪnˈvent]   erfinden 2D2
invest *** [ɪnˈvest]   investieren 7B1/T
   investment *** [ɪnˈvestmənt]   Investition L04

J

joke ** [dʒəʊk]   Witz 2B2
junction ** [ˈdʒʌŋkʃ(ə)n]   Kreuzung, Autobahnkreuz 3B2/T
jungle * [ˈdʒʌŋgl]   Dschungel, Urwald 9D1
junk * [dʒʌŋk]   Müll, Schund 2E2
   junk mail [ˈdʒʌŋk ˌmeɪl]   unerwünschte Post, Reklamesendungen 7D1

K

kangaroo [ˌkæŋgəˈruː]   Känguru RCU10
karaoke [ˌkæriˈəʊki]   Karaoke 10C1
kedgeree [ˈkedʒəri]   anglo-indisches Gericht bestehend aus (meist geräuchertem) Fisch, Reis, Eiern und Butter 2H2
kerosene [ˈkerəˌsiːn]   Kerosin 7E2
kick ** [kɪk]   Kick, Spaß 5H5
kid ***vb [kɪd]   Spaß machen, (etwas) nicht ernst meinen 4C2/T
kill *** [kɪl]   töten, umbringen 10A2/T
   kill off [ˌkɪl_ˈɒf]   vernichten, töten, ausrotten 8A1
kindergarten [ˈkɪndəˌgɑːtn]   Kindergarten 6C1/T
kiss *** [kɪs]   Kuss 7A3
   kissing *** [ˈkɪsɪŋ]   Küssen 7A3
kitten * [ˈkɪtn]   Kätzchen 6B1/T
knife, **pl.** *knives* *** [naɪf, naɪvz]   Messer 7D3/T

L

layers [ˈleɪəz]   Schichten 8D1
lazy ** [ˈleɪzi]   faul RCU1
lecture ** [ˈlektʃə]   Lesung; Vorlesung RCU9
leisure (time) ** [ˈleʒə (taɪm)]   Freizeit 2A2
limited *** [ˈlɪmɪtɪd]   begrenzt 4D2
line *** [laɪn]   Menschenschlange 10D1
lipstick [ˈlɪpˌstɪk]   Lippenstift 7D3
liver [ˈlɪvə]   Leber 9A2/T
lobster [ˈlɒbstə]   Hummer 10A1
locked [lɒkt]   abgeschlossen 7C2/T
lonely ** [ˈləʊnli]   einsam 6D3

long-term *** [ˌlɒŋˈtɜːm]   langfristig, dauerhaft 2B2
look after [ˌlʊkˈˈɑːftə]   sich kümmern um 2D2
look up [ˌlʊkˈˈʌp]   nachsehen, suchen 3B1
love affair [ˈlʌv_əˌfeə]   (Liebes)Affäre 2D1
luxurious [lʌgˈzjʊəriəs]   luxuriös, üppig; hier: wohltuend 9B1

M

maid [meɪd]   Dienstmädchen, Zimmermädchen 7B2
mail **vb [meɪl]   per E-Mail schicken, mailen 6D2/T
   mailbox [ˈmeɪlˌbɒks]   Mailbox, Briefkasten 7D1
make up vb [ˌmeɪkˈˈʌp]   sich ausdenken, erfinden 5A3
make-up * n [ˈmeɪkˌʌp]   Make-up 7D3/T
market *** [ˈmɑːkɪt]   Markt RCU1
marriage *** [ˈmærɪdʒ]   Ehe 6A4
mature ** [məˈtʃʊə]   reif 2B2
may *** [meɪ]   können 3A2/T
mean *** [miːn]   bedeuten, heißen, meinen 6C1/T
melodies [ˈmelədiz]   Melodien 1E2
melt ** [melt]   schmelzen 8C1
mess ** [mes]   Durcheinander 3D1/T
might *** [maɪt]   könnte 2D2
migrants [ˈmaɪgrənt]   Migranten 9A2
mind *** [maɪnd]   etwas ausmachen, stören 3D1/T
mirror *** [ˈmɪrə]   Spiegel 2C2
monkey * [ˈmʌŋki]   Affe 9D1
monotonous [məˈnɒtənəs]   monoton 4A3
mother tongue [ˈmʌðə ˌtʌŋ]   Muttersprache 1A2
motorist * [ˈməʊtərɪst]   Autofahrer/in 3B2/T
mugger [ˈmʌgə]   Straßenräuber/in 7C1
mumble [ˈmʌmbl]   murmeln, nuscheln 5A3
muscle *** [ˈmʌsl]   Muskel 9B1
mussel [ˈmʌsl]   (Mies)Muschel 10A1
mutton [ˈmʌtn]   Hammel(fleisch) 10A1

N

nasty [ˈnɑːsti]   schlimm, hässlich 9C2/T
neck *** [nek]   Nacken, Hals 9B1
negotiating ** [neˈgəʊʃiˌeɪtɪŋ]   verhandeln 1B2
the Netherlands [ˈneðələnz]   Niederlande 7A2
network *** [ˈnetˌwɜːk]   Netzwerk 5E1
   networking [ˈnetˌwɜːkɪŋ]   Networking, Vernetzung 2A1
night porter [ˈnaɪt ˌpɔːtə]   Nachtportier 4A4/T
noodles [ˈnuːdlz]   Nudeln 7A3
no-shows [ˈnəʊˌʃəʊz]   No-show: jemand, der nicht (oder zu spät) erscheint 3E1
notebook computer [ˌnəʊtbʊk kəmˈpjuːtə]   Notebook 7E1/T
nuclear family [ˌnjuːkliə ˈfæmli]   Kernfamilie 6A3
number * [ˈnʌmbə]   Anzahl 2A1
nylon * [ˈnaɪlɒn]   Nylon 8B2

O

occasionally *** [əˈkeɪʒn(ə)li] gelegentlich 5B1

official *** [əˈfɪʃ(ə)l] offiziell 1B2

only child [ˌəʊnli ˈtʃaɪld] Einzelkind 6A4

operate *** [ˈɒpəˌreɪt] operieren 2D2

opinion *** [əˈpɪnjən] Meinung 2A1

originally *** [əˈrɪdʒn(ə)li] ursprünglich 3H2

otherwise *** [ˈʌðəˌwaɪz] sonst, ansonsten 1H5

ought to *** [ˈɔːt tə] sollten 1C2

outfit [ˈaʊtfɪt] Outfit, Kleidung 8D1

outgoing [ˌaʊtˈgəʊɪŋ] kontaktfreudig 4C1

outsider ** [aʊtˈsaɪdə] Außenseiter/in 6D3

overbook [ˌəʊvəˈbʊk] überbuchen 3E1

owing to [ˈəʊɪŋ tə] infolge, wegen 3B2/T

oyster [ˈɔɪstə] Auster 10A1

P

pageboy [ˈpeɪdʒˌbɔɪ] hier: Brautführer 6A1/T

palm ** [pɑːm] Handinnenfläche 9B1

paradise * [ˈpærədaɪs] Paradies RCU10

patchwork family [ˌpætʃwɜːk ˈfæmli]
  Patchwork-Familie 6A4

patient ** [ˈpeɪʃnt] Patient/in 2D1

peanut butter [ˌpiːnʌt ˈbʌtə] Erdnussbutter 10H2

pedal * [ˈpedl] Pedale 5H1

pen friend [ˈpen ˌfrend] Brieffreund/in 6D2/T

percentage ** [pəˈsentɪdʒ] Prozentzahl 2E1

perch [pɜːtʃ] Flussbarsch 10A1

perfection * [pəˈfekʃn] Perfektion 5E1/T

persuade *** [pəˈsweɪd] ermutigen, auffordern 10B3

pet hates ** [pet ˈheɪts] Gräuel, Dinge, die man
  auf den Tod nicht ausstehen kann 2B2

phrase *** [freɪz] Satz, Wendung 1A2

pickpocket [ˈpɪkˌpɒkɪt] Taschendieb/in 7C1

pickup truck [ˈpɪkʌp ˌtrʌk] Pick-up, kleiner Lieferwagen
  mit Pritsche 8A1

(Great) Plains ** [pleɪnz] die Great Plains (USA) 8A1

playground * [ˈpleɪˌgraʊnd] Spielplatz 8A2

pocket *** [ˈpɒkɪt] Tasche (in Kleidungsstücken) 8D1

poison * [ˈpɔɪzn] Gift 9C1

polite * [pəˈlaɪt] höflich L03

poll ** [pəʊl] Umfrage 2A1

pollution *** [pəˈluːʃn] Verschmutzung 8B1

Post-it [ˈpəʊstˌɪt] selbstklebender Notizzettel 1A1

postman * [ˈpəʊstmən] Briefträger/in 7B2

posture [ˈpɒstʃə] (Körper)Haltung 9B1

pour *** [pɔː] gießen, schütten 9B1

power station [ˈpaʊə ˌsteɪʃn] Kraftwerk 8B1

pow-wow [ˈpaʊˌwaʊ] Pow-Wow
  (Treffen nordamerikanischer Indianer) 8A1

prairie [ˈpreəri] Prärie 8E1

prawn [prɔːn] Garnele 10A1

pretty ** [ˈprɪti] ziemlich 1A1

prize draw [ˈpraɪz ˌdrɔː] Ziehung 7B3

profile ** [ˈprəʊfaɪl] Profil 2B1

promenade [ˌprɒməˈnɑːd] promenieren RCU9

protect *** [prəˈtekt] schützen RCU4

psychotherapist [ˌsaɪkəʊˈθerəpɪst]
  Psychotherapeut/in 7B3

punctual [ˈpʌŋktʃuəl] pünktlich 4C1

Q

queue * [kjuː] (Menschen)Schlange 10D1

quote * [kwəʊt] Angebot, Kostenvoranschlag 10B2

R

railroad [ˈreɪlˌrəʊd] Eisenbahn 8A1

raindrops [ˈreɪnˌdrɒps] Regentropen 6B1/T

rainforest * [ˈreɪnˌfɒrɪst] Regenwald 8B1

rancher [ˈrɑːntʃə] Betreiber einer Ranch 8A1

range *** [reɪndʒ] hier: Reihe 9B1

raven [ˈreɪvn] Rabe RCU4

raw ** [rɔː] roh RCU4

real *** [rɪəl] echt, wirklich 2A1

recently *** [ˈriːsntli] kürzlich 2A1

recession ** [rɪˈseʃn] Rezession 3B2

recognize *** [ˈrekəgˌnaɪz] erkennen RCU2

refuse *** [rɪˈfjuːz] sich weigern, verweigern,
  ablehnen 10B1

  refuseniks [rɪˈfjuːznɪks] hier: Menschen, die sich
  weigern, das Internet zu nutzen 2E2

relationship *** [rɪˈleɪʃnʃɪp] Beziehung 2B2

relieved [rɪˈliːvd] erleichtert 6E1

religious *** [rəˈlɪdʒəs] religiös 10A2

representative *** [ˌreprɪˈzentətɪv] Vertreter/in; hier:
  Mitarbeiter/in 9D3

research *** [rɪˈsɜːtʃ] Forschung 3A2

reservation ** [ˌrezəˈveɪʃn] Reservat 8A1

restless * [ˈrestləs] unruhig 2B2

restore *** [rɪˈstɔː] wiederherstellen 9B1

reuse [riːˈjuːz] wiederverwerten 8B2

review [rɪˈvjuː] Kritik 5B1

revolution *** [ˌrevəˈluːʃn] Revolution 2A1

rewarding [rɪˈwɔːdɪŋ] lohnend 4A3

rhythm ** [ˈrɪðəm] Rhythmus 5D2

  rhythmic [ˈrɪðmɪk] rhythmisch 9B1

richness [ˈrɪtʃnəs] Reichtum 8A1

rise *** [raɪz] ansteigen 3H3

rob ** [rɒb] ausrauben, bestehlen 7C2/T

  robber * [ˈrɒbə] Räuber/in 7C1

rock ***n [rɒk] Fels 9C2/T

roll up *** [ˌrəʊl ˈʌp] hochkrempeln 8D1

romance * [rəʊˈmæns]   Romanze 5D2/T
roundabout * [ˈraʊndəˌbaʊt]   Kreisverkehr 3C2
route *** [ruːt]   (Reise-)Route, Strecke, Linie 3B2/T
rub ** [rʌb]   reiben RCU7
rubbish ** [ˈrʌbɪʃ]   Müll 8H2/T
rude *** [ruːd]   unhöflich, unverschämt L03

S

safety *** [ˈseɪfti]   Sicherheit 4A2
salmon [ˈsæmən]   Lachs 10A1
same-sex marriage [ˌseɪmseks ˈmærɪdʒ]
   Ehe von gleichgeschlechtlichen Partnern 7D1
sarcasm [ˈsɑːkæz(ə)m]   Sarkasmus 2B2
satnav [ˈsætnæv]   Satelliten-Navigationssystem 7E1/T
save *** [seɪv]   sparen, retten 8B1, 2D2
scandalous [ˈskænd(ə)ləs]   skandalös, Skandal- RCU6
(be) scared ** [skeəd]   Angst haben 7C2/T
   scary * [ˈskeəri]   unheimlich, gruselig 5C1/T
scene *** [siːn]   Szene 5C1/T
sea bass [ˈsiː ˌbæs]   Seebarsch 10A1
sea level [ˈsiː ˌlevl]   Meeresspiegel 8C1
seafood [ˈsiːˌfuːd]   Meeresfrüchte 10A1
seagull [ˈsiːˌgʌl]   Möwe 8E2
secret ***adj [ˈsiːkrət]   geheim 2D1
   secret ***n [ˈsiːkrət]   Geheimnis 6D2
secure ** [sɪˈkjʊə]   gesichert, sicher 4A2
   security *** [sɪˈkjʊərəti]   Sicherheit 4A2
seldom ** [ˈseldəm]   selten 5B1
self-help [ˌself ˈhelp]   Selbsthilfe Co2C3
sense of humour [ˌsens_əv ˈhjuːmə]   Sinn für Humor 2B1/T
sensitive *** [ˈsensətɪv]   sensibel 4C1
separate *** [ˈsep(ə)rət]   trennen 6D2/T
share *** [ʃeə]   teilen 2A1
shave *n [ʃeɪv]   Rasur RCU4
shift ** [ʃift]   Verschiebung, Verlagerung, Umschwung 2A1
shipwreck [ˈʃipˌrek]   Schiffswrack 5C2
shopkeeper * [ˈʃɒpˌkiːpə]   Ladenbesitzer/in 3B2
shoplifter [ˈʃɒpˌlɪftə]   Ladendieb/in 7H8
shoulder *** [ˈʃəʊldə]   Schulter 9B1
shrimp [ʃrɪmp]   Shrimps, Krabben 10A1
sick *** [sɪk]   krank 2D2, 5H5
silver wedding anniversary ** [sɪlvə ˌwedɪŋ_ænɪˈvɜːs(ə)ri]   Silberhochzeit 6A4
sketch * [sketʃ]   Zeichnung 8A2
skill *** [skɪl]   Fähigkeiten, Können 1A1
skin *** [skɪn]   Haut 9B1
sky-high [ˌskaɪˈhaɪ]   schwindelerregend, unermesslich 8B2/T
slow down [ˌsləʊ ˈdaʊn]   langsamer werden 8B1
slum [slʌm]   Slum 5E1
smart ** [smɑːt]   intelligent 1E1

snake * [sneɪk]   Schlange 9A4
soap [səʊp]   hier: Seifenoper, Soap 2C1
   soap opera [ˈsəʊp ˌɒp(ə)rə]   Seifenoper, Soap 2A1
solar panel [ˌsəʊlə ˈpænl]   Solarzellen 7E2
sound engineer [ˈsaʊnd endʒɪˌnɪə]   Toningenieur/in, Tontechniker/in 7B2
southbound [ˈsaʊθˌbaʊnd]   Richtung Süden 3B2/T
spend *** [spend]   verbringen RCU4
spill ** [spɪl]   verschütten 10D1
spoil ** [spɔɪl]   verderben RCU3
sprain [spreɪn]   verstauchen 9A4
square *** [skweə]   Platz 2C1
staff *** [stɑːf]   Personal 3D2
stamp ** [stæmp]   Briefmarke 7D3
stand *** [stænd]   aushalten 4B1/T
star *** [stɑː]   die Hauptrolle spielen RCU6
steeply [ˈstiːpli]   steil 3H3
stepmum (stepmother) [ˈstepˌmʌm]   Stiefmama (Stiefmutter) 6A4
stiff ** [stɪf]   steif 9B1
stimulating [ˈstɪmjʊˌleɪtɪŋ]   anregend 4A1
sting * [stɪŋ]   stechen 6B1/T
stitch [stɪtʃ]   nähen 9C2/T
straightforward ** [ˌstreɪtˈfɔːwəd]   aufrichtig, offen 2H3
strange *** [streɪndʒ]   seltsam, merkwürdig 7A3/T
strengthen ** [ˈstreŋθ(ə)n]   stärken 9B1
strike *** [straɪk]   Streik RCU3
string *** [strɪŋ]   Band, Schnur 6B1/T
stroke ** [strəʊk]   Schlag; hier: Bewegung 9B1
(be) stuck [stʌk]   feststecken 5A1/T
stupid ** [ˈstjuːpɪd]   dumm 9A3
subtitle [ˈsʌbˌtaɪtl]   Untertitel RCU2
successful at [səkˈsesfl_æt]   erfolgreich darin 2B1/T
suffer *** [ˈsʌfə]   leiden 6E1
summer peace camp [sʌmə ˈpiːs ˌkæmp]   Sommerfriedenscamp 1A1
superstitious [ˌsuːpəˈstɪʃəs]   abergläubisch 7A3/T
supervisor * [ˌsuːpəˌvaɪzə]   Leiter/in (der Umfrage) 3A2
support *** [səˈpɔːt]   unterstützen 8B1
suppose *** [səˈpəʊz]   vermuten, annehmen 6C1/T
suspense [səˈspens]   Spannung 5C2
sustainable [səˈsteɪnəbl]   nachhaltig 8D1
switch off *** [ˌswɪtʃ_ˈɒf]   ausschalten 3D1/T

T

tap ** [tæp]   klopfen 1E2
   tap dancing [ˈtæp ˌdɑːnsɪŋ]   Steppen 1A1
tepee [ˈtiːpiː]   Tipi (Zelt der nordamerikanischen Indianer) 8A1
tetanus [ˈtet(ə)nəs]   Tetanus 9C2/T
theme *** [θiːm]   Thema 1B2
therefore *** [ˈðeəfɔː]   darum 3D2

thriller ['θrɪlə]   Thriller 5B2/T

tidy * ['taɪdi]   sauber, ordentlich; aufgeräumt 3D1/T

time off [ˌtaɪm‿'ɒf]   frei 3A1

tiring ['taɪrɪŋ]   ermüdend 4A1

titbit ['tɪtbɪt]   Kleinigkeit 5B2/T

tool *** [tuːl]   Werkzeug 5A1

treat *** [triːt]   behandeln 2B2

   treatment *** ['triːtmənt]   Behandlung 9B1

tremendous ** [trə'mendəs]   gewaltig, enorm 8H3

trend *** [trend]   Trend, Tendenz, Entwicklung 2A1

   trendy ['trendi]   modisch RCU1

trout [traʊt]   Forelle 10A1

(a) try ** [ə 'traɪ]   ein Versuch 3A2/T

U

unemployed *** [ˌʌnɪm'plɔɪd]   arbeitslos 7B3

unexpected ** [ˌʌnɪk'spektɪd]   unerwartet 9D1

unique *** [juː'niːk]   einzigartig 1E2

universal ** [ˌjuːnɪ'vɜːsl]   allgemein gültig, universell RCU2

unsociable [ʌn'səʊʃəbl]   ungesellig 1H5

update * ['ʌpdeɪt]   Aktualisierung 2D1

upset ** [ʌp'set]   hier: verdorben 9C1

user *** ['juːzə]   Nutzer 2A1

V

vaccination [ˌvæksɪ'neɪʃn]   Impfung 3B1, 9C3

valuable *** ['væljʊbl]   wertvoll 7C2/T

varied * ['veərɪd]   abwechslungsreich, vielfältig 4A3

veal [viːl]   Kalb(fleisch) 10A1

veggie burrito [ˌvedʒi bə'riːtəʊ]   vegetarisches Burrito 3D1/T

venison ['venɪs(ə)n]   Reh(fleisch) 10A1

verse ** [vɜːs]   Vers, Strophe 6B2

videoconferencing ['vɪdiəʊˌkɒnf(ə)rənsɪŋ]
   eine Video-Konferenz durchführen 3H3

vision *** ['vɪʒn]   Vision 5E1/T

voicemail ['vɔɪsmeɪl]   Mailbox-Nachricht 4C2

voucher ['vaʊtʃə]   Gutschein 3E1

W

walls [wɔːlz]   Wände 5E1/T

wasp * [wɒsp]   Wespe 9A4

waste ** [weɪst]   hier: wegwerfen RCU8

waves *** [weɪvz]   Wellen 9E2

wedding *** ['wedɪŋ]   Hochzeit 6A4

weekly ** ['wiːkli]   wöchentlich 8B2/T

well-paid [ˌwel'peɪd]   gut bezahlt 4A1

well-respected [ˌwelrɪ'spektɪd]   sehr angesehen RCU3

wet ***vb [wet]   nass machen RCU9

whether *** ['weðə]   ob 6A3

which *** [wɪtʃ]   welche, welcher, welches 8D1

whiskers [ˌwɪskəz]   Schnurrhaare (z.B. bei Katzen) 6B1/T

whisper ** ['wɪspə]   flüstern 10E4

witness ** ['wɪtnəs]   Zeuge/Zeugin 7C3

wonder **vb ['wʌndə]   sich fragen 7B1/T

work *** [wɜːk]   funktionieren 2B2

   work out [ˌwɜːk‿'aʊt]   trainieren 1D1

   workmate ['wɜːkˌmeɪt]   Kollege/Kollegin 4B1

Z

zip * [zɪp]   Reißverschluss 7C2/T

Acknowledgements

The authors and publishers are grateful to the following copyright owners for permission to reproduce artwork, photographs, illustrations and texts.

Illustrations: Bettina Kumpe, Braunschweig

Cover: *left*: © Stockbyte; *middle*: © Kristi J. Black/Corbis; *right*: ©ThinkStock

Photos: **Page 9:** *left*: © Getty Images; *middle:* © iStockphoto; *right*: © Imago **Page 10:** *top: left*: © iStockphoto; *right*: © Panthermedia; *piano man, artist, woman:* © iStockphoto; *sudoku:* © Superbild/BSIP; *cook:* © CHROMORANGE; *tap dancers:* © Teutopress / Süddeutsche Zeitung Photo; *woman:* © iStockphoto **Page 12:** *image:* © CHROMORANGE **Page 14:** *1 and 2:* © iStockphoto; *3:* © Panthermedia **Page 15:** *image* © Panthermedia **Page 17:** *left to right:* © CHROMORANGE ; © iStockphoto, © Granada TV **Page 18:** *photo:* © Panthermedia **Page 19:** *left:* © iStockphoto; *right:* © A1PIX Ltd. **Page 20:** *all images:* © Panthermedia **Page 21:** *background:* © iStockphoto; *image Coronation Street:* © Granada TV **Page 22:** *all images* © Panthermedia **Page 25:** *left to right* © Panthermedia; © Fotolia; © iStockphoto **Page 26:** *Irene, David, Murat:* © Panthermedia; *Sylvia:* © Superbild / Phanie; *Pierre:* © Lufthansa **Page 28:** *cell phone* © Panthermedia **Page 29:** *hand-held satnav:* GPS©etrex; *compass:* © iStockphoto; *cell phone:* © Nokia; *map book:* © Backroad Mapbooks; *in-car satnav:* © Garmin **Page 30:** *image:* © UpperCut Images A/F1online **Page 33:** *image:* © iStockphoto **Page 34:** *image:* © iStockphoto **Page 35:** *all images:* © iStockphoto **Page 37:** *left:* © iStockphoto; *right:* © Getty Images / Digital Vision; *bottom:* © iStockphoto **Page 38:** *image:* © iStockphoto **Page 40:** *cell phone:* © Nokia; *man:* © iStockphoto **Page 41:** *image:* © iStockphoto **Page 43:** *left* © Alamy; *middle:* © iStockphoto; *right:* © Getty Images / Blend Images **Page 45:** *shelf:* © Panthermedia; *woman:* © iStockphoto; *iPad:* ©Apple inc **Page 46:** *all images:* © iStockphoto **Page 47:** *"Küss mich, Dummkopf"," Dick und Doof":* © Finest Images; *Dean Martin, Jerry Lewis:* © Picture-Alliance ;*"Illuminati", "Sinn und Sinnlichkeit", „Der Dritte Mann":* © Cinetext; *"Der unsichtbare Dritte"* © ddp-images **Page 49:** *musician:* © iStockphoto, **Page 51:** *left to right:* © Panthermedia; © iStockphoto; Getty Images / Image Source **Page 52:** *image:* © Alamy / Jijo Kunily **Page 54:** *all images:* © iStockphoto **Page 55:** *family:* © Panthermedia **Page 56:** *Samantha and Hans-Peter:* © Panthermedia; *Don:* © iStockphoto; *Robert:* © Imago **Page 59:** *image:* © Adrian Reynolds/AGE/F1online **Page 60:** *image:* © Gerhard Westrich/laif **Page 61:** *left to right:* © RWE; © Panthermedia; © iStockphoto **Page 62:** *image:* © iStockphoto **Page 63:** *background:* © Getty Images / PhotoAlto / Laurence Mouton **Page 64:** *image:* © "Who Wants To Be A Millionaire?" **Page 66:** *image:* © Darcy Padilla / Redux / laif **Page 67:** *image:* © iStockphoto **Page 69:** *left image:* © www.theuniformproject.com; *middle and right image:* © iStockphoto **Page 70:** *typewriter, sewing machine, tepees and pickup truck:* © iStockphoto; *bison:*© picture-alliance / dpa; *Native American woman:* © Alamy; *milkman:* © Getty Images / Hulton Archive **Page 72:** *bicycles:*© Deutsche Bahn AG; *Smart:* © Mercedes Benz; *remaining images* © iStockphoto **Page 73:** *The Arctic:* © Aurora Photos; *remaining images* © iStockphoto **Page 74:** *image:* © www.theuniformproject.com **Page 75:** *images:* © www.theuniformproject.com **Page 77:** *left image:* © picture alliance / Photoshot; *middle and right image:*© iStockphoto **Page 79:** *Pilates:* © Getty Images / Frare Davis Photography; *Abhyangam:* © iStockphoto **Page 80:** *image:* © iStockphoto **Page 85:** *image:* © iStockphoto **Page 87:** *left:* © Cultura Images / F1 online; *middle and right:* © iStockphoto **Page 88:** *image:* © iStockphoto **Page 89:** *image:* © iStockphoto **Page 90:** *all images:*© iStockphoto **Page 91:** *image:* © Lufthansa **Page 92:** *image:* © iStockphoto **Page100:** *1 and 2:* © Finest Images; *3:* © Rue des Archives / Süddeutsche Zeitung Photo; *4, 5, 6 and 7:*© Action Press **Page 101:** *teenager with cell phone and talking couple:* © Panthermedia; *people playing cards:* © A1PIX Ltd.; *remaining images:* © iStockphoto **Page 102:** *image:* © Munich Airport **Page 103:** *dictionary:* © Macmillan **Page 104:** *image:* © El Sistema **Page 106:** *MP3 player:* © Trek Store; *cell phone:*© Samsung; *iPad:* ©Apple inc; *in-car satnav:* © Garmin; *laptop:* © Acer; *Amish people:* © age fotostock / LOOK-foto **Page 107:** *Top:* © iStockphoto; *bottom:* © Panthermedia **Page 108:** *all images:* © iStockphoto **Page 110:** *all images:* © Winter Love Song **Page 111:** *image:* © iStockphoto **Page 112:** *image:* © iStockphoto **Page 112:** *image:* © iStockphoto **Page 120:** *all images:* © iStockphoto **Page 124:** *all images:* © Panthermedia **Pages 54 and 139:** *"My Favorite Things" music:* © Richard Rogers, *text:* Oscar Hammerstein II, EMI Music Publishing Germany GmbH